HMH | into Reading™

my Book 2

Authors and Advisors

Alma Flor Ada • Kylene Beers • F. Isabel Campoy
Joyce Armstrong Carroll • Nathan Clemens
Anne Cunningham • Martha C. Hougen
Elena Izquierdo • Carol Jago • Erik Palmer
Robert E. Probst • Shane Templeton • Julie Washington

Contributing Consultants

David Dockterman • Mindset Works®
Jill Eggleton

Printed in the U.S.A.

ISBN   978-1-328-51703-6

7   8   9   10   11   12   0029   27   26   25   24   23   22   21

4500825758   B C D E F G

HMH

into Reading™

myBook 2

Welcome to myBook!

Do you like to read different kinds of texts for all kinds of reasons? Do you have a favorite genre or author? What can you learn from a video? Do you think carefully about what you read and view?

Here are some tips to get the MOST out of what you read and view:

Set a Purpose. What is the title? What is the genre? What do you want to learn from this text or video? What about it looks interesting to you?

Read and Annotate. As you read, underline and highlight important words and ideas. Make notes about things you want to figure out or remember. What questions do you have? What are your favorite parts? Write them down!

Make Connections. How does the text or video connect to what you already know? To other texts or videos? To your own life or community? Talk to others about your ideas. Listen to their ideas, too.

Wrap It Up! Look back at your questions and annotations. What did you like best? What did you learn? What do you still want to know? How will you find out?

As you read the texts and watch the videos in this book, make sure you get the MOST out of them by using the tips above.

But, don't stop there . . . decide what makes you curious, find out more about it, have fun, and never stop learning!

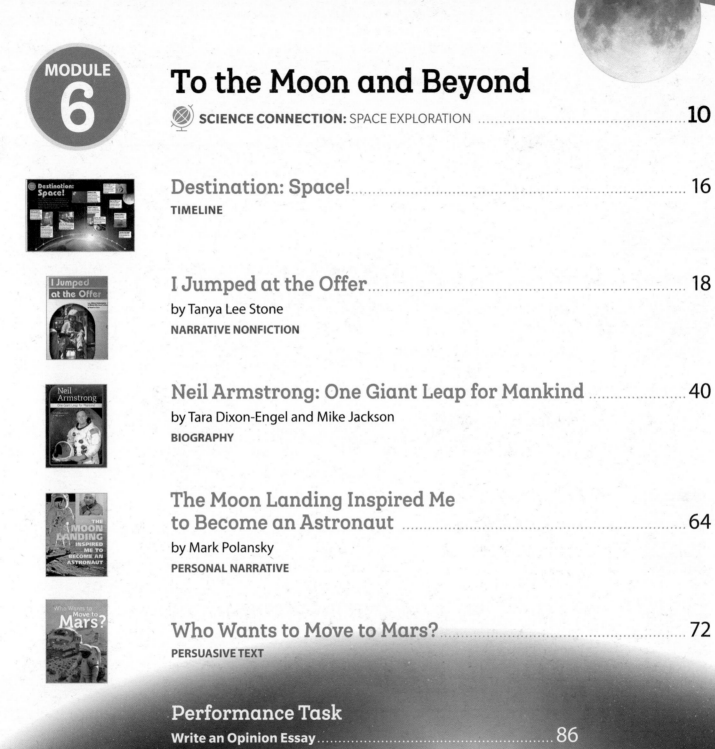

MODULE 6

To the Moon and Beyond

MODULE 8

Champions of the Game

 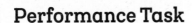

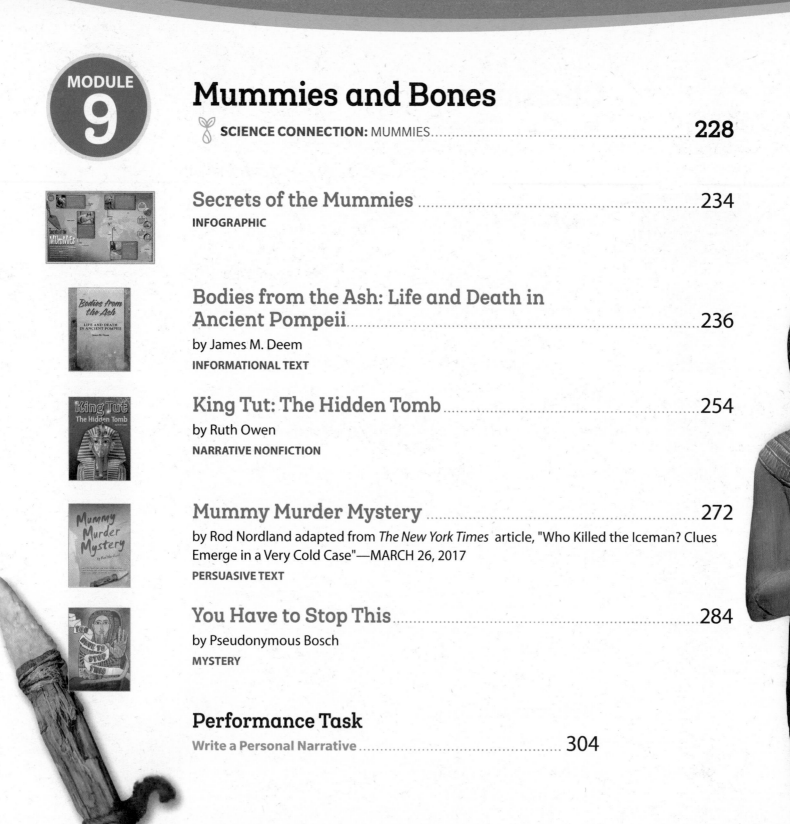

MODULE 9

Mummies and Bones

Get Out the Vote

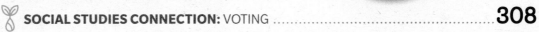

WE MARCH TOGETHER
CATHOLIC
JEWS
PROTESTANT
FOR DIGNITY
AND BROTHERHOOD
OF ALL MEN UNDER GOD
NOW!

To the Moon and Beyond

"Space is the new ocean, and I believe
the United States must sail on it."

—John F. Kennedy

? Essential Question

What does it take to explore outer space?

Get Curious
Video

Words About Space Exploration

The words in the chart will help you talk and write about the selections in this module. Which words about space exploration have you seen before? Which words are new to you?

Add to the Vocabulary Network on page 13 by writing synonyms, antonyms, and related words and phrases for each word about space exploration.

After you read each selection in this module, come back to the Vocabulary Network and keep building it. Add more boxes if you need to.

WORD	MEANING	CONTEXT SENTENCE
craters (noun)	Craters are bowl-shaped indentations on a surface, such as the moon or a volcano.	The moon's craters were likely formed by asteroids or meteors crashing into it.
satellite (noun)	A satellite is a human-made object that's been placed in space to collect information or for communication.	The first satellite in space was only 22.8 inches in diameter.
orbit (verb)	An object is said to be in orbit when it's moving in a circular motion around a planet, moon, or star.	The International Space Station has been in orbit around Earth since 1998.
launched (verb)	If you've launched a rocket or satellite, it means you've sent it into space.	Over the years, NASA has launched many rockets into space.

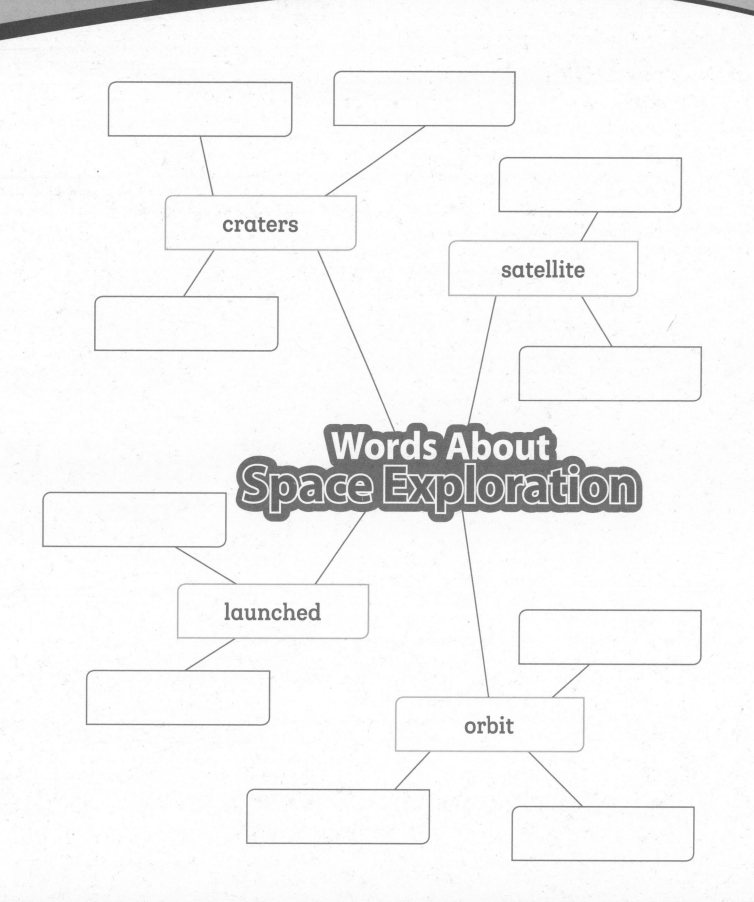

Words About
Space Exploration

craters

satellite

launched

orbit

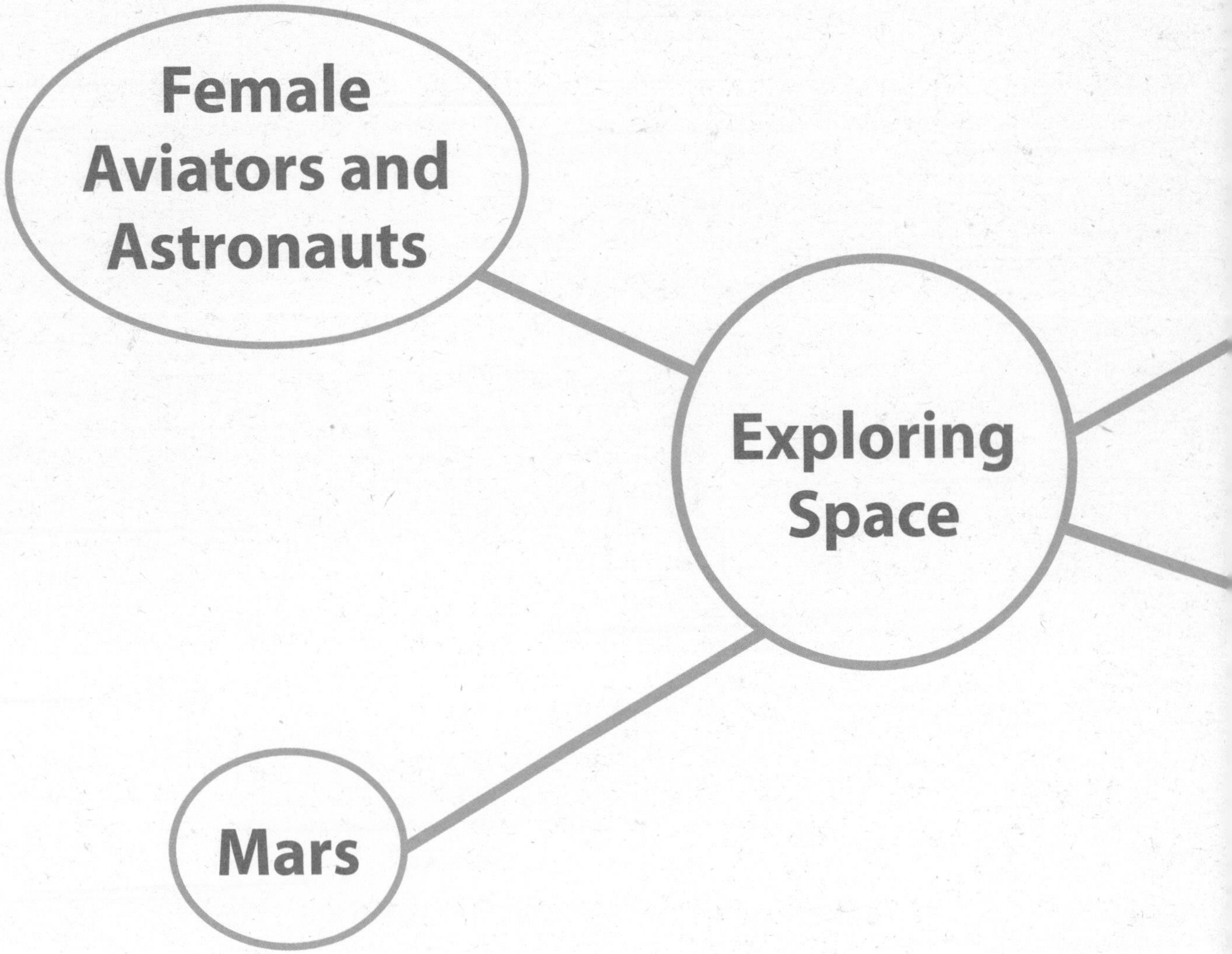

Female Aviators and Astronauts

Exploring Space

Mars

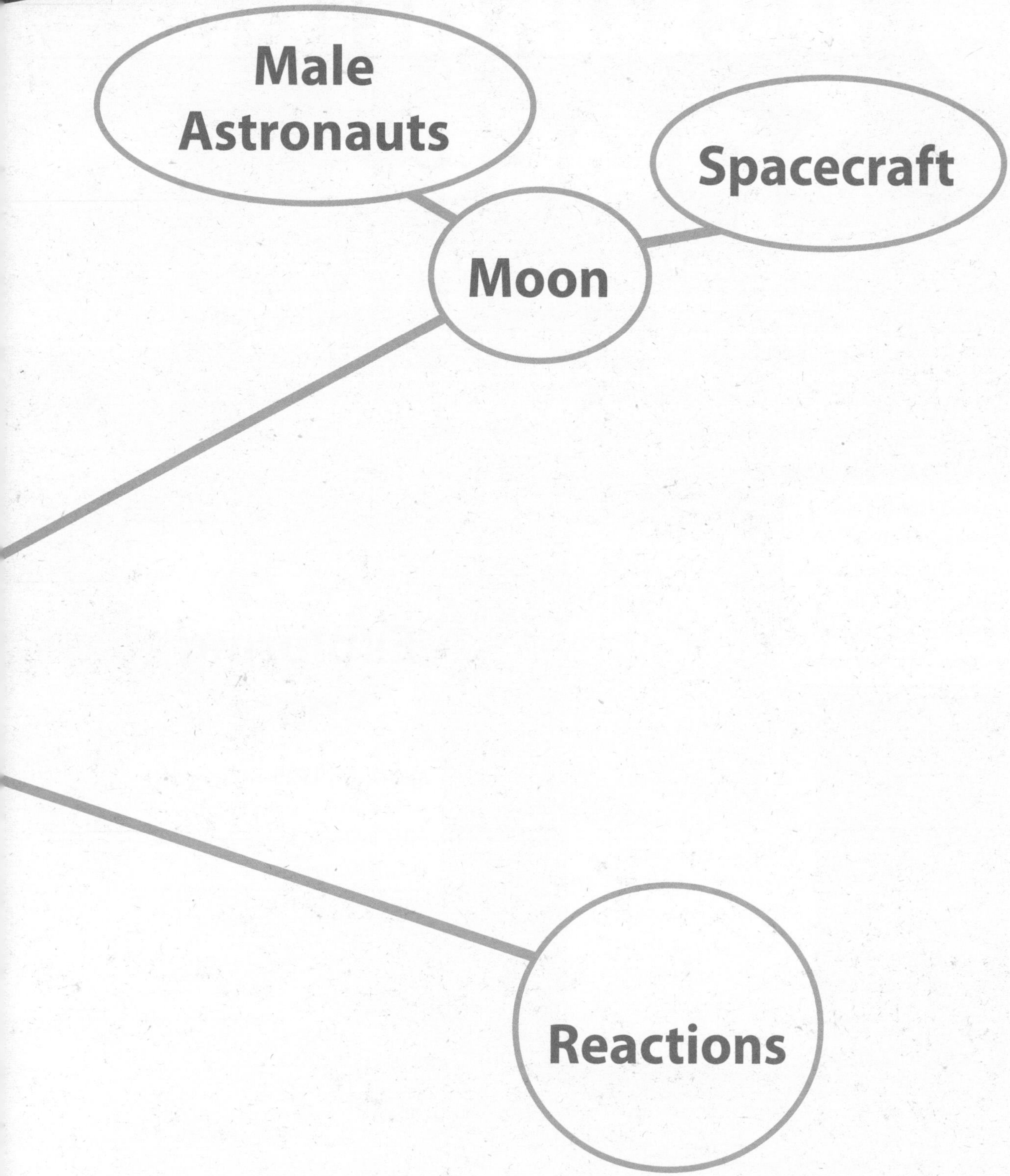

Male Astronauts

Spacecraft

Moon

Reactions

Short Read

Destination: Space!

Humans have gazed at the night sky since prehistoric times and wondered what was out there. As our knowledge advanced, we began to build tools for observing the moon, stars, and planets. Eventually, we developed the technology to send equipment— and then people—into space. What follows are just a few major milestones in the history of space exploration.

Sometime during the 11th century AD: Chinese inventors from the Sung Dynasty build the first rockets. These early rockets are propelled by gunpowder and used in warfare.

1610: Italian astronomer Galileo Galilei becomes the first person to observe the night sky through a telescope. During his career, he discovers craters on Earth's moon and is the first to spot the moons of Jupiter.

March 16, 1926: Robert Goddard launches the first successful liquid-fueled rocket. Three years later, he launches the first rocket carrying scientific tools.

July 20, 1969: The world watches in wonder as the American crew of NASA's Apollo 11 mission become the first humans to land—and walk—on the moon.

October 4, 1957: The Soviet Union launches Sputnik 1—the first human-made satellite—into orbit around Earth. This event marks the beginning of the Space Race between the US and the USSR.

August 7, 1959: NASA launches a small satellite called Explorer 6, which captures the first photographs of Earth from space.

April 12, 1961: Soviet cosmonaut (the Russian term for astronaut) Yuri Gagarin becomes the first man in space.

May 14, 1973: The first US space station, Skylab, is launched into orbit around Earth, where it will remain for six years.

January 4, 2004: The first Mars Exploration Rover, NASA's Spirit, lands on Mars.

Sometime in the 2030s: Humans land on Mars? NASA and other organizations say it can be done.

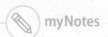

Prepare to Read

> **GENRE STUDY** **Narrative nonfiction** gives factual information by telling a true story.

- Narrative nonfiction presents events in sequential, or chronological, order. This helps readers understand what happened and when.

- Authors of narrative nonfiction may organize their ideas using headings and subheadings. The headings and subheadings tell readers what the next section of text will be about.

> **SET A PURPOSE** **Think about** the title and genre of this text. The title of this selection quotes a person from the text. Who might have said these words? Write your ideas below.

Meet the Author:
Tanya Lee Stone

CRITICAL VOCABULARY

ideal

productivity

extravagant

consumption

isolation

qualify

objectivity

option

induces

justify

I Jumped at the Offer

from **Almost Astronauts:**
13 Women Who Dared to Dream

by Tanya Lee Stone

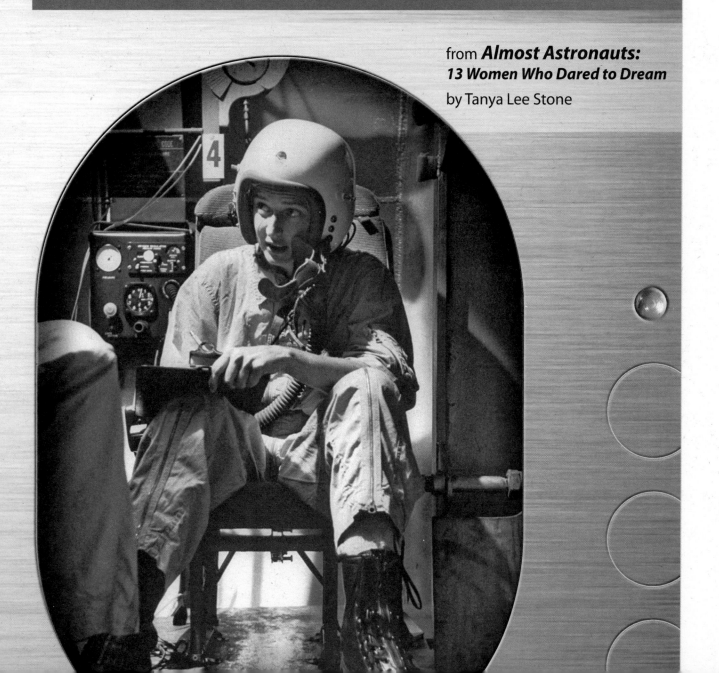

NASA

1960

1   We have turned back the clock.

2   John F. Kennedy has just been elected president.

3   Three years earlier, the Soviet Union (now Russia) launched a satellite called Sputnik. It was the first time anyone, anywhere, had sent *anything* into orbit around Earth. People all over the world were talking about it. The United States was determined to get into the game.

4   And it did. In 1958, the year after Sputnik went up, the National Aeronautics and Space Administration (NASA) was created. President Kennedy put beating the Russians in the race to explore space right at the top of his to-do list.

5   NASA put together a winning team for their Mercury program—a program designed to orbit a man around Earth. Seven male jet test pilots, the best of the best, went through extensive testing and training to be selected as the first group of American astronauts.

6   They were dubbed the Mercury 7 and hailed as heroes. Their faces beamed out from the September 14, 1959, cover of *Life* magazine. The article's headline: THE ASTRONAUTS—READY TO MAKE HISTORY. Confident, strong, clean-cut men ready to take on the world. And beyond.

On May 25, 1961, President John F. Kennedy gave a historic speech declaring, "I believe that this nation should commit itself to achieving the goal, before this decade is out, of landing a man on the moon and returning him safely to the earth." In the background are (left) Vice President Lyndon B. Johnson and (right) Speaker of the House Sam T. Rayburn.

7   This is what bravery looked like.

8   When the author Tom Wolfe wrote about these men, he called his book *The Right Stuff*. It was a phrase he coined to describe a quality that jet test pilots and those first astronauts seemed to embody. Men who continually risked their lives to test the boundaries of what new aircraft and spacecraft could do, who were ready to die in the name of their mission, their country. Wolfe wrote, "But it was not bravery in the simple sense of being willing to risk your life. The idea seemed to be that any fool could do that. . . . No, the idea here . . . seemed to be that a man should have the ability to go up in a hurtling piece of machinery and put his hide on the line and then have the moxie, the reflexes, the experience, the coolness, to pull it back in the last yawning moment—

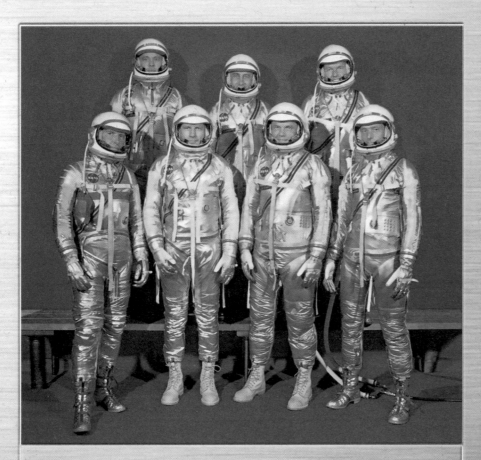

The Mercury 7 astronauts. Left to right at front: Walter M. "Wally" Schirra, Donald K. "Deke" Slayton, John H. Glenn Jr., and Scott Carpenter. Left to right at rear: Alan B. Shepard Jr., Virgil I. "Gus" Grissom, and Gordon Cooper Jr.

This portrait of the wives of the Project Mercury astronauts was taken on September 21, 1959.

and then to go up again *the next day*, and the next day, and every next day. . . . *Manliness, manhood, manly courage* . . . there was something ancient, primordial, irresistible about the challenge of this stuff."

9   On September 21, another smiling group shot graced the cover of *Life*: the seven wives of the seven astronauts. Their tagline: "Astronauts' Wives: Their Inner Thoughts, Worries." The women talked about how they shared their hopes and fears with one another. Interior photos showed them doing many wifely, motherly chores: bathing the kids, doing dishes, riding bikes with their children, playing cards, and waiting for their husbands to return. They even posed by a full-scale red steel model of the space capsule.

10   This is what loyalty looked like.

11   It was a nice, neat package that the media presented. Women in their proper place, supporting their menfolk, keeping the home fires burning.

12   Of course, these images did not represent all women—especially after World War II. In the 1930s, as many Americans struggled to make a living, most white Americans believed that women shouldn't work unless they had to, shouldn't take jobs away from the men. Certainly, that did not apply to all—African American women, for example, especially in the South, often worked for white families, and the poorest families, black or white, expected daughters to help out in any way they could. Yet still, the ideal—the image in the movies and the women's magazines and in common conversation—was of a wife who did not work outside the home. But the war required an attitude change. Men shipped off, and jobs were left open, right when companies desperately needed to increase their productivity.

---

ideal   Something that is ideal is perfect.
productivity   Productivity is the effectiveness of a company's efforts.

Someone had to keep the factories rolling so that all of the military equipment could be built and sent overseas.

13   So all different kinds of women, even those who were well off or married, went to work in steel mills, factories, and shipyards. They built boats, planes, and munitions. They joined the Red Cross, the Women's Army Corps (WAC), and the WASP (Women Airforce Service Pilots).

14   Women were called to duty. They jumped in where they were needed. They did their country proud.

15   Then the men came back from overseas.

16   And women were called to duty again. But this time, it was to restore the ideal of the traditional family. Even the WASP had their wings clipped; their organization folded. They had proven that women could fly, but the question then became, *Should* they fly? The answer was no. After the war, the men wanted their planes and their jobs back. And they got them.

17   Most men who had fought in the war wanted to leave that grim scene behind and return to a nice home, a sweet wife, a growing family. As the economy improved, there were more jobs available, and many men were able to support their families on their salaries alone. Many women agreed that their place was the home. But others had tasted independence, had felt the satisfaction of earning their own money, supporting their families, excelling at jobs outside of the home. They didn't want to give all that up and did not like this change in the national mood. They still had hopes and dreams beyond serving up hot casseroles for their men returning home from work. Nevertheless, from the late 1940s through much of the 1950s, these women were viewed as misfits unable to adapt to their "natural" roles.

During World War II, the government created posters such as this one to encourage women to do their part and join the Women's Army Corps (WAC).

The Women Airforce Service Pilots (WASP) were considered civil service employees—not military personnel—even though they risked their lives for their country during World War II in noncombat missions, ferrying planes from the factories to the men at military bases overseas.

18   In 1959, when the Mercury 7 men were put forth as the ideal picture of bravery and heroism, most Americans were ready to agree. But there were women who wanted to see themselves in that same picture—as astronauts on the cover of a magazine.

Enter Randy Lovelace

19   Randolph Lovelace was the chairman of NASA's Life Sciences Committee.

20   He was the doctor who put the Mercury 7 men through all of their testing.

21   He was a scientist who believed that women are as capable as men, and he wanted to prove it.

22   Lovelace was a realist, keenly aware that women were often pigeonholed—thought of as interested only in getting married, raising children, and generally being nurturing, pleasant people who wouldn't ruffle too many feathers.

23   In this social climate, a woman wanting to become an astronaut was going to take a lot of heat. She might even be treated as a joke.

24   Lovelace knew that if women were ever going to be let into the space program, he was going to have to prove, beyond a shadow of a doubt, not just that they were up to the job, but that they were *more than* up to the job. And he believed they were.

25   He also believed that women could save the space program a lot of money. They are generally smaller and lighter than men, so they need less oxygen and would take up less room in a spacecraft. Female astronauts would be cost-effective, saving NASA nearly $1,000 per pound! But he knew he was going to have a tough time selling NASA on the idea.

26   Lovelace wasn't the only person to have this same thought. In fact, his was one of three plans being cooked up in 1959 to test women's suitability for spaceflight. This may seem odd, considering the overall status of women at this time, but at least one of the plans—put forward by *Look* magazine—was as much about image as science. The magazine may have been competing with its rival, *Life*, and looking for a fresh story to capture the mood of the nation as it headed toward the new decade, the 1960s. The other two plans had more scientific goals in mind.

27   *Look* thought that showing a woman going through some of the astronaut testing would make an interesting magazine story. And NASA cooperated. They allowed a top-notch pilot named Betty Skelton to operate an orbital-flight simulator—a mock spacecraft cockpit. She was then spun around in a centrifuge, a machine that spins a pilot around and around at high speed, preparing him or her for strong acceleration forces in space. She took the tilt-table test, in which she lay on a table that shifted quickly back and forth between flat and upright at a 65-degree angle. She had her body fluids and functions measured and examined repeatedly. These tests were some of the same tests that men like John Glenn and Scott Carpenter had taken—Mercury 7 men.

28   When the story ran, Betty Skelton was *Look*'s cover girl, looking fabulous in a sleek silver space suit. The headline read SHOULD A GIRL BE FIRST IN SPACE? Inside, the bulk of the piece was made up of photos of Betty and the Mercury 7 boys joking around—apparently they called her No. 7½—while she took her tests and sported a way-too-large man's flight suit.

Pilot Betty Skelton

29   None of Skelton's results were included in the article, but, to the writer's credit, he did indicate how well she had done: "She is just a petite example of the anatomical fact that women have more brains and stamina per pound than men." But Skelton was mainly portrayed as soaking up the atmosphere of the male pilots, taking in what they had to teach her, as if she were part of some sort of extravagant career-day presentation. The article also suggested that the best woman for the job might be the "scientist-wife of a pilot," ready to relegate the flying to the men and act as caretaker for the other—presumably male—crew members.

30   In the end, *Look* got their high-interest story and NASA was able to glamorize their space program for the general public. The whole thing was an exercise in public relations. Skelton was never actually considered a potential astronaut candidate by anyone. And she knew it.

31   So why did she do it? Skelton said, "I felt it was an opportunity to try to convince them that a woman could do this type of thing and do it well." And she was right. Skelton's test results were recorded, one of the first times a woman's abilities were measured with the same equipment and technology used on men.

In addition to setting records as an aerobatic champion, pilot Betty Skelton also broke land speed records in a race car. Her airplane, *Little Stinker*, is on display at the Smithsonian Air and Space Museum.

32   Ruth Nichols was another exceptional pilot who had been setting aviation records for decades. The air force invited her to Wright Air Development Center, in Dayton, Ohio, to take some of the astronaut tests and see how she fared. Unlike testing conducted for the *Look* magazine piece, this testing was not for public consumption. But like Skelton, Nichols performed extremely well.

33   Nichols felt free to speak up for her gender. "I put in a very strong urge that women be used in spaceflights. When I was out at Wright Field, they thought of this with horror, and they said, 'Under no circumstances.'"

extravagant   Something that is extravagant is excessive or expensive.
consumption   If something is for consumption, people can hear or read about it.

34   The researchers told Nichols that women could not go into space because not enough was known about how they would fare under difficult conditions. To Nichols this just showed that scientists needed to hurry up and focus on testing women. But the air force had no interest in that approach. They were quite content to treat her results as interesting notes to file away and ignore. In fact, when word of how well she had done got out, it soured the whole project.

35   The air force contact behind Nichols's testing had been Brigadier General Donald Flickinger. Flickinger was a man who was willing to take chances and who shared some of Lovelace's ideas. The two men had been friends for a long time. Flickinger was the one who had suggested Lovelace to NASA for the testing of the Mercury 7 men.

36   Flickinger got in touch with his old friend.

37   Lovelace's NASA connections were solidly in place. He knew how to put the astronauts through their paces, and he had a research facility at his disposal.

38   Flickinger had air force funds.

39   They put their heads together and named their idea for a female testing program Project WISE (Woman in Space Earliest). In casual conversation, Flickinger often referred to it as a "girl astronaut program." Now all they needed was the perfect test subject.

September 1959— Enter Jerrie Cobb

40   Slender, with sky-blue eyes, twenty-eight-year-old Jerrie Cobb had been flying airplanes since she was twelve years old. It was in her blood. She had already logged more than 7,000 hours in the air—far more than John Glenn's 5,000 hours and Scott Carpenter's 2,900 hours. She had ferried military aircraft all over the world and set the world altitude record, as well as a world light-plane speed record. And the records she broke were among all pilots—not just women pilots.

When Jerrie Cobb met Randy Lovelace, she was already a record-breaking pilot.

41   All she had ever wanted was to keep going higher, faster, farther.

42   On this particular morning, she was in Miami, Florida, with her boss, Tom Harris, for the annual Air Force Association meeting.

43   At seven a.m., they were taking a walk on the beach when two men came out of the surf after their morning swim. Harris recognized them and waved them over. Jerrie didn't know them on sight, but she certainly knew their names when she heard them: Donald Flickinger and Randy Lovelace.

44   Everyone in aviation knew that Flickinger had his hand in the future of human spaceflight and that Lovelace had worked with the NASA astronauts.

45   Flickinger and Lovelace hadn't heard of Jerrie Cobb. But here was a world-record-setting, award-winning, *ponytailed* pilot. They were immediately intrigued.

46   This was the woman they were waiting for. The perfect test subject, standing right in front of them on the beach.

47   Was it luck? Being in the right place at the right time? That was part of it. But mostly, they got the impression that Jerrie Cobb might just have the Right Stuff.

48   They invited her back to the Fontainebleau Hotel to talk.

49   They asked her if there were other young, physically fit female pilots.

50   They told her that medical tests had shown that women withstand isolation and pain better than men do. But there was no data to show how women would hold up in space-fitness testing.

51   They wanted those data.

---

isolation   To be in isolation is to be alone.

28

52   Cobb got a chill up the back of her neck.

53   Here were men with air force and NASA affiliations wanting to know if she would be their first subject for female astronaut testing. Would she like to volunteer to show how women might fare in space? Would she like to help give women the chance to prove their worth?

54   Jerrie had had plenty of experience dealing with discrimination in aviation. As a pilot looking for work, she had been told flat out, "No airline passenger will ever fly with a woman in the cockpit." Even her father, who supported her desire to be a pilot, had told her, "Honey, it's no career for a woman. ... A girl doesn't have a chance." The male pilots always got hired first and got the best flying jobs. She was often stuck with the lower-paying jobs the guys didn't want.

55   She didn't care. She belonged in the air.

56   And there, standing right in front of her, were men who might just have the power to turn her wildest dreams of flight into reality.

57   Cobb's eyes filled with tears. She didn't waste a breath. "I jumped at the offer," she said later.

58   For a while, things went as planned. Flickinger, Lovelace, and Cobb worked together to identify female pilots who would qualify as testing subjects.

59   But trouble lay ahead.

60   Flickinger's superiors at the air force were still ruffled about the Ruth Nichols incident. The release of her information to the public implied that the air force was in favor of testing females, which they were not. They told Flickinger that they did not want to conduct any further testing of women for spaceflight.

61   Flickinger sent Cobb a letter of apology. Project WISE was over. But neither Flickinger nor Lovelace, nor especially Cobb, let that stop them.

62   Flickinger encouraged Lovelace to proceed without him, and Lovelace put his own foundation behind the project. The idea was to keep their activities quiet until they had enough data to present a solid

qualify   If you qualify for something, you have the training, skill, or ability for a specific purpose.

and convincing case to NASA. The space race pitted American science, medicine, and technology against the science, medicine, and technology of the Russians. It was—or was supposed to be—a contest in which reason, objectivity, tests, and measurements would rule. So if Lovelace could run impeccable tests and come up with unquestionable results, NASA would have to listen.

63   Lovelace gave Cobb a directive: Don't tell anyone what they were doing until the time was right. This was in keeping with how he handled the Mercury 7 testing. He didn't like to show his hand until he was ready.

64   He also told her to start training. She was going to need it.

65   Cobb got moving, making sure she was in her best physical shape for testing. Every morning, she was up at five a.m. and out the door, running laps in her bare feet around the vacant lot next to her house. Then it was off to work. The laps started up again when her workday ended. So did stints on a stationary bicycle. She ran five miles a day and rode twenty miles a day on the bike.

66   Extra sleep was on the schedule, too, as was lots of protein—steak and hamburgers became regulars on her breakfast menu.

67   And then the day arrived. Five months after that fateful meeting on the beach, Cobb got word to report to the Lovelace Clinic, in Albuquerque, New Mexico. It was time to prove that women were up to the job.

68   Failure was not an option.

69   If she failed, they might never test another woman.

70   NASA might never get a persuasive report from an influential member of their team filled with data making the case for women as astronaut candidates.

71   The pressure was on.

---

objectivity   If you have objectivity about something, you can think about it without emotion.

option   An option is a choice.

February 14, 1960

72 Astronaut testing, phase one.

73 In secret, Jerrie Cobb traveled to New Mexico—not to her parents' home for a visit, as coworkers were told.

74 In secret, she became the first.

75 The first woman to have the blood tests. And X-rays—more than a hundred. The first to blow into a tube to test her lungs. Jerrie later wrote: "It's the lung-power equivalent of showing muscle strength by hitting a sledgehammer on a scale."

76 The first to have freezing water injected into her ears. This test froze the inner ear bone, which induces vertigo—a particularly dangerous sensation for pilots because this extreme dizziness completely destroys one's sense of balance and orientation. When the water hit her inner ear, Jerrie's hand fell off the chair arm and she couldn't lift it back up. She went into a whirl. They timed her to see how long it took for her eyeballs to stop spinning, for her to come out of vertigo. The pain of that test was bad. But not nearly as bad as the dread of watching the syringe coming back for more, to repeat the horrendous test on her other ear.

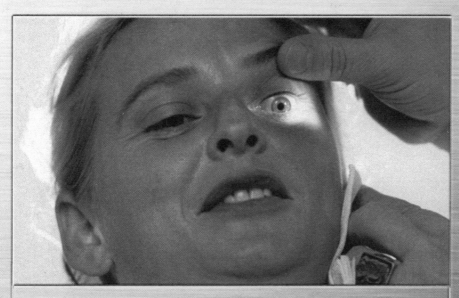

Doctors determined the vertigo effect by examining Cobb's eye.

induces If something induces a reaction, it causes it to happen.

77   The first to have three feet of rubber hose snaked down her throat. To drink radioactive water.

78   The first to have probes poke her head to record her brain waves.

79   The first to take the bike test, pedaling until the point of exhaustion. She knew she would keep going until they told her to stop.

80   The first to be rocked back and forth, back and forth, on a tilt table, having her heart rate and blood pressure measured every few minutes. Many people pass out during this test. Cobb didn't even get dizzy.

81   The first to be flown to a secret government location in the mountains of Los Alamos and be slid inside the belly of a machine that measured the amount of radiation in her body.

82   "Here's the chicken switch," a technician told her. It was pointed out in case panic came over her and she needed to get out. Any chance she'd flip it? None.

83   The first to be peppered with psychological questions designed to prod her, annoy her, make her angry and lose her cool. One hundred and ninety-five questions, to be exact.

Cobb during the tilt-table test

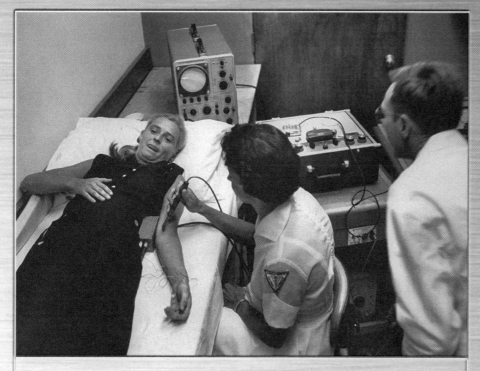

Cobb is poked and prodded.

84   Questions like: What's your favorite hobby? Why? That doesn't seem like a worthwhile activity—why would you want to waste your time doing that?

85   Questions designed to provoke.

86   Questions designed to rattle.

87   Jerrie never lost her cool. Not once.

88   In secret, she was the first woman to take all eighty-seven of the physical tests the Mercury 7 men had taken.

89   The first woman to be told that she had passed the Mercury astronaut tests—and, the doctors added, with fewer complaints than the guys.

90   The first to open the door for others to walk through.

91   When Jerrie was little, she had to endure a painful doctor's visit to clip the membrane of her tongue. She was reminded of that time during her tests and later reflected, "At five, I'd been given soda pop as a reward. This time I was hoping for something far, far greater."

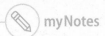

August 19, 1960

92   Lovelace was at an international space conference in Stockholm and he was ready to make his surprise announcement.

93   Jerrie had been told to lie low until two things happened—until he made his Stockholm speech and until the August 28 issue of *Life* magazine hit the newsstands, complete with an article and photos about her phase-one testing.

94   Lovelace delivered his news, telling the world about Cobb's outstanding test results. She had "successfully completed the tests given to the seven men in the United States man-in-space project." He added, "We are already in a position to say that certain qualities of the female space pilot are preferable to those of her male colleague." He also disclosed that "no definite space project [exists] for the women."

Randy Lovelace discusses the testing with Jerrie Cobb.

95   Back in New York, where Jerrie Cobb was staying, it was the middle of the night.

96   Her phone started ringing. Her parents' phone started ringing. Her friends' and colleagues' phones started ringing. And they didn't stop. The world wanted to know who this woman was.

97   By the next morning, the news was all over the papers. So was her photograph. Shy, soft-spoken Jerrie Cobb was smack in the middle of a media frenzy. Later, she said she felt as if she headed the FBI's "most wanted" list.

98   *Life* magazine and *Sports Illustrated* both ran features on her the following week. The *Life* article was particularly powerful, chock-full of photographs of Jerrie hooked up to machines and instruments. People could see, with their own eyes, a woman being tested in exactly the same ways the Mercury 7 had been—taking all the Project Mercury tests—and excelling.

99   Some cheered her on. Others complimented Cobb but couldn't resist taking jabs. The *Los Angeles Times*: "The scientists haven't even figured out how to get a man to the moon yet, but already they've opened the trip to women. That shows how far the craftier sex has come." Headlines such as MOON MAID'S READY, NO. 1 SPACE GAL SEEMS A LITTLE ASTRONAUGHTY, and 20 YEARS A PILOT, WANTS TO BE AN "ASTRONETTE" all made light of the situation.

100   Editorial cartoons poked fun.

101   Reporters included her physical measurements alongside her test results.

102   Or they dropped the test results completely, asking her what kind of meats she liked to cook and marveling at how slim, blond, and dimpled a pilot could be. "[That] has nothing to do with flying. I never read about men pilots who had their measurements listed in stories about them," Cobb later said.

103   NASA was not convinced. They were not even interested. The organization announced that it "has never had a plan to put a woman into space, it doesn't have one today, and it doesn't expect to have any in the foreseeable future."

NASA

Jerrie Cobb poses next to a Mercury spaceship capsule.

104   But why? Flickinger commented on why the air force didn't want to continue testing women: "The consensus of opinion . . . was that there was too little to learn of value."

105   Some claimed it would take too much time and cost too much money to redesign pressure suits for women. Flickinger told Lovelace, "One of the major objections made . . . was that we could not justify the expense of altering the PPSs [partial-pressure suits] to fit the girls."

106   Lovelace was not deterred by any of this. And the media was embracing Cobb. As far as they were concerned, she was America's first "lady astronaut."

justify   To justify something is to prove that it is worthwhile or necessary.

Collaborative Discussion

Look back at what you wrote on page 18. Tell a partner two historical facts that you learned from this text. Then work with a group to discuss the questions below. Refer to details and examples in *I Jumped at the Offer* to explain your answers. Take notes for your responses. When you speak, use your notes.

1 How did World War II play a role in improving women's independence in America?

Listening Tip

Pay close attention to the members of your group when they speak. Look at each speaker to show that you are listening.

2 Which men helped Betty Skelton, Ruth Nichols, and Jerrie Cobb prove that women could be good astronauts? What did they do, and what risks were involved for them?

Speaking Tip

As you speak, glance at each member of your group. If anyone looks confused, invite that person to ask you a question.

3 On page 28, the author refers to Jerrie Cobb as a "*ponytailed* pilot." Why does the author describe Cobb in this way, and what effect does it have?

Write an Opinion Paragraph

The text *I Jumped at the Offer* described how three women—Betty Skelton, Ruth Nichols, and Jerrie Cobb—took difficult astronaut tests. They proved that women were just as well suited for space travel as men.

In your opinion, what made these women just as qualified as men to become astronauts? Which strengths and personality traits did they possess that would help them to become good astronauts? Write a paragraph that states your opinion, and support it with evidence from the text.

PLAN

List and briefly explain three qualifications that a woman during the 1950s and 1960s would need to be a good astronaut. Refer to *I Jumped at the Offer* as you decide which strengths and personality traits to include.

WRITE

Now write your opinion paragraph about why Betty Skelton, Ruth Nichols, and Jerrie Cobb from *I Jumped at the Offer* were just as qualified as men to become astronauts.

✓ Make sure your opinion paragraph

- ☐ begins with an opinion about the women's qualifications.

- ☐ includes at least three pieces of text evidence that support your opinion.

- ☐ ends with a sentence that persuades the reader to agree with your opinion.

- ☐ uses a firm yet friendly tone.

Prepare to Read

GENRE STUDY A **biography** is the story of a real person's life written by someone other than that person.

- Biographies include third-person pronouns such as *he, she, him, her, his, hers, they, them,* and *their*.
- Biographies include photographs from the subject's life.
- Authors of biographies present events in sequential, or chronological, order. This helps readers understand what happened in the person's life and when.

SET A PURPOSE **Think about** the title and genre of this text. What do you think the phrase "one giant leap for mankind" means? Write your ideas below.

Meet the Author:
Tara Dixon-Engel

CRITICAL VOCABULARY

implications

aeronautics

priorities

aloofness

engage

simulators

Neil Armstrong

One Giant Leap for Mankind

by Tara Dixon-Engel
& Mike Jackson

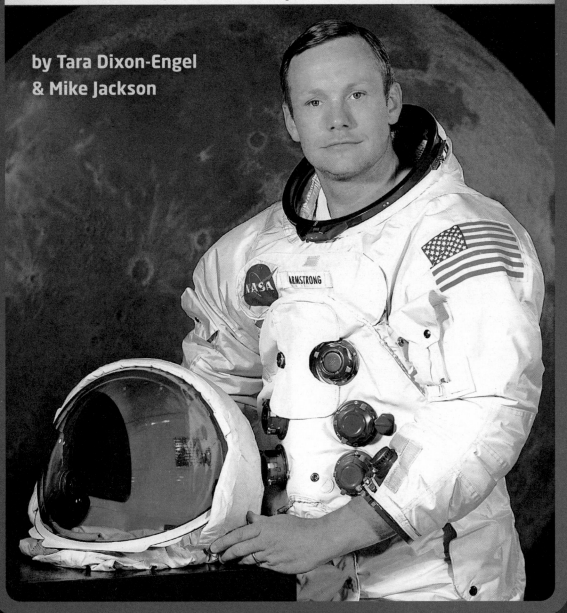

From Fiction to Reality

1   On July 20, 1969, the smooth blackness of space was broken by a spidery silver machine that dropped slowly toward the gray powdery surface of the moon. At a distance, it might have been mistaken for a child's toy, molded from paper clips, tin cans, and scraps of aluminum foil. Close up, the odd little spacecraft was a miracle of modern technology, and a testament to American initiative and determination.

2   It was a scene that had been played out countless times in hundreds of science-fiction tales over the years. But suddenly it was no longer the stuff of fiction. This was reality. Men from Earth were about to set foot on the surface of the moon.

3   Our fascination with the moon is as old as humankind itself. Since the dawn of time, we have scanned the night sky wondering about the milky white globe that chased away the sun at day's end.

4   Now a shy, yet driven young man from Ohio named Neil Armstrong was about to discover its secrets. As commander of *Apollo 11*, he and his crew had traveled thousands of miles to get to this point in the solar system. No one ever doubted that Neil would leave his mark in *this* world, but few could have predicted that he would leave his mark on the powdery surface beyond our world as well.

We came in peace for all mankind.

—PLAQUE LEFT ON THE MOON

Left: One of the most famous test pilots ever, Chuck Yeager, stands next to the Bell X-1 in which he broke the sound barrier on October 14, 1947.

Below: Sputnik, this beeping sphere launched by the Russians in October 1957, was the first satellite of its kind.

Higher, Faster, Farther

The Race for Space

5   Many things were happening in the world—and out of it—that were pushing America to push its pilots and its aircraft designers. In October 1957, Armstrong and the rest of the country had been caught by surprise when the Russians launched the first human-made satellite into space.

6   This metallic, beeping sphere was nicknamed Sputnik by the Russians (known then as the Soviet Union or the USSR—Union of Soviet Socialist Republics). The translation of the word *sputnik*—"little traveler"—seemed pretty harmless, but the implications of the Soviet Union having an "eye in the sky" were anything but.

7   America was locked in a Cold War with the Soviet Union. The two countries had completely different political and economic beliefs, and each viewed the other as a potential opponent in nuclear war. When Soviet premier Nikita Khrushchev told Westerners, "We will bury you," Americans had good reason to fear this sprawling and determined superpower.

implications   The implications of a statement or an event are the conclusions that can be drawn, but are not directly stated.

Military pilots all, the Mercury Seven pose for a NASA publicity shot. From the left: Scott Carpenter, navy; Gordon Cooper, air force; John Glenn, marines; Gus Grissom, air force; Wally Schirra, navy; Alan Shepard, navy; and Deke Slayton, air force.

8   Sputnik quickly coaxed America's behind-the-scenes air and space research out into the open. By 1958, NACA—the National Advisory Committee for Aeronautics—had been rechristened NASA—the National Aeronautics and Space Administration— and the organization was moving full-tilt toward something big. The space race was on.

9   While NACA had focused on advancing our nation's aeronautical technology within Earth's atmosphere, NASA was looking beyond the horizon, way beyond. The new agency would be adding space-related research and development to its list of priorities. Shortly after changing its name and its mission, NASA would begin interviewing and testing pilots from across the country—the best of the best—for a new and dangerous assignment. NASA was on the hunt for astronauts!

10   In 1958, the space agency was still gearing up for the next two years of change and challenge. Young Neil Armstrong was not yet interested in being either an astronaut or an astronaut candidate. He was just happy to be living out the test pilot's credo of *Higher, faster, and farther* on a daily basis.

aeronautics   Aeronautics is the science of air travel.
priorities   Things that are priorities are very important.

11   Armstrong quickly earned a reputation as a brilliant engineer—and as someone who carefully guarded everything he did and said. His deep and abiding shyness was sometimes mistaken for arrogance or aloofness. He was fiercely protective of his privacy and was never one to engage in idle chitchat. Everything he did and said seemed to have a purpose behind it. Milt Thompson, one of his fellow pilots at NACA, would later comment that "I knew him . . . but I didn't know him."

12   Armstrong had a quiet determination and a distrust of strangers outside his "clan" or circle of intimate family and friends.

13   Armstrong watched with detached interest in 1959 when NASA paraded the seven astronauts of Project Mercury before a public that was hungry for some kind of Cold War victory. Project Mercury, which began in 1958, was the first installment of America's space program and involved its first effort to launch humans into space. It would be followed by projects Gemini and Apollo. The objectives of Project Mercury, which made six manned flights from 1961 to 1963, were:

- To orbit a manned spacecraft around Earth.
- To investigate man's ability to function in space.
- To return both man and spacecraft safely back to Earth.

14   By 1963, all of the goals for Project Mercury had been successfully met.

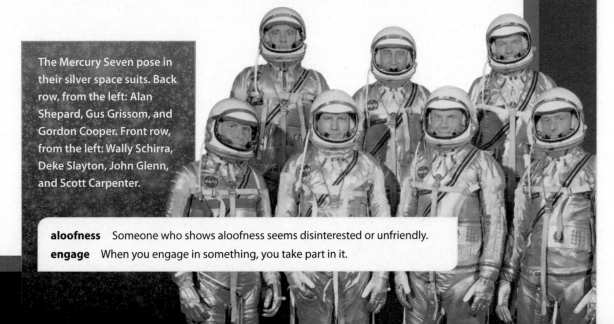

The Mercury Seven pose in their silver space suits. Back row, from the left: Alan Shepard, Gus Grissom, and Gordon Cooper. Front row, from the left: Wally Schirra, Deke Slayton, John Glenn, and Scott Carpenter.

aloofness   Someone who shows aloofness seems disinterested or unfriendly.
engage   When you engage in something, you take part in it.

Up in the Air

15 The early 1960s were a dynamic and exciting time in American technology, especially flight and space technology. As Armstrong threw himself into his test-piloting work, the Mercury Seven astronauts were making demands regarding their pending spaceflights. They wanted control of the spacecraft— they wanted to actually fly it. As a result, the program began to change from launches, where the astronaut was present but the flight was mainly controlled from the ground, to the active participation of skilled professional pilots.

The Space Race Heats Up

16 On April 12, 1961, America got a shock much bigger than the one delivered by Sputnik. This time the Russians announced that they had achieved yet another first: A Soviet cosmonaut named Yuri Gagarin had become the first human being to fly in space. Aboard his spacecraft, *Vostok 1*, Gagarin had orbited Earth one time.

Russian cosmonaut Yuri Gagarin became the first man in space on April 12, 1961. Up to that point, America had only managed to launch a few monkeys.

The United States responded to Yuri Gagarin's flight by quickly launching Alan Shepard, pictured here, aboard a Mercury Redstone rocket for a brief suborbital hop on May 5, 1961.

17   American scientists were caught off guard. Most people assumed that Sputnik had been a fluke. Most people assumed that America had far more technological skill than the Soviet Union. Suddenly it became very clear that the USSR was a serious contender in the space race. America could not afford to be casual, but it was not yet ready to send a man into orbit. The best NASA could offer was to attempt to launch a man into space for a brief visit. He would not circle Earth as Gagarin had done, but at least he would get a taste of weightlessness and the challenges of space travel. Something had to be done. Russia was clearly gaining the lead. The world now turned its attention toward the United States to see how it would respond.

18   The response was Alan Shepard. On May 5, 1961, NASA launched Shepard and his *Freedom 7* Mercury capsule into the sky for a fifteen-minute suborbital hop. It wasn't as impressive as Gagarin's actual orbit of Earth, but it showed that America was not going to sit back and let Russia claim the heavens.

19   Shortly after Shepard, Gus Grissom made a slightly longer suborbital launch in the *Liberty Bell 7* Mercury spacecraft. Once again, it was a successful flight, except that Gus's capsule hatch blew shortly after splashdown, causing the spacecraft to sink and prompting a hasty helicopter rescue of one soggy, frustrated astronaut.

NASA's New Challenges

20 The first two Mercury flights were enough to give America hope that NASA could effectively respond to the Russian challenge. They also were encouraging to Neil Armstrong, who continued to monitor the space race and consider the role he might play in conquering these new frontiers.

21 Although Armstrong still preferred the idea of winged aircraft, even for space travel, his interest was piqued with John Glenn's orbital flight on February 20, 1962. For almost an hour and a half, Glenn and his *Friendship 7* spacecraft circled Earth at 17,544 miles per hour, achieving three full orbits (two more than the Russians!) before splashing down southeast of Bermuda.

22 America's space program had finally come of age, and there was no turning back. NASA now began eyeing the challenges of extended space flight.

John Glenn—shown in front of *Friendship 7*—was the first American to orbit Earth. The spacecraft made three full orbits on February 20, 1962.

Becoming an Astronaut

23 In mid-September 1962, Neil was formally introduced to America as one of "the New Nine," as the second astronaut group was dubbed. Also making the cut were Air Force Major Frank Borman, Navy Lieutenant Charles "Pete" Conrad, Navy Lieutenant Commander James Lovell Jr., Air Force Captain James McDivitt, civilian Elliott See Jr., Air Force Captain Thomas Stafford, Air Force Captain Edward White III, and Navy Lieutenant Commander John Young.

24 Although America worshipped the astronauts as if they were rock stars or movie idols, their day-to-day work was anything but glamorous. The New Nine immediately went back to school so that they were fully prepared for their upcoming spaceflights. Time was something they had little of as they rushed from hands-on training to survival school, classroom studies on topics such as orbital mechanics, publicity appearances, and continuing proficiency training in jet aircraft such as the T-33, T-38, and F-102.

25 They "enjoyed" periodic flights in an aircraft endearingly dubbed "the vomit comet." This was a Boeing KC-135 that could create periods of weightlessness by climbing steeply into the air then dropping into a sharp dive that simulated zero gravity for a few seconds. The experience gave astronaut trainees the opportunity to see how their bodies would react to weightlessness.

The New Nine astronauts were introduced to the public in late 1962. Pictured from the left, back row, are Elliott See, James McDivitt, James Lovell, Edward White, and Thomas Stafford; front row, Charles Conrad, Frank Borman, Neil Armstrong, and John Young.

Reaching for the Moon

26 With renewed commitment to excellence and safety, the NASA team threw itself into the Apollo program in the hope of achieving John F. Kennedy's goal: putting a man on the moon by the end of the 1960s. Armstrong's time was consumed by training and by the development of flight simulators.

27 In October 1968, *Apollo 7*, the first manned Apollo mission, was launched. The mission was largely a confidence builder. The spacecraft had been completely redesigned, and NASA wanted the public to know that the program was back on track. Former Mercury astronaut Wally Schirra commanded the eleven-day Apollo mission, accompanied by newcomers Donn Eisele and Walter Cunningham.

28 *Apollo 7* was a success if by no other measure than that it launched, flew, and came home in one piece. Schirra and his crew performed with typical skill and commitment, despite developing head colds in mid-flight.

29 Armstrong served on the *Apollo 8* backup crew and watched with interest as his colleagues did the impossible. The Apollo spacecraft had only one successful mission under its belt, which was nowhere near the magnitude of a trip to the moon. Likewise, the powerful Saturn V booster—the rocket launcher that would propel the Apollo spacecraft beyond the atmosphere—had only been tested a couple of times and had demonstrated more than its share of problems.

simulators   Simulators are devices that artificially create the effect of being in certain conditions, such as being in space.

Earthrise, shot from the *Apollo 8* spacecraft. This remains one of the most stunning photos in human history.

Privately, there were those at NASA who questioned the safety and sanity of the mission. Armstrong, however, saw the wisdom of the decision, noting that "the time schedule was becoming an overbearing issue. To get the job done by the end of the decade, we needed to take giant steps and really make lots of progress on each flight, and this was the only way."

The Assignment of a Lifetime

30   Soon after, Deke Slayton, NASA's Director of Flight Crew Operations, summoned Armstrong to his office. There he shared the historic news that Neil would command the *Apollo 11* mission—and that, if *Apollo 8* returned safely and all went well on 9 and 10, Armstrong would likely be captaining the first moon landing.

31   Although Armstrong had been handed an assignment unlike any in history, he was careful to keep everything in perspective. Many events had to unfold with great precision in order to make *Apollo 11* the moon landing. "A lot of things we just didn't know at that point and I think I did not really expect that we'd get the chance to try a lunar landing on that flight," Neil recalled. "Too many things could go wrong on [*Apollo*] 8, 9 or 10, or whatever."

32   Slayton talked to Armstrong at length about who his crewmates should be. They decided on Edwin "Buzz" Aldrin and Mike Collins.

The prime crew of *Apollo 11*: From the left are astronauts Neil Armstrong, commander; Michael Collins, command module pilot; and Edwin "Buzz" Aldrin Jr., lunar module pilot.

Armstrong tries on his space suit.

Armstrong and Aldrin simulate collecting lunar samples in a training camp.

33   Nineteen sixty-nine began with considerable fanfare and optimism, as President Lyndon Johnson awarded medals to the triumphant crew of *Apollo* 8 while NASA made public the names of the *Apollo* 11 crew—and the fact that they would be training for a possible lunar landing.

34   For Neil Armstrong, always the calm and focused engineer, it was business as usual. He and his crewmates threw themselves into training for what would certainly be the longest—and arguably the most significant—flight of the twentieth century.

Preparing for Launch

35   After spending Fourth of July weekend 1969 with his family, Armstrong went into quarantine with the other two astronauts so they wouldn't pick up any bugs that might delay the launch. Everyone was acutely aware that the eyes of the world were on this mission. The three astronauts held a nationally televised press conference on July 14, but they spoke from a private room and were interviewed over closed-circuit television by journalists.

36   Jan Armstrong brought her sons Ricky and Mark to Florida for the launch. She planned to view it from a friend's boat in the Banana River, several miles away.

37   At 4:10 on the morning of July 16, Deke Slayton tapped on the door to the astronauts' quarters and summoned them to their last Earth-bound breakfast for a while. Steak and eggs had become the traditional meal on launch day, with a strong cup of coffee to wash it all down. Then began the lengthy and often uncomfortable process of outfitting the astronauts for space travel. The bulky space suits were just the finishing touch. The astronauts needed to be outfitted with numerous layers of material and gadgets—including unpleasant devices that would allow them to use the bathroom in space without making a mess. Remember, in zero gravity, everything floats!

38   As the astronauts climbed into the NASA van that would take them to their spacecraft, thousands of anxious spectators crowded the beaches, streets, and yards in the Cape Canaveral/Cocoa Beach area. In the viewing stands, a mile from launchpad 39A, sat U.S. congressmen, governors, and special guests, including Armstrong's brother, Dean, and his sister, June Hoffman.

39   Back in Wapakoneta, Ohio, Neil's parents were watching their television set. They were hardly alone. All over America, parents were waking their children. Families were huddled in front of the "boob tube" waiting for the historic moment when *Apollo 11* would leave Earth and begin its journey to the moon.

Armstrong, Collins, and Aldrin on launch day

Launch day captured the attention of everyone in America. The viewing stand hosted dignitaries including Vice President Spiro T. Agnew, far right, along with former President Lyndon B. Johnson (center) and his wife, Ladybird.

Liftoff

40 At 6:52 a.m., Armstrong stepped into the *Columbia* and took the left seat. In the Apollo spacecraft, as in airplanes, the commander flew "left seat" while the copilot flew "right seat." Mike Collins settled into the right seat position, as the man who would be flying the command module while Buzz and Neil were on the lunar surface. Buzz, the lunar module pilot, took his place in the middle.

41 All the months of training, frustration, and preparation had come down to this one moment. In a matter of seconds, the historic journey would begin. The astronauts were confident but hardly relaxed. Even they could not know with certainty how the trip would end. Would they come back triumphant? Would they come back at all?

42 At roughly 9:32 a.m., the giant engines of the Saturn V rocket sprang to life and the towering spacecraft summoned all of its 7.6 million pounds of thrust and slowly lifted off the pad.

43 "Lift off! We have lift-off!" came the announcement from an exuberant Mission Control in Houston.

44 Throughout the launch, Armstrong's hand had stayed near the abort handle. If there was any sign of trouble, he was to twist the handle and trigger the escape tower that would blast the command module out of harm's way. And trouble could come in many forms. The crew of

Apollo 11 was sitting high atop what amounted to a 363-foot-tall bomb, loaded with kerosene, hydrogen, and oxygen. A major malfunction could result in a massive fireball that would be seen all over central Florida.

45   But Armstrong soon reported to Mission Control that the launch was a smooth one. "That Saturn gave us a magnificent ride," he told Houston.

46   Back on Earth, Jan and the boys prepared to head back to Texas—but not before chatting with the press about the launch. Exhausted and eager to get home, Jan remained positive for the public: "It was a tremendous sight. I was just thrilled."

47   Up in space, Neil and his crew were getting down to the business of flying a spaceship. It would take almost three days for them to reach the moon and begin their lunar orbit.

48   On the night of July 19, the astronauts slept fitfully. It was impossible not to be edgy and alert. Only sixty-six years earlier, Orville and Wilbur Wright had tested a small, odd-looking flying machine over the sands of Kitty Hawk, North Carolina. The next morning, Armstrong and Aldrin would be testing a small, odd-looking flying machine over the dusty surface of a dark and airless world. There would be no second chance.

Left: *Apollo 11* launches into a crisp blue Florida sky, as thousands crowd the streets and beaches to watch.

Right: Neil Armstrong practices for the moon landing in a lunar module simulator.

The *Eagle* Has Landed

49 Mike Collins was now, officially, the loneliest person in history. Never had a human being been more cut off from his fellow man than Collins was as Armstrong and Aldrin climbed into the lunar module (LM), undocked, and began their descent to the lunar surface. All alone inside the command module, Collins was 250,000 miles from Earth and sixty miles above his traveling companions.

The Risk of Exploration

50 At this point, no one was taking anything for granted. In fact, Collins's training had included how to return home solo if Armstrong and Aldrin were lost somewhere between the command module and the moon. It was not something Collins wanted to think about—especially as he sat alone in the orbiting command module and eyed the hostile, ashen landscape some sixty miles beneath him—but he was a professional and he had to be ready for anything.

51 The two LM passengers were also well aware of the risks of the moon shot. In fact, they had frankly discussed the possibility that they might not make it through the mission alive.

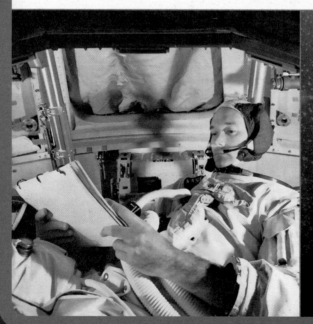

Mike Collins studies the *Apollo 11* flight plan during simulation training at Kennedy Space Center.

52   But the astronauts of *Apollo* 11 understood what all explorers know: that discovering new horizons and divergent paths cannot be done without risk. Someone has to be willing to step forward and assume that risk. Someone has to be willing to offer his or her own life to move humankind to a new vantage point.

A Decision Under Pressure

53   As Armstrong and Aldrin maneuvered the LM closer to the moon, they stayed in radio contact with Mike Collins in the command module and with Mission Control in Houston. Fellow astronaut Charlie Duke was serving as capcom (capsule communicator) at Mission Control for this mission. It was Duke's job to relay information between the astronauts and the technical experts in Houston who were monitoring every aspect of the LM's descent.

54   In an instant Aldrin and Armstrong's concentration was broken by the scream of an alarm inside the tiny LM.

55   "Program alarm," Armstrong announced to Mission Control. "It's a 1202."

56   More than a quarter million miles away, the guys in Houston were scrambling to determine the seriousness of a 1202 alarm. So many things could go wrong on this complex mission, and it would only take one problem to wreck the landing—or worse.

Staff at Mission Control in Houston, Texas, monitor the lunar module's descent to the moon.

57   Flight Director Gene Kranz paced tensely as his staff researched the origins of a 1202 alarm. Twenty-six-year-old Steve Bales, the guidance officer for that day, was consulting with his associates Gran Paules and Jack Garman. The Mission Control computers were frustratingly slow at spitting out any usable data, but Bales and Garman were certain they had an answer.

58   "Give us a reading on the 1202 program alarm." Neil Armstrong's voice carried just a hint of urgency, detectable even across the void of space.

59   Again Kranz raised an eyebrow in the direction of his guidance officer. Steve Bales's voice cracked slightly as he announced with as much certainty as he could muster in the nineteen seconds he'd had to make a decision, "We're go on that, flight"—meaning that the alarm was not anything serious.

60   The controllers had agreed that the alarm was a minor glitch— just a matter of the computer system "thinking" it was overloaded. Years later, Bales would acknowledge that, while certain of his decision, he was *only* certain in the context of their Earth-bound simulations. Everything happening up on the moon was completely new. All bets were off and, for the moment at least, the future of the American space program rested on nineteen seconds of consideration by a twenty-six-year-old and a twenty-four-year-old.

61   "We've got you . . . we're go on that alarm," Charlie Duke radioed to the LM.

62   "Roger," Armstrong replied and turned his attentions back to the complexities of landing the LM.

63   Seconds later the alarm blared again. And once more Houston reassured the astronauts that all was well.

The *Apollo 11* mission patch with an American bald eagle settling on the moon's surface visually reflects the success of the *Eagle's* landing.

Right: Flight Director Eugene Kranz would make the final decision on whether conditions were suitable for the LM to actually land on the moon's surface.

Left: The *Apollo 11* command and service module is photographed through the window of the lunar module on its way to the moon's surface.

64 As the LM drew closer to the lunar surface, Armstrong could see that their anticipated landing site was peppered with huge rocks. In order for the duo to return safely to the command and service module, the *Eagle* had to land on a flat, smooth area. Armstrong saw no such terrain from his tiny window.

65 It was time to override the automatic landing system and manually fly the *Eagle* to safer terrain. But with sixty seconds of fuel remaining, it would take total concentration and two cool heads to pull victory from the jaws of disaster.

Landing the *Eagle*

66 Aldrin recited the computer readouts as Armstrong quietly maneuvered the LM over the rocky terrain.

67 "Thirty seconds," came Charlie Duke's urgent reminder from Houston. Dust from the moon powdered up around the feet of the LM as it sank toward a flat surface that Armstrong had finally spied from the *Eagle*.

68   "Contact light!" Buzz called out, signaling that the LM's feet were almost on the ground. After a few seconds, Charlie Duke radioed back, "We copy you down, *Eagle*."

69   A second of silence hung tensely in the air before Neil Armstrong radioed back the historic words, "Houston, Tranquility Base here. The *Eagle* has landed."

70   "Roger Tranquility. We copy you on the ground," the capcom radioed back. "You got a bunch of guys about to turn blue. We're breathing again. Thanks."

71   And then, for a brief moment, there were no polished professional engineers manning the panels at Mission Control; there was only a crowd of excited kids, whooping, hollering, and slapping one another on the back.

72   Across America, people were similarly celebrating and breathing sighs of relief. Most adults and many children would forever recall where they were and what they were doing the moment that man first landed on the moon.

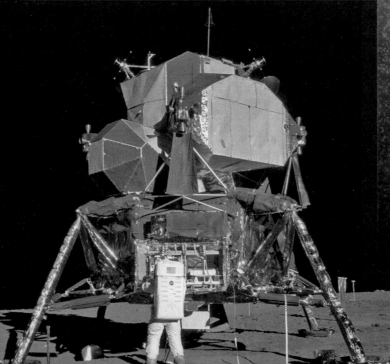

Above: Mission Control in Houston, TX, celebrates *Apollo 11*.

Left: The Lunar Module *Eagle* on the moon

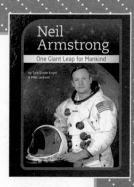

Collaborative Discussion

Look back at what you wrote on page 40. Tell a partner two things you learned from this text. Then work with a group to discuss the questions below. Refer to details and examples in *Neil Armstrong: One Giant Leap for Mankind* to explain your answers. Take notes for your responses. When you speak, use your notes.

1 What events had to happen over many years so that Neil Armstrong could land on the moon? Consider events from other countries, the United States, and Armstrong's own life.

2 On page 45, a fellow pilot says of Armstrong, "I knew him . . . but I didn't know him." What does he mean by that, and why was this quotation included in the text?

3 If you were Mike Collins, what would you have thought and felt as you remained alone in the space shuttle while the *Eagle* made its way to the moon? Use details from the text to support your response.

Listening Tip

Listen to the details a speaker gives when answering a question. Think of different, yet related, details that you can add.

Speaking Tip

When it is your turn to add to the discussion, say each word clearly. Use a speaking pace that is not too fast or too slow.

Write a Job Listing

PROMPT

Neil Armstrong had qualities that made him a very successful astronaut. NASA recognized these qualities before Armstrong ever went into space.

Write a job listing to help NASA find future astronauts. Include the physical, technical, and personal traits that would help to identify the best people for the job.

PLAN

Brainstorm five traits that a person needs to be a good astronaut. Include at least one physical, one technical, and one personal trait on your list. Refer to *Neil Armstrong: One Giant Leap for Mankind* to help you come up with ideas.

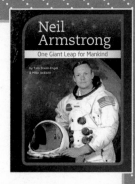

WRITE

Now write your job listing for future astronauts based on details from *Neil Armstrong: One Giant Leap for Mankind.*

✓ Make sure your job listing

- ☐ begins by identifying the employer and the job.

- ☐ identifies five traits that a person needs to become an astronaut.

- ☐ includes at least one physical, one technical, and one personal trait.

- ☐ is brief with a formal tone.

Prepare to Read

GENRE STUDY **Personal narratives** tell about an important event in a real person's life.

- Personal narratives include first-person pronouns such as *I, me, my, mine,* and *we.*

- Some personal narratives include a theme or lesson learned by the author.

- Authors of personal narratives often present events in sequential, or chronological, order. This helps readers understand what happened in the person's life and when.

SET A PURPOSE **Think about** the title and genre of this text. What do you know about the moon landing and astronauts? What would you like to learn? Write your ideas below.

Meet the Author:
Mark Polansky

CRITICAL VOCABULARY

inevitable

module

ascent

legacy

THE MOON LANDING

INSPIRED ME TO BECOME AN ASTRONAUT

by Mark Polansky

1969

"ABOVE ALL, I REMEMBER THE MOON LANDING."

1   I turned 13 that year, the last year of the '60s. I recall so much from that decade, even if I didn't understand it at the time. The U.S. Civil Rights movement in full bloom. A young American president assassinated. The Vietnam War's escalation. The Cold War.

2   Above all, I remember the moon landing.

3   In my middle school, black and white TVs rolled into classrooms whenever there was a launch of American astronauts. Out came the rabbit ears (a TV antenna for those unable to fathom the world without cable, satellites, and Wi-Fi), the TV turned on, and we'd watch the shuttles launch live. Astronauts became my heroes, and when the inevitable question came as to what I wanted to do when I grew up, the answer was easy.

4   By the summer of 1969, the whole world knew that the United States was sending astronauts to the moon—two of the three Apollo 11 crew members were going to land on, walk on, and return home from it. Was this possible? I later learned President Richard Nixon had

---

inevitable   Something inevitable is certain to happen.

prepared a speech in the event the crew didn't make it home.

5   That summer, my mom packed my suitcase for my annual summer visit with my grandmother and aunt in Manhattan. It was July: there would be baseball games, museums, movies. Yet, this visit was fated to be a bit different from the others. On July 20, 1969, I sat in the mezzanine of Yankee Stadium. I don't remember who was playing that day, but I remember that the game was interrupted by news that the Apollo 11 lunar module had landed on the moon.

6   The stadium erupted in cheers; everyone stood and broke out into an impromptu rendition of "America the Beautiful." That evening, I stayed up, rewarded by the sights and sounds of Neil Armstrong and Buzz Aldrin descending Apollo 11's ladder and stepping onto the moon for the first time.

7   We know the facts about the Apollo program and missions, but do you ever wonder what Neil, Buzz, and command module pilot Michael Collins thought about before, during, and after the mission? Did they worry? Did the experience change them? If so, how? Though I never walked on the moon, almost 32 years after that day in Yankee Stadium, I earned a chance to understand it.

2001

8   On February 7, 2001, I strapped into my seat as the pilot of STS-98 onboard the Space Shuttle Atlantis. Was I worried? Yes. About my safety? No. As the launch clock counted down, I thought through my responsibilities for the eight-and-a-half minute ascent and the rest of my mission. So many men and women had put their blood, sweat, and tears into preparing the vehicle, our precious cargo (the U.S. laboratory Destiny), and into training us. I had to do my job—and do it well—or I would let the whole team down. This mission wasn't about me.

9   A little while after I reached orbit, I finally was able to unstrap, float to the shuttle mid-deck, and remove my launch suit. As I began to drift, a crewmate grabbed me, pressed my face to a window, and told me to look back at the Earth.

module   A module is a self-contained part of a spacecraft that can operate away from the rest of the spacecraft.

ascent   An ascent is an upward movement.

67

"TO PROTECT THE EARTH, WE MUST WORK TOGETHER."

10   It was the first moment that I had had a chance to observe it from space. As I looked at the majesty of our planet from 200 miles above, I was overcome with emotion. I thought of my fiancé and parents, but especially my dad. His health was failing, and I had been concerned that he might not make it to my launch. I was ecstatic knowing he did. He passed away four months later.

11   Over three shuttle missions, I always found time to view Earth—a reminder that the mission was not about me. Watching the world go by at roughly five miles per second creates a unique perspective: It's nearly impossible to tell where one country's border ends and another begins.

12   What did Neil and Buzz think about when they walked the moon? Every anniversary of their landing brings forth vivid boyhood memories for me, but it's also a time when I can't help but reflect on what I learned as an astronaut. Two men were put on the moon through the work of thousands. To protect Earth, we must work together in the same way. Humans have to teach ourselves to co-exist peacefully and sustainably— that's the true legacy of Apollo 11.

legacy   A legacy is the ongoing impact of something from the past.

Collaborative Discussion

Look back at what you wrote on page 64. Tell a partner two things you learned from this text. Then work with a group to discuss the questions below. Refer to details and examples in *The Moon Landing Inspired Me to Become an Astronaut* to explain your answers. Take notes for your responses. When you speak, use your notes.

1. Reread page 67. Why do you think those in the stadium chose to sing "America the Beautiful"? What might they have been thinking and feeling?

2. Why do you think it is meaningful to the author that from space, it is "nearly impossible to tell where one country's border ends and another begins"?

3. How has the author's view of space travel and exploration changed over the course of his life? Use examples from the text to support your ideas.

 Listening Tip

Sometimes, a group member might speak too softly. If that happens, politely ask the person to speak a little louder.

 Speaking Tip

Do not speak until your group leader calls on you. Then make sure you speak clearly and make eye contact with each group member.

Write a Thank You Email

PROMPT

Mark Polansky was thirteen years old when Neil Armstrong landed on the moon. That achievement, and other achievements of American astronauts, inspired Polansky to become an astronaut himself.

What if Polansky could have thanked Neil Armstrong during one of his NASA missions? Write a thank you email that Polansky could have sent to Armstrong from space to express his gratitude to Armstrong for inspiring him to become an astronaut.

PLAN

Make notes about how Neil Armstrong inspired Polansky and reasons Polansky is grateful that he became an astronaut based on details in *The Moon Landing Inspired Me to Become an Astronaut.*

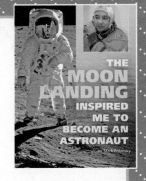

WRITE

Now write your thank you email by Mark Polanksy from *The Moon Landing Inspired Me to Become an Astronaut.*

✔ Make sure your thank you email

☐ is addressed to Neil Armstrong, and is signed by Mark Polansky.
☐ includes an expression of thanks to Armstrong.
☐ explains how Armstrong inspired Polansky.
☐ describes what Polansky likes about being an astronaut.
☐ is written from Polansky's point of view.

Notice & Note
Extreme or Absolute Language

Prepare to Read

GENRE STUDY **Persuasive texts** give an author's opinion about a topic and try to convince readers to believe that opinion.

- Authors of persuasive texts may organize their ideas by explaining causes and effects.

- Persuasive texts include evidence, such as facts and examples, to support the author's viewpoint.

- Persuasive texts include strong language and techniques to convince readers to believe their viewpoint. This text includes language that appeals to readers' emotions, such as excitement and curiosity.

SET A PURPOSE **Think about** the title and genre of this text. Why might people want to live on Mars? Why would someone try to convince others to move to Mars?

CRITICAL VOCABULARY

colonize

anticipates

enabling

mania

plague

prohibitive

venture

ordeal

barriers

entice

Build Background:
Mars

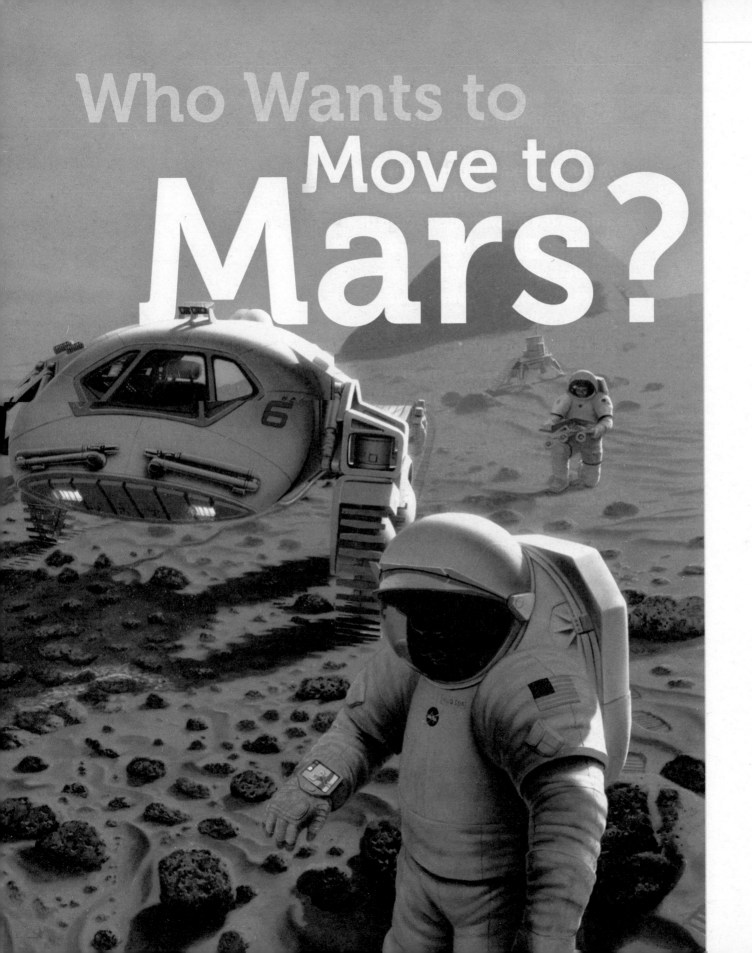

Who Wants to Move to Mars?

1   Once we worried about Martians invading Earth. Now some Americans believe earthlings should invade Mars and establish a colony there. Who exactly thinks this and why? Chris Impey is an astronomer who is among the individuals leading the charge to **colonize** Mars. Impey predicts we'll establish a colony there by 2045. He believes we need a "fallback planet" in case Earth becomes uninhabitable.

2   Stephen Petranek agrees with Impey about the fallback planet. Petranek is a journalist who writes about science and technology. He has written a book titled *How We'll Live on Mars*. Just as its title suggests, Petranek's book lays out his ideas about how reaching and living on Mars could be possible.

3   Along with individuals such as Impey and Petranek, several organizations hope to send people to Mars, some with the goal of establishing a settlement there. Here is a look at three of them.

colonize   To colonize a place means to go there and take control of it.

Mars One

4   The Mars One project is a Dutch nonprofit founded by entrepreneur Bas Lansdorp and physicist Arno Wielders. As explained on its website, "Mars One aims to establish a permanent human settlement on Mars." The plan is to start by completing a series of unmanned cargo missions, which will deliver rovers, a communications satellite, living units, and other equipment and supplies needed to make Mars inhabitable.

5   In the meantime, a crew of astronauts will be selected and trained here on Earth. Who will they be? Mars One hopes to recruit volunteers from around the world, in the hopes that their project will inspire global unity. When the crewmembers are ready—and Mars has been made ready for them—the first manned mission will launch. The Mars One leadership team anticipates that this will happen in 2031.

6   Unlike some Mars-related enterprises, the Mars One team has no intention of becoming involved in space tourism, or sending humans to Mars for exploration purposes only. "The Mars One crews will go to Mars not to simply visit, but to live, explore, and create a second home for humanity," the team explains. "The first men and women to go to Mars are going there to stay."

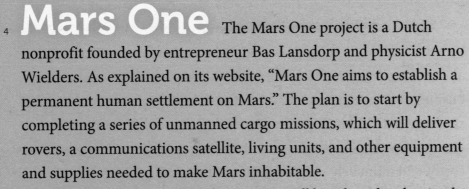

Bas Lansdorp of the Mars One project

anticipates Someone who anticipates an event is aware of what will happen and takes action to be prepared for it.

SpaceX

7 SpaceX is a private company founded in 2002 by entrepreneur Elon Musk. Musk—who is also the founder of PayPal and co-founder of the Tesla automotive company, among other businesses—is among the wealthiest people in America. As a lifelong space enthusiast, Musk decided to invest some of his considerable fortune in SpaceX, with the goal of making space travel easier and less costly, and ultimately enabling humans to colonize Mars. Musk believes that becoming interplanetary should be the next step in human development. "Fundamentally the future is vastly more exciting and interesting if we are a space-faring civilization and a multi-planet species than if we are not," he explains. Like many other would-be space colonists, Musk also thinks that the ability to live on other planets might someday be essential to our survival.

8 So far, SpaceX has had some successes in developing and launching spacecraft. In 2012, the SpaceX Dragon became the first commercial spacecraft to deliver cargo to the International Space Station. In 2017, the company launched several rockets into orbit. Musk has plans to someday deliver a greenhouse to Mars for growing food. He predicts that SpaceX will establish its first Mars colony—of about 80,000 people—by 2040.

Elon Musk of Space X

enabling If someone is enabling you to do something, they're allowing or helping you to achieve it.

NASA

9   **NASA** No doubt you're familiar with the National Aeronautics and Space Administration. NASA has been at the forefront of space exploration since the 1960s, when it sent the first humans to the moon. Now NASA wants to be the first to send humans to Mars.

10   Currently, NASA is testing a new rocket called the Space Launch System (SLS). It will be capable of launching humans and cargo out of Earth's orbit.

11   Because NASA is a U.S. government organization, it is dependent on federal funding to support its work. If funding permits, NASA hopes to put humans in orbit around Mars sometime in the 2030s. Landing on Mars will happen some time after that.

12   More so than most groups planning missions to Mars, NASA is interested in expanding our scientific knowledge. The group wants to investigate the science and technology involved in getting humans to Mars and keeping them alive there. NASA also wants to explore and learn as much as possible about Mars itself.

NASA's Space Launch System

THE DEBATE:
Should We Colonize Mars?

13 So, are Mars One, SpaceX, NASA, and others headed in the right direction? Is putting humans on Mars really a worthy goal? Here is a look at the arguments for both sides of the issue.

No! **Mars mania is a foolish fantasy.**

14 In recent years, business people, scientists, and thrill seekers alike have become interested in the idea of sending humans to Mars to explore and even settle on the planet. A trip to Mars might sound like the adventure of a lifetime. And colonizing another planet might seem like a convenient solution to the environmental and other woes that plague Earth. But building a human settlement on Mars is a wholly unrealistic idea. Even just visiting the planet is a dubious prospect.

15 First of all, just getting to Mars from Earth would be enormously difficult.

16 No matter how carefully planned and executed, the journey would be fraught with danger. Accidents during launch and landing are possible. Entering Mars's atmosphere would be risky in several ways. Throughout the trip, power outages, equipment failures, and software glitches would be possibilities. That is true of any high-tech

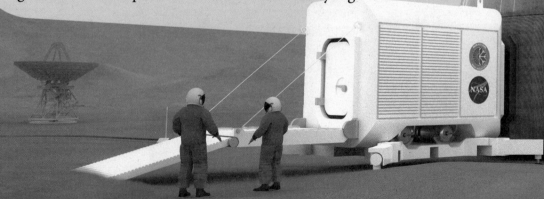

mania If you have mania for something, you have great enthusiasm for it.
plague If you're plagued by bad things, they cause you great discomfort.

environment, but in outer space, such problems could quickly become life threatening.

17   Even if everything went as smoothly as possible, the journey to Mars would be most people's idea of a nightmare. It would last anywhere from six to nine months, depending on both planets' positions in their orbits. That's a very long time to spend in very close quarters with several other people.

18   Passengers would not be riding in luxury, either. The space capsule would be small and tightly packed. Each traveler's personal space—for the entire lengthy journey—would be approximately the size of an SUV. You'd have only freeze-dried space food to eat and little to do for entertainment.

19   You would spend the journey floating upside down and sideways. And that's just one effect of traveling in zero gravity. Over time, your muscles would begin to atrophy and your bones would grow brittle. Your heart, lungs, and digestive system would not function as well as they do on Earth.

20   When you finally arrived on Mars, much bigger problems would await. You would need a spacesuit to survive outdoors for more than a few seconds. Your life as a colonist would be spent entirely indoors—in a habitat yet to be built—when not in your suit.

21   The average temperature on this cold and barren planet is minus 81 degrees Fahrenheit. In addition to the frigid cold, Mars has dust storms about every two years. They last for weeks and block 99 percent of the sun's light. Mars has no breathable air, no liquid water, and no source of food. Most likely, no life exists there. If Mars does support life forms, they are probably just microorganisms.

An artist's rendering of a possible Mars settlement

22   The only water on Mars is frozen beneath the surface. To use it, colonists would need to dig up frozen soil and heat it to melt and extract the icy water. This process would be complicated and require expensive equipment.

23   Creating breathable air would be an even bigger challenge. Frozen water in the soil is also the only source of oxygen on Mars. If the water were liquefied, the oxygen (in the H_2O) could be separated from the hydrogen. This oxygen could be combined with nitrogen extracted from the thin atmosphere of Mars. The result would approximate the air on Earth. But imagine going through all that just to breathe!

24   These are just a few of the obstacles to creating a permanent human settlement on Mars. Then there is the prohibitive cost. The team at Mars One would like to pretend it could send humans to Mars for six billion dollars. But NASA has estimated that such a venture would cost at least 100 billion dollars. Instead of spending an astronomical sum to colonize a hostile planet, why not invest that money to improve life on Earth? Perhaps then we would find ourselves with no need for a "fallback planet."

Sunrise on planet Mars

prohibitive   Something prohibitive is extremely expensive or unaffordable.
venture   A venture is a risky project or undertaking.

Yes!   We *can* colonize Mars, so we *should* colonize Mars.

25   Is colonizing Mars a ridiculous idea? Skeptics have noted that just getting there would be an ordeal. And the first colonists on Mars would face a life of hard work, numerous challenges, and no luxuries. Not only that, but this life might cost more than one billion dollars per person! All of these points are correct. But do they mean we should rule out the notion of sending humans to Mars? Of course not!

26   Colonizing Mars would be difficult, indeed. But it would not be impossible. We have already sent robots to Mars, and we have the know-how to send humans, too. We also know how to make Mars livable once we arrive. We *can* colonize Mars, therefore we should.

27   After all, danger and discomfort have never been barriers to expanding human horizons. Back in the fifteenth and sixteenth centuries, sailing the oceans to unknown lands was nearly as risky and uncomfortable as a journey to Mars. Sailors frequently died from starvation, disease, and storms at sea. But, that did not stop Ferdinand Magellan's fleet of sailors, the first to circumnavigate the globe.

28   Imagine our world today if no one had ever left home to explore faraway lands. Space is now our final frontier, and those who are willing to deal with the hardships should be encouraged to study and explore it firsthand. There are so many reasons that it is worth all the trouble!

29   For one thing, the possibility of joining a Mars mission might entice some of our brightest young minds into STEM fields. As astronomer Neil deGrasse Tyson points outs, the lure of Mars could encourage an "entire generation of students in the educational pipeline to want to become scientists, engineers, technologists, and mathematicians. The next generation of astronauts to land on Mars is in middle school now."

---

ordeal   An ordeal is generally an unpleasant experience.

barriers   Barriers are obstacles or things that make it difficult to achieve a goal.

entice   To entice someone to do something is to persuade them by offering pleasure or advantage.

30   Another reason to colonize Mars is that the best way to search for life there is in person. No, we're not going to find the humanoid Martians that populate fiction. But even living microorganisms buried deep below the surface of Mars would be a monumental discovery. Imagine confirming that life exists on another planet!

31   What's more, exploring another planet could lead to discoveries that improve life here on Earth. Space exploration has already benefited us in many different ways. Satellite imaging systems in space help us monitor natural disasters on Earth. Technology developed for the International Space Station is used to purify drinking water in developing nations. Hardware developed for use in space is now used to perform surgeries and detect cancer. Those tiny digital cameras in our cell phones were originally developed by NASA.

32   Those are just a few of many examples. And the trend is likely to continue.

33   Sending humans to Mars will undoubtedly advance our medical knowledge as we observe how the human body responds to life in space. The challenge of growing crops on Mars may improve earthly farming techniques. And who knows what else we could learn? But the most compelling argument for colonizing Mars is this: It might ensure the survival of our species! War, disease, and climate change may someday threaten our home here on Earth. The future could bring other threats we haven't yet imagined.

34   Most of the leading voices in favor of colonizing Mars argue that humankind needs a fallback planet. Those voices are right. We can colonize Mars and so we should. Our future may depend on it!

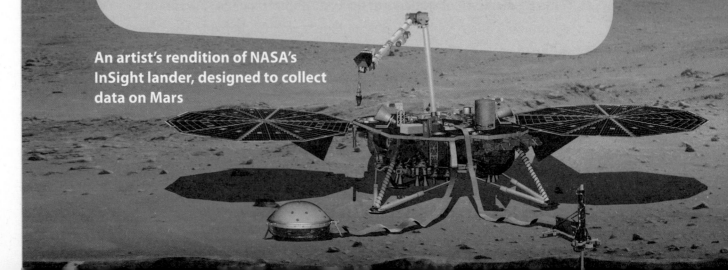

An artist's rendition of NASA's InSight lander, designed to collect data on Mars

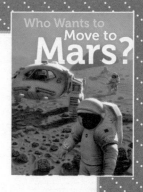

Collaborative Discussion

Look back at what you wrote on page 72. Tell a partner two things you learned from this text. Then work with a group to discuss the questions below. Refer to details and examples in *Who Wants to Move to Mars?* to explain your answers. Take notes for your responses. When you speak, use your notes.

1 Which of the three organizations that wants to explore Mars has the best plan? Why?

2 The argument for living on Mars says that because we *can*, then we *should*. Why is this or isn't this a good reason?

3 Would you want to live on Mars? Use details from the text to support your decision.

Listening Tip

Notice the facial expressions and physical gestures of the speakers in your group. This will help you to understand their ideas.

Speaking Tip

When you speak, make eye contact with the members of your group. This will help you to know whether they understand you.

Write a Letter to the Editor

PROMPT

Who Wants to Move to Mars? describes three separate plans to explore and research Mars. It also presents opposing opinions about whether we should colonize, or live on, Mars. After reading the article, you probably have your own opinion about exploring and colonizing Mars!

Write a letter to the editor that shares your opinion about whether people should explore and colonize Mars. This letter will appear in your local newspaper, so you will want to persuade all of the newspaper's readers, not just the editor. Remember that readers will have different amounts of knowledge on the subject.

PLAN

Identify your opinion and list three pieces of information to support it. Refer to *Who Wants to Move to Mars?* as you form your argument.

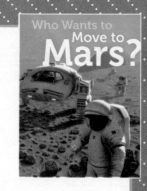

WRITE

Now write your letter to the editor about Mars exploration and colonization using details from *Who Wants to Move to Mars?*

✓ | **Make sure your letter to the editor**

☐ clearly states your opinion.
☐ supports your opinion with facts and details from the text.
☐ uses persuasive language.
☐ invites readers to take action or learn more.

Essential Question

What does it take to explore outer space?

Write an Opinion Essay

PROMPT Think about what you learned about space exploration in this module.

In the last 75 years, achievements in space travel and exploration have been impressive. Interest in space is still growing, and there will surely be more progress made in the future. Write an opinion essay about what people, skills, equipment, and other resources will be necessary for future space travel and exploration. Support your opinion with evidence from at least two of the module's texts.

I will write an opinion essay about _____.

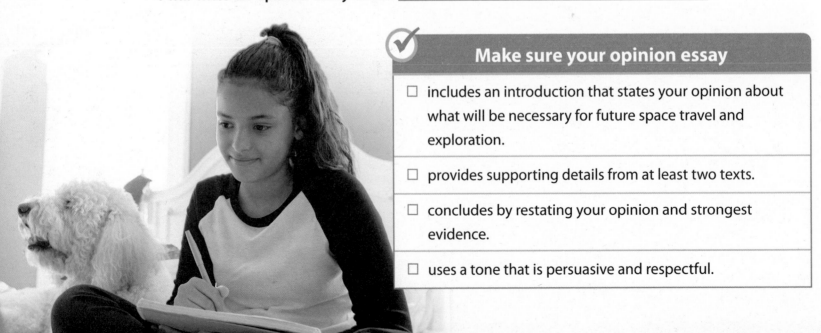

✓ Make sure your opinion essay

- ☐ includes an introduction that states your opinion about what will be necessary for future space travel and exploration.

- ☐ provides supporting details from at least two texts.

- ☐ concludes by restating your opinion and strongest evidence.

- ☐ uses a tone that is persuasive and respectful.

What will be the goals of future space travel and exploration? What will be necessary to meet these goals? Revisit the texts and identify details to help you answer these questions and shape your opinion.

In the chart below, write the topic of your opinion essay (What is necessary for future space travel and exploration?). In the top box, write your opinion about the topic. In the next four boxes, record details from the texts that support your opinion. Use Critical Vocabulary words where appropriate.

My Topic: _____

DRAFT ⋯⋯⋯⋯⋯⋯⋯⋯⋯⋯⋯⋯⋯⋯⋯⋯⋯ Write your opinion essay.

Begin by writing an **introduction** that states your opinion about what will be necessary for future space travel and exploration.

In the **middle paragraphs** of your essay, support your opinion with evidence from at least two texts.

For your **conclusion**, use persuasive language as you restate your opinion and strongest evidence.

The revision and editing steps give you a chance to look carefully at your writing and make changes. Work with a partner to determine whether you have explained your ideas clearly to readers. Use these questions to help you evaluate and improve your article.

✓ PURPOSE/ FOCUS	ORGANIZATION	EVIDENCE	LANGUAGE/ VOCABULARY	CONVENTIONS
☐ Does my essay clearly state my opinion? ☐ Does my essay persuade readers to agree with my opinion?	☐ Does my essay include an introduction and a conclusion? ☐ Does the middle of my essay support my opinion?	☐ Do I use evidence from at least two texts? ☐ Does my text evidence strongly support my opinion?	☐ Do I choose words that are specific and precise? ☐ Do I include Critical Vocabulary words when appropriate?	☐ Have I used correct spelling? ☐ Have I used correct verb tenses?

PUBLISH ·· Share your work.

Create a Finished Copy Make a final copy of your opinion essay. You may wish to include an illustration. Consider these options to share your opinion essay.

1. Publish your essay on a classroom or school blog.

2. Submit your essay to the youth section of a local newspaper or news website.

3. Share your essay in a small group and try to convince others to agree with your opinion about the topic.

Into the Deep

"The sea is home to creatures whose weirdness rivals that of the strangest sci-fi aliens anyone ever imagined."

—Sy Montgomery

? Essential Question

What fascinates us about our seas and shorelines?

Get Curious
Video

Words About Ocean Exploration

The words in the chart will help you talk and write about the selections in this module. Which words about ocean exploration have you seen before? Which words are new to you?

Add to the Vocabulary Network on page 93 by writing synonyms, antonyms, and related words and phrases for each word about ocean exploration.

After you read each selection in this module, come back to the Vocabulary Network and keep building it. Add more boxes if you need to.

WORD	MEANING	CONTEXT SENTENCE
inhabit (verb)	If you inhabit a place, you live in it.	Many types of fish and other creatures inhabit the ocean.
aquatic (adjective)	A plant or animal that is aquatic lives in or around water.	Scientists who study aquatic plants and animals use special equipment to explore the ocean.
invertebrates (noun)	Invertebrates are animals that lack a vertebral column, or spine.	Invertebrates found in the ocean include the octopus, starfish, and jellyfish.
vast (adjective)	Something vast is very large.	I felt very small as I looked out over the vast ocean.

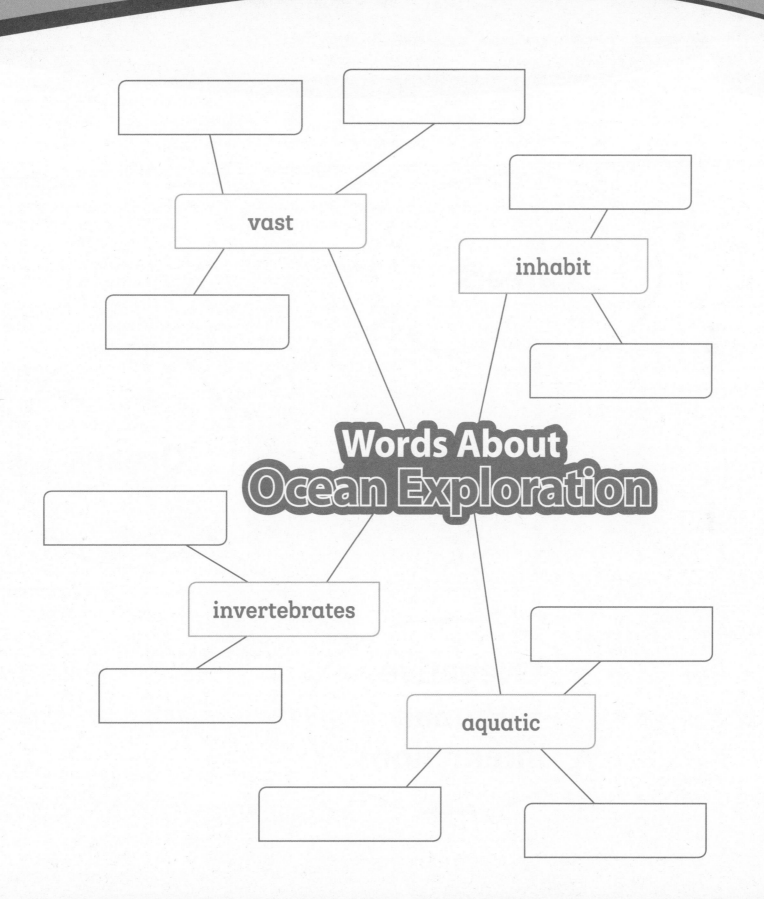

vast

inhabit

Words About Ocean Exploration

invertebrates

aquatic

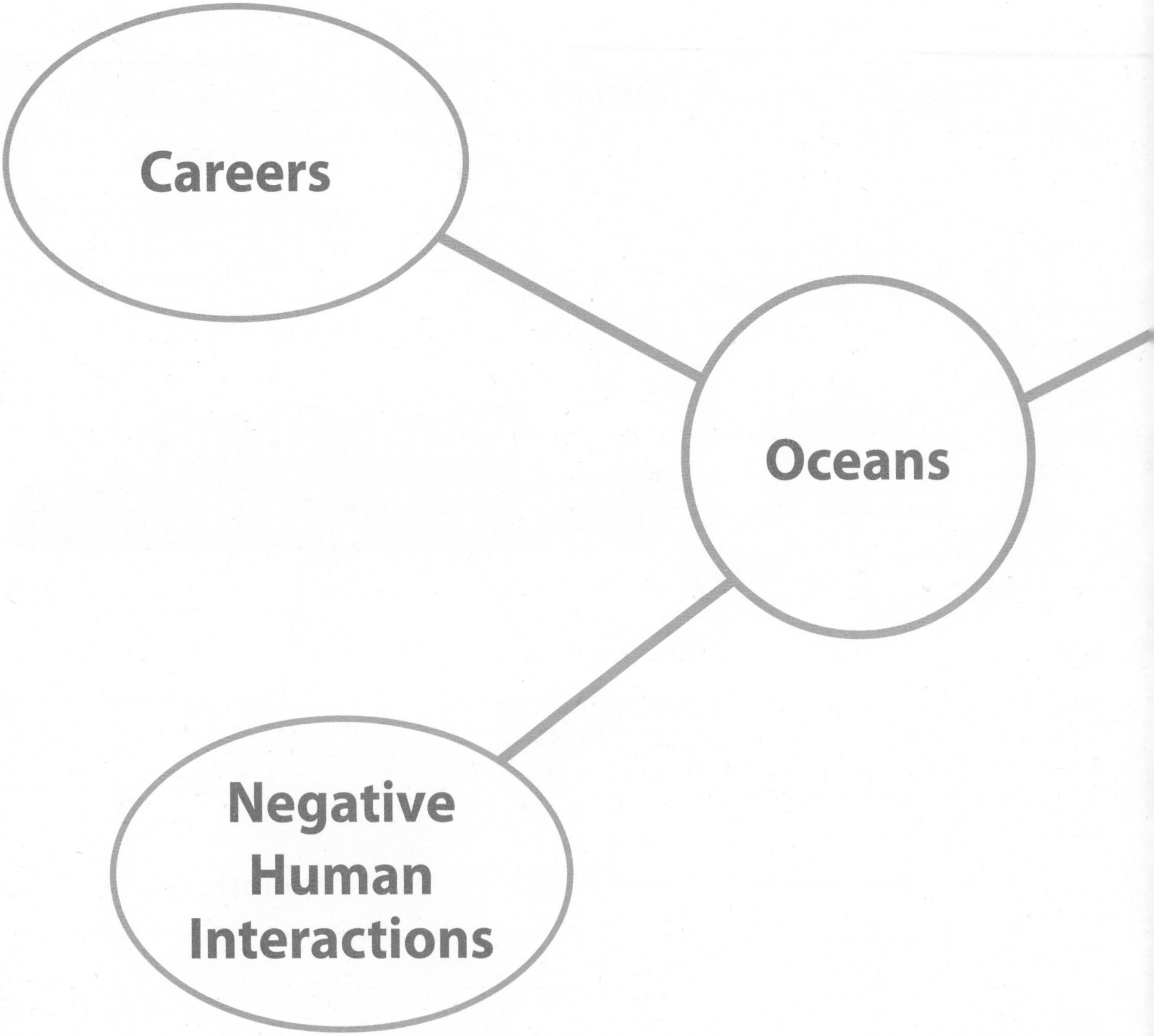

Careers

Oceans

Negative Human Interactions

Positive Human Interactions

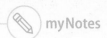

Short Read

IN THE ZONE

Earth's five oceans—Atlantic, Pacific, Indian, Southern (sometimes called Antarctic), and Arctic—cover 70 percent of its surface and contain about 97 percent of all the water on the planet. These vast bodies of water make up 99 percent of all living space on Earth. They provide a home to more than one million known plant and animal species. In addition, some scientists estimate that anywhere from one million to 8 million undiscovered species might inhabit the oceans!

The oceans have three main zones.

The **epipelagic zone** (surface to 660 feet deep) Also known as the **sunlit zone,** this is the brightest and warmest of the zones. The widest variety of marine life dwells here. The presence of sunlight makes photosynthesis possible, so plants can live here. It's the only zone where plants live.

Algae is often called seaweed. It is a term for a diverse group of aquatic organisms that have characteristics of both plants and animals.

The **mesopelagic zone** (330 to 3,300 feet deep) This area is also known as the **twilight zone** because very little sunlight penetrates. The animals that live here have special adaptations for surviving in the dark, such as large eyes for better vision or bioluminescence. That means they glow in the dark.

Swordfish can grow up to 14 feet long and swim as fast as 50 miles per hour.

The **bathypelagic zone** (3,300 to 13,100 feet deep) No sunlight reaches the **midnight zone.** The water here is black, the water pressure is intense, and the temperatures are extremely cold. This zone and the even deeper areas below it encompass 90 percent of the oceans. Yet, they support the fewest life forms by far. Vampire squid, deep sea dragonfish, and giant tubeworms are among the strange-looking creatures that inhabit this zone.

Giant tubeworms make their home on the bottom of the Pacific Ocean. With no mouths or digestive systems, they feed on bacteria that grow inside them.

ARCTIC OCEAN

ATLANTIC
OCEAN

PACIFIC
OCEAN

PACIFIC
OCEAN

INDIAN
OCEAN

SOUTHERN OCEAN

The leatherback sea turtle is the largest of all living turtles.

With almost no natural predators, the Great White shark is the most fearsome shark in this zone.

Rare coelacanths are called "living fossils" because they have been around since dinosaurs walked the earth.

The dwarf lantern shark is smaller than a human hand. Lantern sharks are bioluminescent.

While its body is just six inches long, the deep sea dragonfish has an oversized mouth filled with sharp, fang-like teeth. A light-producing barbel protrudes from the dragonfish's chin. Like a fishing lure, it attracts prey.

Mysterious giant squid are among the most intelligent invertebrates in the ocean. They can grow up to 60 feet long and have the largest eyes of any marine animal— the better to see with at extreme depths.

Prepare to Read and View

GENRE STUDY **Narrative nonfiction** gives factual information by telling a true story.

- Science texts also include words that are specific to the topic.
- Narrative nonfiction often includes visuals, such as photographs and maps.

The Camouflaged Octopus

Informational videos present factual information in visual and audio form. A narrator explains the topic as images on the screen change to support the narration.

SET A PURPOSE **Think about** the title and genre of this text and video. What would you like to learn about octopuses? Explain below.

**Meet the Author:
Sy Montgomery**

CRITICAL VOCABULARY

realm

quarry

probing

manipulation

classifying

disruption

perplexing

mollusks

unfurl

The Octopus Scientists

Exploring the Mind of a Mollusk

by Sy Montgomery

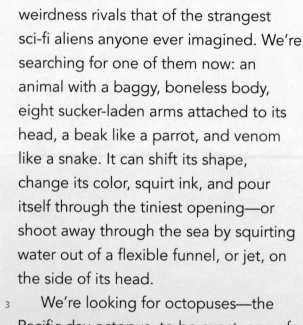

1   The ocean is the world's largest wilderness, covering 70 percent of the surface of the globe. But this vast blue territory is even bigger than it looks from land, or even from space. It's a three-dimensional realm that accounts for more than 95 percent of all livable space on the planet—and most of it is unexplored.

2   The sea is home to creatures whose weirdness rivals that of the strangest sci-fi aliens anyone ever imagined. We're searching for one of them now: an animal with a baggy, boneless body, eight sucker-laden arms attached to its head, a beak like a parrot, and venom like a snake. It can shift its shape, change its color, squirt ink, and pour itself through the tiniest opening—or shoot away through the sea by squirting water out of a flexible funnel, or jet, on the side of its head.

3   We're looking for octopuses—the Pacific day octopus, to be exact, one of perhaps 250 octopus species on the planet. Pacific day octopuses grow to more than four feet long. They're not rare or endangered. Should be pretty easy to find, right?

4   "Pttttttthhhth!"

5   A spout like a small whale's shoots from a snorkel as Jennifer Mather pulls her silver-haired head from the water. She looks through her prescription facemask and waits for the rest of us to surface from the sea. Soon we answer her with a chorus of spouts.

6   Jennifer pulls the snorkel from her mouth. "Find anything?" she asks.

> **realm** The term *realm* is used by scientists to describe a region of the earth's surface.

7   Around us stretches a tropical paradise of palm-fringed mountains. The island's waters teem with fish in neon colors and fantastic shapes. Honeymooners seek its warm blue sea, white beaches, and Polynesian food. But that's not what draws our team of six from three countries to the shallows here surrounding Moorea, a fifty-square-mile, roughly heart-shaped island twelve miles northwest of its much larger neighbor, Tahiti, in the South Pacific.

8   No—we are out here looking for holes. Because where there's a hole, there might be an octopus.

9   "That hole in the middle of that dead coral looks good," says Jennifer, pointing. Near it, she has found an empty shell. She holds it up to show us. That makes *two* pieces of evidence that suggest we could be closing in on our quarry. But it won't be as easy as it might seem.

10   What does our octopus look like? Well, that's the problem: *Octopus cyanea* (it's named after Cyane, a water nymph in Greek mythology) might be fat and red, skinny and white, tall and brown, or a combination of colors and shapes. It might have stripes or spots or splotches—and then, the next second, it might look completely different. Or become utterly invisible.

quarry Quarry is something that is hunted.

101

11   Not only can it squeeze its three-foot-long arms and melon-size body through a hole the size of a thimble, it can also hide in plain sight. In addition to changing color to match its surroundings, it can instantly sprout little projections all over its skin called papillae (pa-PIL-ay) to make it look exactly like a piece of algae or coral or rock.

12   Which is what the octopuses in this part of Opunohu Bay may be doing at this very moment—if they're here at all.

13   "Octopuses are hard to find," concedes Jennifer. Though she works at the University of Lethbridge in the center of Canada, far from any ocean, she's been probing the mysteries of these quirky, changeable animals for forty years. She's conducted experiments with the giant Pacific octopus, which can grow to more than one hundred pounds, in the Seattle Aquarium. She's studied the five-inch-long pygmy octopus in Florida and the common octopus in Bermuda. And she's watched the Pacific day octopus before, off the islands of Hawaii, and the common octopus off the Caribbean island of Bonaire.

probing Probing is researching something for the purpose of answering questions.

14   Everything about them fascinates her, but especially this: "Octopuses are smart," she says—and that's thought to be rare for invertebrates (in-VERT-a-brits). Invertebrates include insects, spiders, worms, snails, starfish, and clams; they have no bones, and usually have a very small brain. (Starfish and clams have no brain at all!)

15   Octopuses are in fact related to snails and clams—they're all mollusks. Most mollusks have shells—but not octos. That makes the octopus an unprotected packet of tasty protein for predators. Almost anything big enough can eat an octopus: along with its cousin, the squid, it is the main prey of marine mammals, sharks, and many fish. Humans eat them too.

Crabs, like this hermit crab, are among octopuses favorite foods.

An octopus can jet away faster than a human swimmer can follow.

16   But what the octopus lacks in protective shell it makes up for in smarts. Actually, having no shell might be the very reason octopuses are so smart: they have to be. If you're a clam, you can just sit around, wait for food to float to you, and depend on your shell to protect you. Without a shell, octopuses can lead more active lives, but also face dangers that demand snap judgments. If a hungry shark approaches, should the octopus hide in a hole? Change color or shape? Release a smokescreen of ink? Or squirt a hanging blob of ink that looks like an octopus—while the octopus itself jets away?

17   To both hunt and hide, an octopus must choose wisely among many options, and it has a big brain to help it do so. Jennifer, a professor of psychology, is interested in how these intelligent invertebrates make decisions. That's why she's invited a team of octopus experts here to Moorea: to find out how octopuses decide what to eat, while avoiding being eaten themselves.

18   What good can come from studying the life of an octopus?

19   Jennifer points out that people are already using knowledge of octopuses to model "soft" robots, which roam over rough ground much better than vehicles with wheels. And that's only a beginning. "Octopuses' arms are full of suction cups that are marvels of manipulation," she notes. "How come we're not copying them? Well, because we don't understand them."

manipulation   Manipulation is the act of handling something, usually with skill.

20   Dripping with seawater, she holds up for our inspection the two-inch shell she has found. "Is this a drill hole?" she asks. "I can't tell."

21   David Scheel leans his six-foot frame down to look. A behavioral ecologist and an expert on the giant Pacific octopus, David is a professor of marine biology at Alaska Pacific University in Anchorage. He's seen lots of drill holes. Drilling is one of several ways the ingenious octopus can get at the tasty meat inside even the strongest shells.

22   Sometimes an octopus can just pop the two halves of a clam's shell open with its strong suckers. With just one of its biggest suckers, one of David's giants can lift up to thirty pounds. Or the octopus might chip at a shell with its beak, which is as strong as a parrot's.

If the shell is too thick, the octo might drill. On its tongue an octopus has a ribbon of teeth called a radula (RAD-jula), an organ unique to mollusks, which the octopus uses to drill holes and other mollusks use to shred prey. And the octo has another trick up its sleeve: it can dissolve the calcium in the shell by squirting it with acid from a gland in the front of its head. Once the hole is deep enough, the octopus can inject venom from a different gland, one in the back of its head, through the hole to paralyze the prey. The venom even starts dissolving the meal, the way meat-tenderizing enzymes work on a juicy steak.

23 But whoever ate the mollusk who lived in this shell apparently didn't drill. "No," says David, after a careful look, "I don't see a hole. But look what I found!" Just minutes ago he was investigating another possible octopus home—a crevice under a rock—and he collected what he found just outside it. He unfolds his palm and reveals the orange claw and shell (also called a carapace) of a crab. The claw was placed on top of the carapace, and both of them on top of a clam shell. Nobody in the sea is tidier than an octopus!

24 Lots of different items may appear on an octopus's menu—everything from clams to snails to fellow octopuses.

(This is a hazard for an octopus seeking a mate; their first date could be dinner, with one of them being the main course!) Giant Pacific octopuses sometimes catch and eat birds. One was seen dining on an otter (who was probably dead when the octopus found it).

25 But crabs are among octopuses' very favorite foods. And the remains of this crab bear the signature of an octopus—as Tatiana Leite, a marine ecologist from Brazil, confirms the moment David hands his find to her. Beneath her facemask, the edges of Tatiana's brown eyes crinkle as she smiles. "Yeah!" she agrees. "It's intact, and the inside is completely clean. A fish would have crunched it all up."

Meet the Octopus Team

Jennifer Mather
AGE: **69**
NATIONALITY: **Canadian**
JOB: **Professor of Psychology, University of Lethbridge, Alberta, Canada**

David Scheel
AGE: **51**
NATIONALITY: **American**
JOB: **Professor of Marine Biology and Director of the Marine Biology Program, Alaska Pacific University, Anchorage, Alaska**

Tatiana Leite
AGE: **37**
NATIONALITY: **Brazilian**
JOB: **Professor of Marine Ecology, Federal University of Rio Grande do Norte, Natal, Brazil**

26   Jennifer, David, and Tatiana share the same mission: to find out what the Pacific day octopuses of Moorea are eating, and why. But each scientist views this mysterious study animal through a slightly different lens. Jennifer, the head of our team, as a psychologist, is convinced that each octopus's personality plays an important role in food choices. She expects that bolder, more adventurous octopuses will venture farther from their dens and choose a wider variety of prey. David's specialty is behavioral ecology. He's fascinated by the dynamics of predators and their prey. He suspects that octopuses prefer big crabs, but those who can't find and catch them make do with smaller prey and a wider menu. As a marine ecologist, Tatiana is especially interested in how an animal's environment affects how it behaves. She predicts that the octopuses who live in a more complex and varied environment will have a more diverse diet.

27   Which of these theories is correct may be important for many different reasons. But one reason is that finding out what octopuses eat and why might help scientists discover whether octopus populations are in danger or not. Octopuses, as we can see, are very difficult to count. That makes it hard to tell whether any octopus species are endangered or declining. The common octopus might be overfished in some waters; other kinds, such as the exceptionally beautiful mimic octopus, could be overcollected for the saltwater aquarium trade. Other threats, such as pollution and global warming, might be hurting octopus species too—either by harming them directly or by affecting their prey. Is there enough food for each octopus species? Nobody knows—or can even begin to find out—until scientists discover exactly what they all eat and why. This study might turn out to be a model for other studies on different octopus species elsewhere.

28   At Jennifer's invitation, each researcher has come here to test his or her own idea, or hypothesis. A new scuba diver from New Hampshire who has never snorkeled before, I've joined the team to write this book about their quest.

29   There's lots to do. We'll be collecting and **classifying** the shells around octopuses' homes. We'll be carefully surveying the plants, animals, and rocks on the sea bottom where the octopuses live. We even plan to give each octopus we find a personality test!

> **classifying**   If you are classifying things, you are dividing them into groups of like things.

Pacific day octopus

30 But first we have to find the shape-shifting, hole-hiding octopuses—animals who are masters of escape and disguise.

31 "I think an octopus had a meal here, without a doubt," says David.

32 The question is: Where is it now?

33 Wet bathing suits. Wet scuba booties. Wet wetsuits. In French Polynesia, it's winter in July. When we're donning wet gear in the morning, even temperatures below 70 feel downright chilly.

34 We worked out our plan the night before. We're heading back to Church Copse to explore an area with numerous gullies and both live and dead coral—the sort of place where Jennifer and Tatiana have seen octopuses in their previous studies at other tropical sites. They will work the shallows while David and I head to deeper waters.

35 We walk into the shallows, don our fins, masks, and snorkels, and start swimming. A brisk ten-minute swim takes David and me past the shallows to where finally the water is over our heads. "Now we look for octopus!" he says—and then dives like a seal.

36 Once I catch up, we round the point together. We continue our octopus search on our way back to join Tatiana and Jennifer in the shallows. David dives, picks up rocks, shines his underwater flashlight into crevices. He's finding plenty of evidence that octopuses live here: beside little caves in dead coral, shells are stacked up one atop the other, with crab claws resting on top, like spoons in a bowl. "Nobody else is going to leave these in a pile!" he says. "The octopus must have just stepped out." He's found more than ten separate piles of food remains, so many that he's stopped collecting them in his bucket, and at least three potential octopus homes. And he keeps looking—even inside a green glass bottle, in case a youngster's hiding there. Back in the States, off the Pacific Northwest coast, a small species known as the red octopus favors beer bottles as homes, especially stubby brown ones. But nobody's home in ours.

37 We see that the sky overhead is bruised with dark clouds. A storm is gathering. So we turn toward shore to

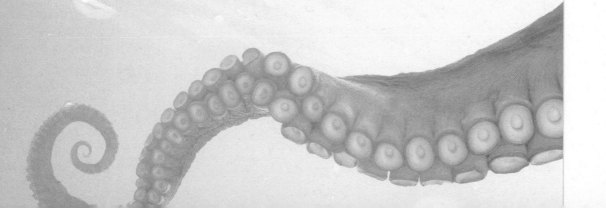

look for Jennifer and Tatiana. There they are! We wave—and they wave back enthusiastically. Only once we're within a hundred yards can we hear what they're shouting at us. "OCTOPUS!"

38   It's 10:10 by the time we catch up. Jennifer pulls her head out of the water just long enough to say "Mmmmnnthth!" She's so excited, she forgets to pull her snorkel out of her mouth at first. Seeing our puzzled expressions, she remembers to remove it. "I'm looking at an octopus!" she says, then pops the snorkel back in and plunges below again.

39   By the time I can locate it, the octopus has retreated into a hole. All I can see are white suckers along one bluish arm, curved inside a small cavern in some dead coral. Jennifer announces that she will name it Kwila after her dog, a half malamute, half border collie she adopted as a puppy.

40   It turns out Kwila is the second octopus of the day! Tatiana was the first to spot one—and she found it during the first ten minutes of their foray. It was hunting, spread across a shallow gully, its skin a beautiful blue-green color. "When it saw me, its head turned brown, and then its arms turned brown," she says, "and then it went down its hole." She named it Cleo, after her white poodle—a dog who has no fewer than three octopus-shaped plush toys to play with.

41   The clouds that were gathering are now hissing down rain. It's cold above water, but from beneath the surface, looking up, the drops look like inside-out dimples and the rain sounds like sizzling grease. Jennifer asks us to make just a few more passes over the shallows. "Look for disruption. Somebody moving rubble around." We agree to turn back at eleven—water is not a good place to be when there might be lightning. We all head toward shore.

disruption A disruption is a disturbance that causes an interruption.

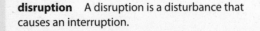

42   The team is confident now. "As soon as we got here," says Tatiana, "I said, 'Yeah! This is the place. We've found our study area!'" Our site reminds her of one of her octopus study areas in Brazil, Tatiana tells us as she sits down in the foot-deep water to remove her fins and walk ashore. David takes one last look—and right beside Tatiana he finds a pile of shells, a hole in the rock—and inside, another octopus! Sticking with the dog theme, he names it Grover, after the beagle his family adopted when he was ten.

43   Before leaving, we mark the three dens so we can find them again. We leave a collection bucket tied to a rock near one and a red bungee cord at another. We haul a flat black rock over to mark the third. In the cold rain, we pile into the truck to return to "base," wash our gear, and take a hot shower. It doesn't matter that nobody has a dry towel.

An octopus peers at us from atop some coral.

How Smart Is an Octopus?

44   Measuring the minds of other creatures is a **perplexing** problem. One yardstick scientists use is brain size—because humans have such big brains. But size doesn't always matter. Think of computers: the first ones were as big as rooms; now they fit in your pocket.

45   Still, octopuses have the largest brains of any invertebrate. A giant Pacific octopus's brain is about the size of a parrot's. That's only as big as a walnut, but scientists now know that a walnut-size brain is enough to allow at least some parrots to add numbers, make jokes, and invent new words.

46   As another measure of intelligence, scientists count nerve cells, or neurons. A human brain has 100 billion neurons. The common octopus (the only octopus species in which anyone has counted neurons) has 130 million in its brain and almost 200 million, or three-fifths of its total neurons, in its arms. As philosopher-diver Peter Godfrey-Smith observed, "It is as if each arm has a mind of its own."

47   Perhaps the most convincing evidence of octopus intelligence comes from what they do—in the wild, in aquariums, and in the laboratory. Octopuses learn new skills fast, and remember what they learn. "We know from many studies that octopuses are smart," says Jennifer. With her Seattle colleague Roland Anderson and others, Jennifer has conducted many of these studies herself. One study showed that octopuses learn and remember individual human faces. One set of volunteers fed captive octopuses fish and squid. Another set, dressed identically, touched the octopuses with a bristly stick, which octopuses don't like. The octopuses quickly learned to approach the people who fed them even when those people had no food. But when they saw the people who had touched them with the bristly stick, the octopuses moved away— or blasted those people with salt water from their funnels!

48   In the wild, octopuses have to solve different kinds of problems all the time. *How can I safely capture that spiny crab? How can I escape that hungry moray eel? What can I collect from my travels to make this coral crevice into a safe den?* (Some octopuses in the wild have been filmed carrying coconut halves to use as portable huts; others use shells as doors to their lairs.) In captivity, they quickly figure out solutions too, such as how to open a container when there's a tasty food item inside.

---

perplexing   If something is perplexing, it's hard to understand or know how to deal with.

112

49 At the New England Aquarium in Boston, to keep the octopuses entertained, Wilson Menashi, an engineer, designed an elaborate set of three clear plastic cubes, each with a different kind of latch on the lid. Once the octopus, inspired by the prospect of eating a tasty crab inside, learned to master opening the first cube, Menashi next placed the first cube within a second cube—and then both of those inside a third with *two* different locks: a bolt that slides into position, and a lever arm like on a canning jar. Most of the dozen octopuses Menashi has known over nearly two decades have learned to open all three boxes within a few minutes, after just a handful of once-a-week tries.

50 But octopuses are individuals, and some are smarter than others. Some come up with solutions to problems that researchers don't anticipate. One eager female octo at the New England Aquarium, Gwenevere, didn't bother with the latches and just crushed the box. She created a small hole through which she grabbed the crab. Another octopus also skipped the latches. He got so excited when he saw the crab, he poured his whole body through the hole Gwenevere had created. Visitors found him squeezed into a perfect cube shape in his exhibit—an octopus-in-the-box.

A meeting of the minds: an octopus sizes up a coral grouper.

The Camouflaged Octopus

As you watch *The Camouflaged Octopus*, notice how the octopus moves, changes colors, and appears to change texture. How does the video help you understand the activities and movement of the octopus? How does the information in this video relate to the text *The Octopus Scientists*? Write your ideas below.

Listen for the Critical Vocabulary words *mollusks* and *unfurl*. Pay attention to how the narrator gives clues to the words' meanings. Take notes in the space below to describe how each word was used.

mollusks   Mollusks are invertebrates, such as snails and octopuses, and have soft bodies.
unfurl   When you unfurl something, such as an umbrella, you unfold it so that it spreads out.

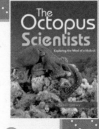

The Camouflaged Octopus

Collaborative Discussion

Look back at what you wrote on page 98. Tell a partner two facts you learned from this text. Then work with a group to discuss the questions below. Refer to details and examples in *The Octopus Scientists* and *The Camouflaged Octopus* to support your ideas. Take notes for your responses. When you speak, use your notes.

1. Reread pages 102–105. Do you think octopus research is important? Cite evidence from the text to support your opinion.

 Listening Tip

Listen for the specific details the speaker uses to answer each question. What details or examples from the text or video can you add?

2. Reread pages 112–113. Why do scientists say octopuses are "smart"? Give an example.

 Speaking Tip

Build your ideas onto what speakers have said before your turn. If you agree with what a speaker has said, say so, and then add your ideas.

3. How does the video help deepen your understanding of what you learned in the text? Cite a detail to support your response.

Write a Script

PROMPT ....

In the text *The Octopus Scientists* and video *The Camouflaged Octopus,* you learned about the Pacific day octopus, which makes its home in the deep ocean. You met four scientists who have spent many hours searching for and studying this "weird" creature.

Now imagine that this fascinating animal will be displayed at an aquarium, and you have been chosen to write a script for a docent, or volunteer, to explain this creature to visitors. What are the most important and interesting facts to include? The docent will not have much time to talk, so your script should be less than one minute long. Use Critical Vocabulary words in your writing.

PLAN ....

Make notes about the most important and interesting facts about the Pacific day octopus. Think about what visitors to an aquarium would want to know.

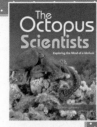

The Camouflaged Octopus

WRITE

Now write your script of interesting facts about the Pacific day octopus from *The Octopus Scientists* and *The Camouflaged Octopus*.

✓ Make sure your script

- ☐ begins with an introduction that captures listeners' attention.

- ☐ includes fascinating facts about the Pacific day octopus.

- ☐ uses Critical Vocabulary from the text and video.

- ☐ includes descriptive language and punctuation so the docent is able to read with expression.

- ☐ is less than one minute long.

Notice & Note
Memory Moment

Prepare to Read

GENRE STUDY **Poetry** uses the sound and rhythm of words to create mental images and inspire feelings in readers.

- Poets use sound effects, such as rhyme (including internal rhyme), rhythm, and meter, to reinforce the poem's meaning.
- Poets sometimes incorporate figurative language, such as similes and metaphors, to develop the ideas in their poems.
- Poets use details that appeal to the senses to describe ideas.

SET A PURPOSE **Think about** the title and genre of this collection of poems. What do you know about poetry? What would you like to learn? Write your ideas below.

**Meet the Author:
Langston Hughes**

CRITICAL VOCABULARY

receptivity

fluctuating

languid

POETRY OF THE SEA

SIX POETS SHARE THEIR VISION OF THE OCEAN AND THE SHORE.

ILLUSTRATED BY MARINA ADAMOVA

NEITHER OUT FAR NOR IN DEEP

by Robert Frost

1 The people along the sand
   All turn and look one way.
   They turn their back on the land.
   They look at the sea all day.

2 As long as it takes to pass
   A ship keeps raising its hull;
   The wetter ground like glass
   Reflects a standing gull.

3 The land may vary more;
   But wherever the truth may be–
   The water comes ashore,
   And the people look at the sea.

4 They cannot look out far.
   They cannot look in deep.
   But when was that ever a bar
   To any watch they keep?

MAGGIE AND MILLY AND MOLLY AND MAY

by e. e. cummings

1 maggie and milly and molly and may
   went down to the beach (to play one day)

2 and maggie discovered a shell that sang
   so sweetly she couldn't remember her troubles, and

3 milly befriended a stranded star
   whose rays five **languid** fingers were;

4 and molly was chased by a horrible thing
   which raced sideways while blowing bubbles: and

5 may came home with a smooth round stone
   as small as a world and as large as alone.

6 for whatever we lose (like a you or a me)
   it's always ourselves we find in the sea

> **languid** If you are languid you are slow and relaxed.

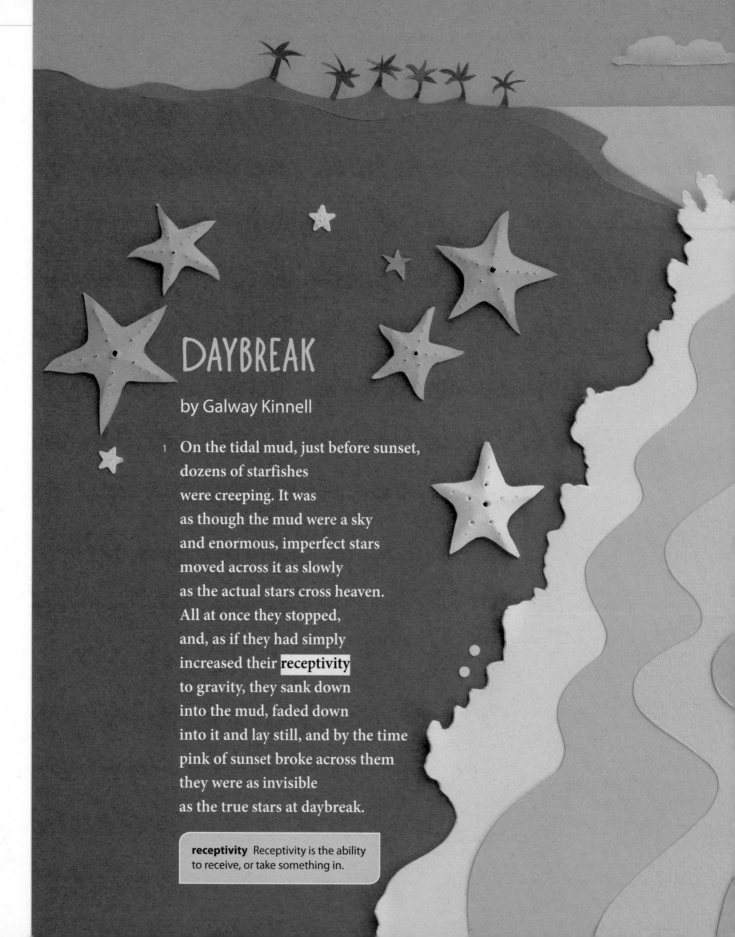

DAYBREAK

by Galway Kinnell

1 On the tidal mud, just before sunset,
dozens of starfishes
were creeping. It was
as though the mud were a sky
and enormous, imperfect stars
moved across it as slowly
as the actual stars cross heaven.
All at once they stopped,
and, as if they had simply
increased their **receptivity**
to gravity, they sank down
into the mud, faded down
into it and lay still, and by the time
pink of sunset broke across them
they were as invisible
as the true stars at daybreak.

receptivity Receptivity is the ability
to receive, or take something in.

A JELLY-FISH

by Marianne Moore

1 Visible, invisible,
A fluctuating charm,
An amber-colored amethyst
Inhabits it; your arm
Approaches, and
It opens and
It closes;
You have meant
To catch it,
And it shrivels;
You abandon
Your intent—
It opens, and it
Closes and you
Reach for it—
The blue
Surrounding it
Grows cloudy, and
It floats away
From you.

> **fluctuating** Something that is fluctuating
> is changing often and in irregular ways.

EARTH DAY ON THE BAY

by Gary Soto

1 Curled like a genie's lamp,
A track shoe from the 1970s among seaweed,
The race long over, the blue ribbons faded,
The trophies deep in pink insulation in the rafters.
Perhaps the former distant runner sits in his recliner.

2 The other shoe? Along this shore,
It could have ridden the waves back to Mother Korea,
Where it was molded from plastic,
Fitted with cloth, shoelaces poked through the eyelets,
Squeezed for inspection.

3 I remember that style of shoe.
Never owned a pair myself.
With my skinny legs I could go side-to-side like a crab,
But never run the distance with a number on my back,
Never the winner or runner up heaving at the end.

4 I bag that shoe, now litter, and nearly slip on the rocks.
Gulls scream above, a single kite goes crazy,
A cargo ship in the distance carrying more
Of the same.

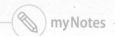

SEA CALM

by Langston Hughes

1 How still,
   How strangely still
   The water is today,
   It is not good
   For water
   To be so still that way.

Collaborative Discussion

Look back at what you wrote on page 118. Tell a partner which one of the poems is your favorite and why. Then work with a group to discuss the questions below. Refer to details and examples in *Poetry of the Sea* to explain your answers. Take notes for your responses. When you speak, use your notes.

1 How did the poets use details to create mental images in the mind of the reader? Give an example.

2 Find an example of a poet using a line break to create meaning. Why did the poet break the line in that way? Explain your answer.

3 How did a poem from *Poetry of the Sea* deepen your understanding of the ocean? Support your response with an example.

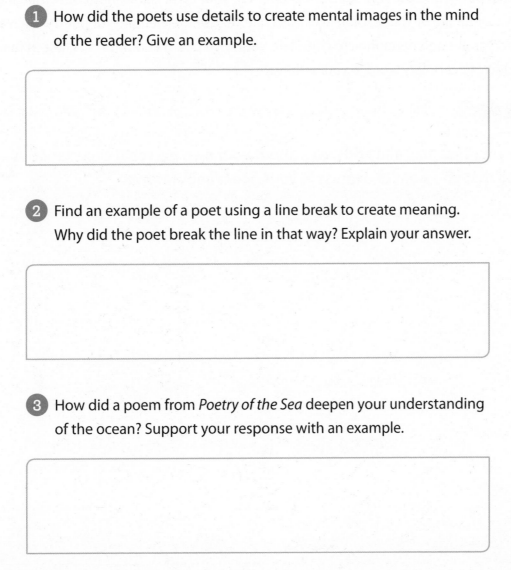

Listening Tip

If you can't hear a speaker easily, politely ask that person to speak a little louder.

Speaking Tip

As you speak, look at the others in your group. If anyone looks confused, invite that person to ask you a question.

Write a Poem

PROMPT

In *Poetry of the Sea*, you read six different poems about the sea and shore. These poets used the sounds and rhythms of words to show images and express feelings. They used figurative language, such as similes, and details that appeal to the five senses.

Now, you write a poem. Which poem in this selection was your favorite? Pick one line from that poem and use it to start a new poem of your own. Think about how that line relates to your life or your experiences with nature. Use the elements of poetry, such as imagery, simile, and metaphor, to complete your own poem about the sea. Use at least one critical vocabulary word in your writing.

PLAN

Write your first line, and add notes about your own personal experience or feeling that you want to express in your poem about the sea.

WRITE

Now write your own poem, inspired by *Poetry of the Sea*.

✓ Make sure your poem

- ☐ begins with a line from one of the poems from *Poetry of the Sea*.

- ☐ expresses a feeling or personal experience about the sea or nature.

- ☐ includes figurative language, such as a simile or metaphor.

- ☐ uses details that appeal to the senses.

Prepare to Read

GENRE STUDY **Informational text** gives facts and examples about a topic.

- Authors of informational texts may organize information by a central idea. The central idea is supported by key details, including facts, definitions, examples, or quotations.

- Informational texts also include detailed photographs that give readers more information.

- Science texts include words that are specific to the topic.

SET A PURPOSE **Think about** the title and genre of this text. What do you know about careers that involve the ocean? What would you like to learn? Write your ideas below.

Build Background:
Preparing for Careers

CRITICAL VOCABULARY

organism

geology

submerged

conduct

extinction

warden

zoology

Ocean Careers

1 The number and types of careers related to the ocean are as vast as the sea itself—
and there is room for talents of all kinds. The first type of ocean career that usually
comes to mind is that of explorer or conservationist. One example is Jacques
Cousteau, the famous French undersea explorer who was also a conservationist—
someone who works to protect and preserve the environment. However, the specific
job of a conservationist represents just one type of career in the marine field.

Jobs in Marine Science

2 Most ocean careers are science related, but within the broad category of "science" there are many branches. One of these branches, marine biology, includes a variety of careers. A marine biologist might work as an ichthyologist [ick-thee-all-o-gist], an expert in the study of fish; a microbiologist, an expert focused on organisms smaller than the naked eye can see; or a marine mammalogist, a researcher studying whales and seals.

3 The terms *geology* and *meteorology* are usually associated with land and its weather conditions, but these two branches of science also include ocean careers. Marine geologists study

the ocean floor, applying knowledge of chemistry, physics, biology, and math to prepare reports and maps that can be used for research on underwater earthquakes that cause tsunamis—or to determine the best place to set up an offshore oil rig.

4 Ocean careers that deal directly with the care of ocean animals usually don't require research. Aquariums around the country employ animal caretakers, tank attendants, and curators of water quality. Fisheries around the world also require scientists, managers, and other kinds of workers.

organism   An organism is any living thing, including animals, plants, fungi, and bacteria.
geology   People who study geology study Earth's structure, surface, and origins.

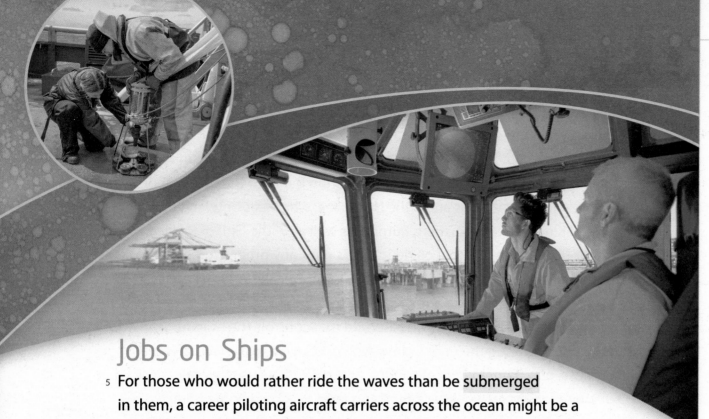

Jobs on Ships

5 For those who would rather ride the waves than be submerged in them, a career piloting aircraft carriers across the ocean might be a good fit. The U.S. Navy, Merchant Marine, and Coast Guard protect our waters, transport our government property, and keep the peace all over the world.

6 There are also plenty of jobs in commercial shipping. In a busy shipping harbor, little tugboats gently tow huge barges and ships into port. On the tugboat, there is a captain who has earned a certification for skills such as leadership, voyage planning, and safety. The captain uses radar to pilot the ship safely and efficiently. Working with the captain is a mate, who also must be certified, and who works on navigation and towing. Even vessels as small as tugboats may also employ a cook and a steward—the person responsible for keeping the ship shipshape!

7 About 90% of the world's goods—shoes, phones, cars, furniture, and more—rely on international shipping to make their way from production to consumer. Often referred to as the maritime industry, there are tens of thousands of jobs in international shipping, from managing ports and ships to working with customers, businesses, and clients all over the world. All these jobs are critical to making international shipping efficient and safe.

> **submerged**   If something is submerged, it is placed below the surface of water or another liquid.

Jobs in Offshore Energy

8 "Offshore energy" is a term for offshore drilling, using wind farms, and tapping other energy sources that are set up in the ocean. As of 2017, there were about 500 offshore oil platforms. Oil platforms are connected to pumps that extract oil and natural gas from beneath the ocean floor. Many of these platforms are in the North Sea, which lies between the United Kingdom and northern Europe, as well as in the Gulf of Mexico.

9 Working on an offshore oil rig is a job unlike any other. Workers are brought in by helicopter and usually work 12-hour shifts. Workers may be in charge of maintenance and repairs or spend their shift in a control room monitoring a computer dashboard that controls the drilling equipment. During their downtime, workers can eat in a small cafeteria, exercise, play games with colleagues, or rest. Workers usually stay offshore for several weeks at a time and then are flown home to take several weeks off.

10 Oil isn't the only offshore energy source that employs people. Offshore wind farms—windmills that are positioned in the ocean—provide a renewable energy source. Most jobs in this growing field are in Europe, where wind farms have been in operation for decades. In the United States, the first offshore wind farm was built off the coast of Rhode Island, and plans are underway for another farm to be built off the coast of southern Massachusetts. New York, New Jersey, and other coastal states also have plans for offshore wind farms in the works in the coming decades.

Fisheries Scientist
Daniel Pauly

WORKPLACE: University of British Columbia, Canada
TITLE: Professor at University of British Columbia; Principal Investigator for Sea Around Us
EDUCATION: PhD in fisheries biology

Daniel Pauly was born in Paris, France, to a French mother and an African American father. When he was very young, Pauly's parents split up. Pauly had an unhappy childhood; he lived apart from his parents with a family that made him work as a servant without pay. He ran away at age 16, leaving France for Germany. Pauly supported himself through high school, and then was reunited with both his mother, in France, and his father's family, in Little Rock, Arkansas. Pauly returned to Germany and worked toward his doctorate in fisheries biology.

Pauly researched and worked in fisheries all over the world—from western Africa to the Java Sea in Indonesia to the University of British Columbia. His special area of focus was helping local scientists in developing countries conduct marine research using inexpensive technology, like calculators, instead of the high-tech, expensive equipment available in Europe. Pauly's work with Sea Around Us includes assessing the impact of fisheries on worldwide marine ecosystems and coming up with solutions. He also helped create FishBase, a website that catalogs information and images of more than 27,000 species. His goal is to empower scientists around the world, regardless of their financial means, to conduct research that could help save ocean species from extinction.

> **conduct** If you conduct something, you organize or do it.
> **extinction** The extinction of a species is the death of all of its remaining living members.

Jobs Outlook

11 In an ideal world, everyone would find a career that corresponds to his or her passions and interests, but there are other factors to consider: how much education is required, how much money can be made, and where the work is located.

High School Graduates

12 Marine careers for high school graduates include jobs in the fishing industry. Being a fisherman involves cleaning and maintenance of the ship, as well as hauling, measuring, cleaning, and storing fish. With more experience, a fisherman might also be required to dive and use a spear to catch fish.

13   Another career for high school graduates is a seafarer—an unlicensed crew member on a commercial ship. To qualify for this type of job, applicants must demonstrate basic physical fitness and have no police record. The main lifestyle requirement for fishermen and seafarers is the ability to be away from home for weeks at a time.

Workers receive on-the-job training and promotions as their skills increase.

14   Other jobs that require only a high school degree include motorboat operators, marine cargo agents, ship's engineers, aquacultural workers, and many other positions. Dredge operators do not need to have a college degree or licensing, and jobs in this field are expected to increase 13% between 2012 and 2022. A dredge operator uses machinery to dig canals and other waterways or clear them of rocks, sand, earth, and other material that would block the movement of ships.

Mapping and Math Careers

Dawn Wright

WORKPLACE: Environmental Systems Research Institute (ESRI)
TITLE: Geological Oceanography Specialist/Chief Scientist
EDUCATION: BS in geology, MS in oceanography, PhD in geography and marine biology

Dawn Wright grew up in Baltimore, Maryland, but also spent time on the island of Maui, in Hawaii. She learned to snorkel and scuba dive, but she was also fascinated by the volcanoes on Hawaii's islands. On Sunday nights as she watched Jacques Cousteau's underwater adventure television program, Wright knew that she had to have a career in the marine sciences.

Today, Wright is the chief scientist for ESRI, an organization that develops products, tools, services, and research partnerships to survey the ocean floor. She works on data modeling and habitat mapping. Her work helps people who work in conservation of ocean life, those who research underwater earthquakes and volcanoes, and those who work in businesses interested in ocean floor geography.

Frank Gonzalez

WORKPLACE: Pacific Marine Environmental Laboratory
EDUCATION: BS in physics; MS, PhD in oceanography

Despite growing up in landlocked San Antonio, Texas, Frank Gonzalez became fascinated by sea life after serving as a U.S. Marine. Gonzalez's hard work and patience in college paid off when he was accepted into a graduate study program in oceanography in Hawaii.

Gonzalez has spent his career studying tsunamis—huge, destructive waves that can be formed by underwater earthquakes. Today, Gonzalez leads a team that creates computer models that simulate tsunami activity. His team has also developed a network of stations in the ocean to report tsunamis as they are happening. Gonzalez's work, which helps report tsunamis in real time, saves lives around the world.

College Certificates and Degrees

15 Many marine jobs, such as commercial diver and motorboat mechanic, are available to those with one to two years of post-high school education. Commercial divers use scuba gear to maintain underwater structures and equipment by, for example, doing welding repairs on an oil rig. Commercial divers may receive special training to defuse underwater bombs. Motorboat mechanics work at docks or marinas, fixing engines, propellers, steering mechanisms, and more. Other jobs that require two-year degrees include electrician, geological data technician, mechanical engineering technician, and many others.

16 With a four-year college degree there are even more options for an ocean career. Fish and game wardens patrol specific areas in order to

protect marine wildlife. They also enforce the laws that set limits for the size and number of ocean animals that can be caught by fishermen.

17 Marine engineers and naval architects are also required to have four-year degrees. These professionals oversee construction and repair of boats and other floating structures.

---

wardens A warden is responsible for enforcing the laws and rules regarding a place, people, or things.

Advanced Degrees

18 For students able to get master's degrees and doctorates in marine sciences, there are many fascinating careers in research. Marine wildlife biologists will conduct research on ocean life, often under the direction of someone with a doctorate degree. They publish their work in scientific journals and can be called on as experts when governments make policies to protect the environment.

However, there's so much more to study in the ocean than wildlife alone. Check out the profiles of professionals with advanced degrees on pages 135, 137, and 140.

Careers in Ocean Sciences

JOB	MINIMUM EDUCATION REQUIRED	MEAN ANNUAL WAGE (2017)
fisherman	no formal credential	$28,530
dredge operator	high school diploma	$46,340
seafarer	high school diploma	$55,590
motorboat mechanic	2-year college degree	$41,350
commercial diver	2-year college degree	$55,270
fish and game warden	4-year college degree	$58,570
wildlife biologist	4-year college degree	$62,290
marine engineer/ naval architect	4-year college degree	$90,970
environmental scientist —federal government	4-year college degree through doctorate	$101,400

Careers in Life Sciences

Sylvia Earle

TITLE: Oceanographer, Explorer, Researcher
EDUCATION: BA, MS, PhD in botany

Sylvia Earle is world-famous for her deep-sea explorations and her expert research on marine algae. In 1979 she set the world record for untethered diving, going 1,250 feet below the surface of the Pacific Ocean.

In her long career, Earle has worked for universities and institutes, written books, and been both the chief scientist of the National Oceanic and Atmospheric Administration (NOAA) and an explorer-in-residence for the National Geographic Society.

Eugenie Clark

WORKPLACE: Mote Marine Laboratory
TITLE: Founding Director
EDUCATION: BA, MA, PhD in zoology

When Eugenie Clark was nine years old, her mother worked at a newsstand on weekends to support the two of them. She would drop off Clark at the New York Aquarium before heading to work. Clark found the sharks she observed irresistible and she brought this fascination to her lifelong career as a zoologist and shark specialist.

Nicknamed "Shark Lady," Clark traveled to the Middle East to search for new fish species and to study sharks. She gave public lectures on sharks, giving context for their role in a healthy marine ecosystem.

Danny Muñoz

WORKPLACE: Aquarium of the Pacific
TITLE: Assistant Curator
EDUCATION: BS in biology

As a child, Danny Muñoz enjoyed taking care of his own home aquariums. Muñoz was certified in scuba diving at age 17 and being able to see the creatures of the sea up close made him all the more certain that he wanted a career in marine biology.

After graduating from college, Muñoz worked at the Miami Seaquarium as an expert in Caribbean species and oversaw the manatee and sea turtle rescue program. Today, he conducts research and maintains exhibits at the Aquarium of the Pacific in Long Beach, California. He also welcomes visitors to the aquarium, a role which is enhanced by his fluency in both English and Spanish.

> **zoology**   Someone who studies zoology studies animals.

Collaborative Discussion

Look back at what you wrote on page 130. Tell a partner two facts you learned from this text. Then work with a group to discuss the questions below. Refer to details and examples in *Ocean Careers* to explain your answers. Take notes for your responses. When you speak, use your notes.

1. Reread page 133. What facts in the text support the idea that there is a demand for workers in international shipping?

    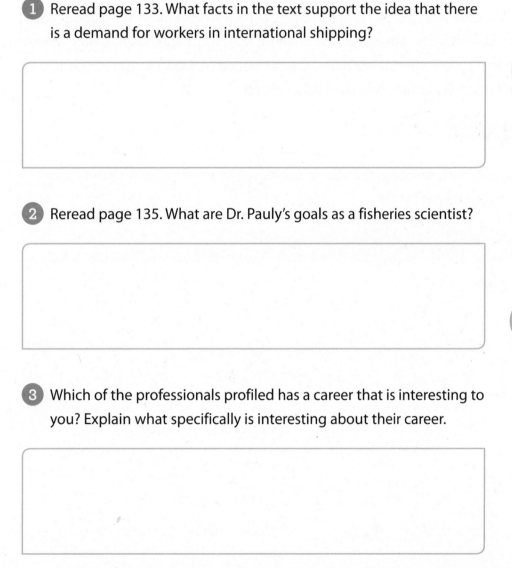

2. Reread page 135. What are Dr. Pauly's goals as a fisheries scientist?

3. Which of the professionals profiled has a career that is interesting to you? Explain what specifically is interesting about their career.

Listening Tip

Be sure the speaker has finished before you volunteer to share your ideas.

Speaking Tip

Wait for your group's leader to call on you. Then, speak clearly and make eye contact with each member of your group as you speak.

Write a List

PROMPT

In *Ocean Careers*, you read about the many different careers that involve the ocean, and the education and training needed to get those jobs. The text contains photographs and a table that add information.

What are three careers mentioned in this selection that you think are the best for your interests, talents, and skills? Write a list, explaining what is interesting about each career, as well as the education and training required. Explain what interests, skills and talents you have that make this career a good fit. Don't forget to use some of the Critical Vocabulary words in your writing.

PLAN

Using the text, photographs, and table, make notes about three ocean careers that interest you.

Now write your list about the three careers that most interest you, using *Ocean Careers* as your source.

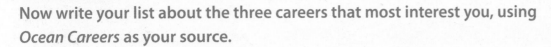

Make sure your list

☐ has a title that summarizes the list.

☐ includes three ocean careers, and the training and education required for each.

☐ explains your talents, skills, and interests that relate to this career.

☐ uses supporting evidence from the selection.

☐ includes at least two Critical Vocabulary words.

Prepare to Read

GENRE STUDY **Persuasive texts** give an author's opinion about a topic and try to convince readers to believe that opinion.

- Persuasive texts include evidence, such as facts and examples, to support the author's viewpoint.

- Persuasive texts can include strong language and techniques to convince readers to believe the author's viewpoint. Authors may appeal to readers' emotions and personal experiences, or use figurative language to support their ideas.

SET A PURPOSE **Think about** the title and genre of this text. How do you think pollution affects the ocean? What would you like to learn about ocean pollution? Write your ideas below.

Meet the Author: Harriet Rohmer

CRITICAL VOCABULARY

pipeline

condense

via

respirators

motivation

commissions

opposition

proposal

oversees

Safeguarding the California Coast

by Harriet Rohmer

Erica Fernandez

*Student and
Environmental Activist
Oxnard, California*

1   When 12-year-old Erica Fernandez volunteered to help clean up the beach in her new hometown, Oxnard, California, she could barely speak English. She had no idea then that within four years, her passionate speeches for the environment and social justice would inspire thousands of people to action—and help change the mind of the governor himself.

2   Back then, in 2003, she was just a kid helping 20 adults take care of the beach. She and her family had recently arrived in California from a small town in Mexico. "I always loved the ocean," she says, "so it made me really sad to see this beautiful beach full of trash. That's why I decided to help." Her dedication impressed the adults in the group. One woman—the only one who spoke Spanish—started explaining to Erica that something far more dangerous than trash threatened the beach.

3   There was a plan to build a processing station for liquefied natural gas (LNG) 14 miles (22.5 kilometers) off the coast of Oxnard. It would be like a giant factory, 14 stories high and three football fields long, floating in the ocean. A pipeline 36 inches (almost a meter) in diameter—as big around as a hula hoop—would transport this highly explosive gas under the ocean to Oxnard, and then right through Erica's community.

4   "At first I couldn't believe it," she says. "I was really shocked. What if there was a leak or an explosion? People could get killed!" She asked around in her community and found out that nobody knew about the project. "We were going to be in danger from this facility, and the company wasn't even telling us about it." Erica started going to meetings with her friends from the beach cleanup to educate herself about what was happening.

pipeline   A pipeline carries gas or oil long distances underground.

5 Behind the new project was the largest mining company in the world, based in Australia. Their plan was to condense natural gas into a liquid by "supercooling" it to around −260° Fahrenheit (−162° Centigrade), and then ship it to their new floating processing station off the Oxnard coast. There, the liquid would be heated up until it was a gas again and would be sent out via pipeline to customers in California and the Western United States.

6 The process would send over 200 tons (181 metric tons) of air pollution per year across the 14 miles (22.5 kilometers) of ocean to Erica's community. Not only that, the station would take in millions of gallons of seawater per day to cool its generators, and discharge the water more than 28 degrees Fahrenheit (15 degrees Centigrade) hotter than the surrounding ocean. This hot wastewater (called "thermal waste") would cause serious harm to the surrounding ecosystem, killing zooplankton (very tiny floating creatures) and small fish critical to the survival of marine mammals and fisheries.

condense To condense something is to change it from a gas to a liquid.
via If you send something via a particular person or thing, that person or thing is taking or carrying it for you.

7   "Their point of view was that it was a cheaper gas," Erica explains. "They never considered the health of the people. They never considered the safety issues. Their idea was just to make money, and that was all."

8   Erica started going door to door in her mainly Spanish-speaking farmworker community. She pointed out where the big gas pipeline was going to cross people's yards and the fields where they worked. Escaping gas could cause an explosion and fire, she explained, and operations out in the ocean would make the air dirtier. People were already suffering because of pollution from a nearby power plant. "Many people had to use respirators to breathe, including my father. I didn't want to end up like that. I didn't think anybody should." Erica's neighbors were worried, but they didn't know what to do.

9   Erica didn't know either, but she cared too much to stay silent. Having grown up in the tiny town of Gómez Farías, in the Mexican state of Michoacán, she had a strong motivation to care for nature. "We grew our own food and raised our own animals. Taking care of nature was part of survival." She wanted to bring that same spirit to her new life in California.

respirators A respirator covers your mouth and helps you breathe.
motivation Your motivation is your reason for caring about something.

149

10   She joined her friends in weekly protests at the office of the natural gas company. Prospects of stopping the project did not look good. The governor was in favor of it, and so were the powerful state commissions that would have to approve it. "The word on the street was that there was nothing we could do."

11   Behind the scenes, however, opposition was growing, and Erica was becoming the spokesperson for the youth of the town. As her English improved, she talked to kids in her high school about what was going on. She regularly walked her neighborhood along the route of the proposed pipeline, using a hula hoop to show people the size of the pipe that would pass by their houses and under their elementary school. She talked to church groups. She talked to the media, and stories about the dangers of the proposed facility began appearing in the press. She gathered a group of young supporters to come with her to demonstrations. Important environmental groups like the Sierra Club took notice and began helping with the campaign.

12   After four years of educating people about the dangers of the natural gas project, Erica was ready for the next step. The California Land Commission, which would rule on the natural gas company permit and review its environmental report, had scheduled a public meeting for April 9, 2007. In an amazing show of opposition to the project, Erica helped bring 3,000 people to a demonstration outside the commission offices. More than 300 of them were high school students.

commissions   A commission is a group formed to make official decisions.
opposition   Opposition to an idea means disagreement with it.

13   Inside, Erica was one of the opposition speakers, representing the youth. "I didn't know if they would listen to me. My English wasn't good and I was only sixteen," she says. As she nervously approached the microphone, she was informed that time was running out. One minute and thirty seconds was all she had. "I couldn't give my prepared speech, so I just spoke from my heart."

14   The result was electrifying. When Erica was finished, people stood up and broke into applause, even though clapping was not allowed at the hearings. One of the commissioners said, "I'm very moved by your testimony, Erica. When I was your age, I was playing video games." The commission voted 2–1 against the proposal.

15   Three days later, Erica spoke at a meeting of the California Coastal Commission, which oversees the well-being of the California coast. Again, her testimony was well received, as were the statements by other speakers from environmental and citizen groups. The commission voted 12–0 to reject the natural gas proposal.

proposal   A proposal is an idea that people discuss and decide on.
oversees   A person or group that oversees an effort is responsible for it.

16   Erica was jubilant, but she also knew that the governor's decision still lay ahead. Unless he also rejected the proposal, it would be approved. It was well known that he favored the project.

17   "We made thousands of phone calls and sent thousands of postcards telling the governor why this facility was a bad idea." In July 2007, the governor made an unexpected move: He vetoed the project. Erica and her friends had won! Other companies have since tried to push through similar projects, but now there are many more environmental requirements for approval—and Erica and the thousands of people she inspired are keeping watch.

18   Only the second person in her family to go to college, Erica wants to become an environmental lawyer so she can fight for the environment and for the rights of communities. She wants other young people to speak out when they see something wrong, even if they feel shy about it at first. She likes to quote the words of her role model, César Chávez: "We are the future. The future is ours."

Collaborative Discussion

Look back at what you wrote on page 144. Tell a partner something you learned from this text. Then work with a group to discuss the questions below. Refer to details and examples in *Safeguarding the California Coast* to explain your answers. Take notes for your responses. When you speak, use your notes.

1. Reread pages 146–149. What problems would the proposed gas processing station cause for local residents and the environment?

2. List the sequence of events that Erica Fernandez participated in that led to the governor rejecting the gas processing project.

3. Erica likes the following quote: "We are the future. The future is ours." Why do you think she likes this quote?

Listening Tip

Be sure the speaker has finished his or her thought before you volunteer to share your ideas.

Speaking Tip

Speak clearly and make eye contact with each member of your group as you speak.

Write a Dialogue

PROMPT

In *Safeguarding the California Coast*, you read about Erica Fernandez's strong opposition to the proposed gas pipeline project. In order to stop the project from happening, she went door-to-door to tell her neighbors about the proposal. Not everyone agreed with her viewpoint. Some neighbors supported the proposal.

Imagine a conversation Erica might have with a neighbor who disagreed with her. Write the dialogue between Erica and a neighbor who supports the gas pipeline proposal. Review the text for ideas and facts that support each person's point of view. Don't forget to use some of the Critical Vocabulary words in your writing.

PLAN

Make notes with facts and ideas for and against the gas pipeline proposal that you find in the text.

Now write your dialogue between Erica and a neighbor who disagrees with her, using evidence from *Safeguarding the California Coast.*

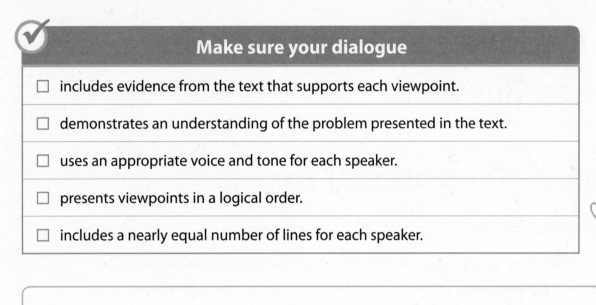

Make sure your dialogue

☐ includes evidence from the text that supports each viewpoint.

☐ demonstrates an understanding of the problem presented in the text.

☐ uses an appropriate voice and tone for each speaker.

☐ presents viewpoints in a logical order.

☐ includes a nearly equal number of lines for each speaker.

Essential Question

What fascinates us about our seas and shorelines?

Write an Informational Article

PROMPT Think about what you learned about the ocean in this module.

Imagine you are a reporter for your local newspaper and you've been assigned to write about oceans—what is fascinating about them, and why we should take care of them. Use evidence from at least two of the selections to write your article.

I will write about _____.

✓ Make sure your informational article

☐ includes an introduction that states what is fascinating about oceans and why people should take care of them.

☐ provides details that support your statement about oceans.

☐ includes text evidence and examples from at least two selections as support.

☐ includes references to visuals and graphics.

☐ provides a clear summary at the end.

How can you explain the wonders of the oceans to a reader? What important information shows what is precious and worth preserving about the sea? Look back at your notes, and revisit the texts and video as necessary.

In the chart below, write your main idea and supporting details about oceans. Then use evidence from the texts and video to outline your article. Use Critical Vocabulary words where appropriate.

My Topic: _____

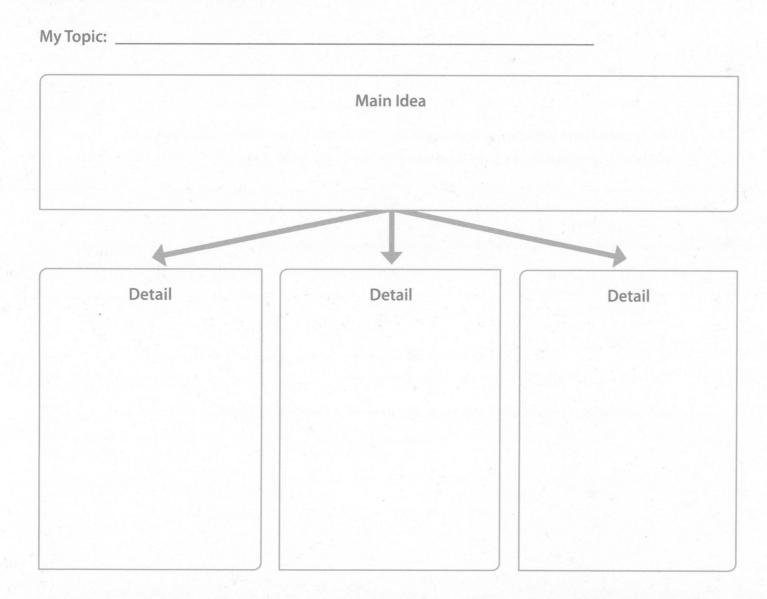

Main Idea

Detail

Detail

Detail

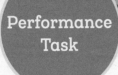

DRAFT ·· Write your article.

Write an **introduction** that clearly states your main idea about what is fascinating about oceans.

For the **body of your article**, use your main idea and details chart to write why people should take care of oceans. Include supporting evidence from the texts.

In your **conclusion**, restate your main idea about what is fascinating about oceans.

REVISE AND EDIT · Review your draft.

The revision and editing steps give you an opportunity to look carefully at your writing and make changes. Work with a partner to determine whether your main idea and supporting details are complete and clear to your readers. Use these questions to help evaluate and improve your article.

✓ PURPOSE/ FOCUS	ORGANIZATION	EVIDENCE	LANGUAGE/ VOCABULARY	CONVENTIONS
☐ Does my article state a clear main idea? ☐ Have I stayed on topic?	☐ Does my introduction state what is fascinating about oceans? ☐ Have I provided a conclusion that restates what is fascinating about oceans?	☐ Does the text evidence I chose support what is fascinating about oceans and why people should care about them?	☐ Did I use linking words to create a smooth flow? ☐ Did I use Critical Vocabulary correctly?	☐ Have I used correct spelling? ☐ Have I capitalized words correctly?

PUBLISH · Share your work.

Create a Finished Copy Make a final copy of your informational article. You may wish to include a photo or illustration. Consider these options to share your article:

1 Collect all the articles and bind them in a science magazine.

2 Publish your article on a school website or social networking page and ask for feedback from readers.

3 Choose a partner and exchange articles. Discuss what you like about each other's article and compare and contrast your thoughts about the ocean.

Champions of the Game

"What I know most surely about morality and the duty of man I owe to sport."

—Albert Camus

? Essential Question

How do sports test an athlete's character?

Get Curious
Video

Words About Sports

The words in the chart will help you talk and write about the selections in this module. Which words about sports have you seen before? Which words are new to you?

Add to the Vocabulary Network on page 163 by writing synonyms, antonyms, and related words and phrases for each word.

After you read each selection in this module, come back to the Vocabulary Network and keep building it. Add more boxes if you need to.

WORD	MEANING	CONTEXT SENTENCE
attributes (noun)	Your attributes are traits or qualities that help define you.	My cousin's positive attributes, such as her determination and focus, helped her win the game.
rivals (noun)	Rivals compete against each other to win something or to prove that they are better.	The two teams had been rivals for many years and always played hard against each other.
leagues (noun)	A league is a group of sports clubs that play against each other for a championship.	My sisters belong to two different softball leagues and compete against each other every Saturday.
statistics (noun)	Statistics are facts or data that are combined and considered together.	I keep statistics on all my favorite players so I can track their progress.

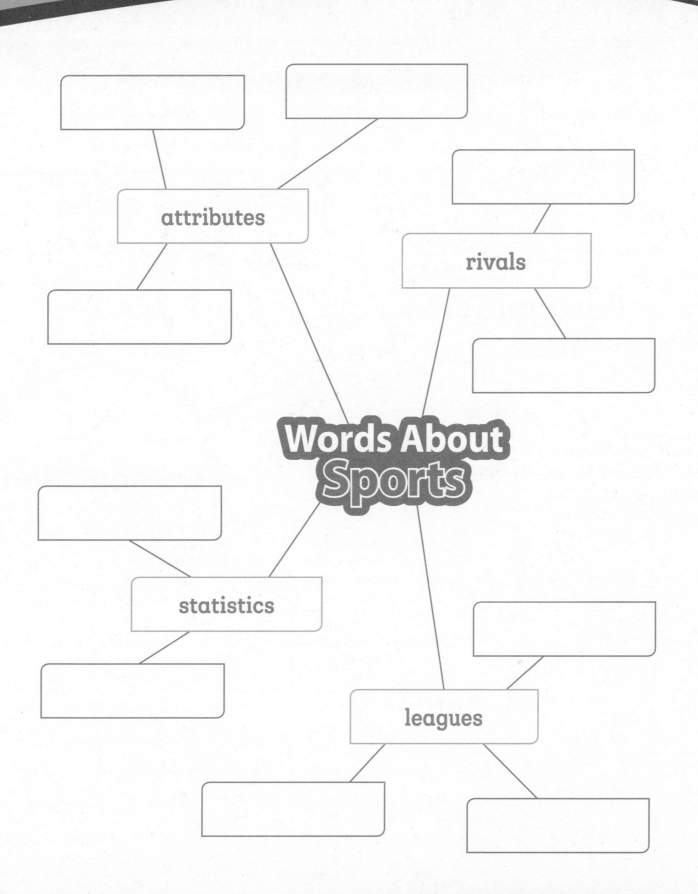

attributes

rivals

Words About
Sports

statistics

leagues

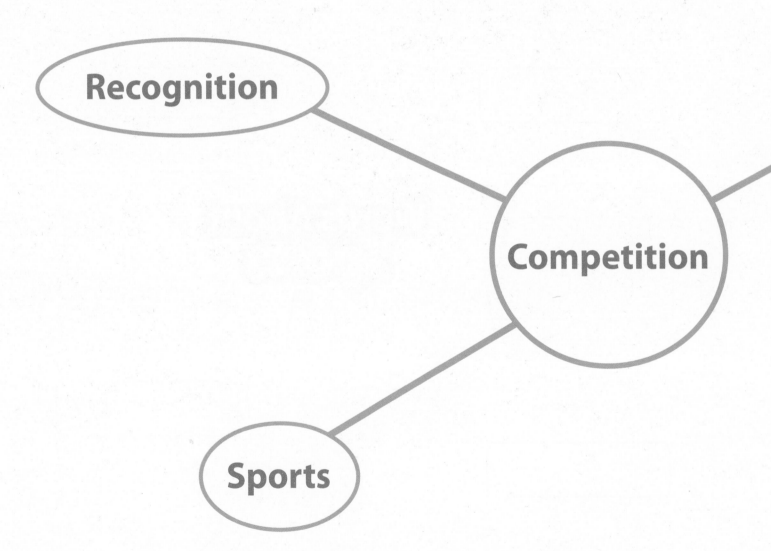

Recognition

Competition

Sports

Athletes

myNotes

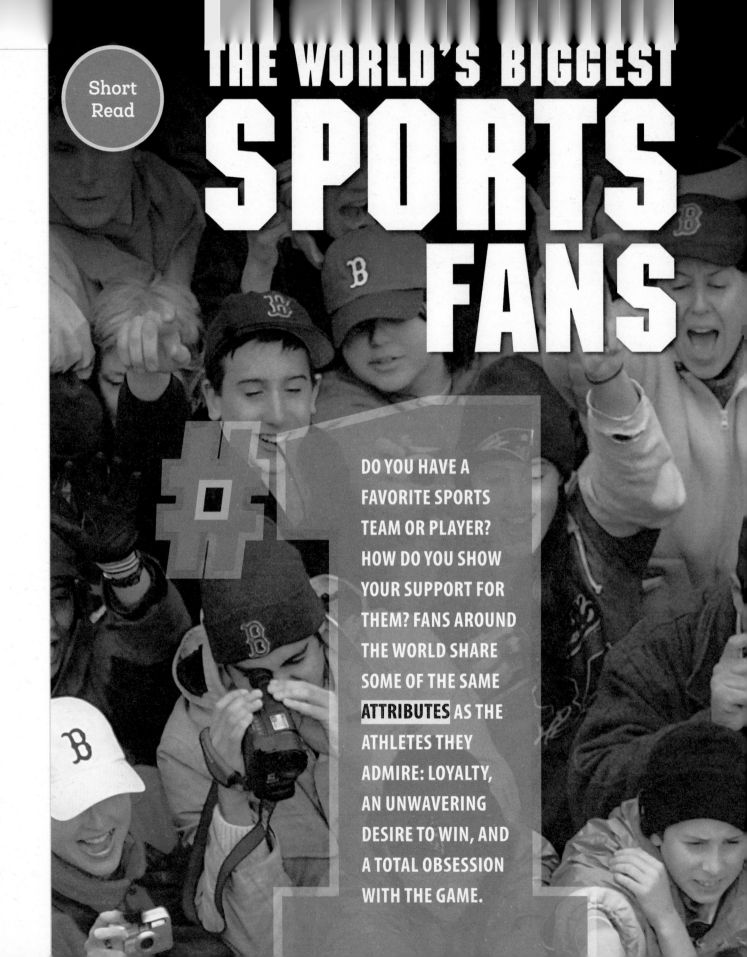

THE WORLD'S BIGGEST SPORTS FANS

#1

DO YOU HAVE A FAVORITE SPORTS TEAM OR PLAYER? HOW DO YOU SHOW YOUR SUPPORT FOR THEM? FANS AROUND THE WORLD SHARE SOME OF THE SAME **ATTRIBUTES** AS THE ATHLETES THEY ADMIRE: LOYALTY, AN UNWAVERING DESIRE TO WIN, AND A TOTAL OBSESSION WITH THE GAME.

WHEN LOSERS FINALLY WIN

Historically, fans of the Boston Red Sox and the Chicago Cubs baseball teams are known for their ability to suffer. The Red Sox, for example, didn't win a single World Series championship from 1918 until 2004. The fans, who call themselves the "Red Sox Nation," believed that they suffered from the "Curse of the Bambino" after the team owner sold baseball great Babe Ruth's contract to the New York Yankees after the 1919 season. The 2004 team, jokingly nicknamed the "Idiots" was a silly, yet amazingly skilled group that was able to defeat the Cardinals in the World Series, ending an 86-year losing streak.

THE CHEESEHEADS

Some fans are so dedicated that they will take an insult and turn it into a point of pride. The Green Bay Packers are a beloved Wisconsin football team, and fans of the team's rivals, the Chicago Bears, used to yell "cheese heads" at the Packers' fans—referring to Wisconsin's long association with cheese and the dairy industry. An inspired Packers fan, Ralph Bruno, created a cheese-wedge hat for himself. He first wore it to a Milwaukee Brewers baseball game. Soon after, he created a company to sell the "cheese heads" to all Wisconsin sports fans.

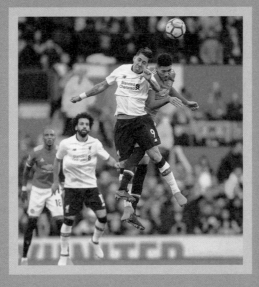

LIVERPOOL VS. MANCHESTER

The Liverpool and Manchester British football (known as soccer in the U.S.) teams are the most successful in England with many trophies and titles over their 100+ year existence. Both teams are wildly popular overseas as well. Manchester United claims that they have 659 million fans worldwide! One way the Premier League (in which Liverpool and Manchester play) measures the popularity of their teams is by the volume of the screaming crowds. In 2014, Manchester won among all premier league teams with fans reaching 84 decibels during the first 60 seconds of the game. That's about as loud as the sound of a train passing 100 feet in front of you.

FANTASY SPORTS

For the truly obsessed sports fan, cheering during real games just isn't enough. Fantasy leagues have become very popular in the last ten years. More than 59 million people in North America play fantasy sports—including 10 million teenagers. Fans choose from real athletes in an online version of a team draft, and create their personal fantasy team. Then, each chosen player's real-game statistics add up to the team performance.

Notice &
Note
Contrasts and
Contradictions

Prepare to Read

GENRE STUDY **Narrative nonfiction** gives factual information by telling a true story.

- Narrative nonfiction presents events in sequential, or chronological, order. This helps readers understand what happened and when.

- Narrative nonfiction may include visuals such as photographs, illustrations, maps, and diagrams to help readers better understand historical facts and details in the text.

SET A PURPOSE **Think about** the title and genre of this text. Have you ever heard of the athlete Babe Didrikson Zaharias? What do you think you might learn by reading this text? Write your ideas in the box below.

CRITICAL VOCABULARY

versatility

unprecedented

lavishly

unadorned

antics

devotion

jalopy

procession

▶ Build Background:
Equality in Sports

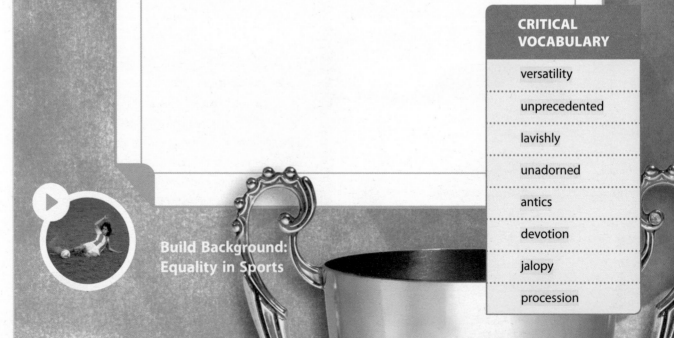

Babe
Didrikson
Zaharias

The Making of a Champion

by Russell Freedman

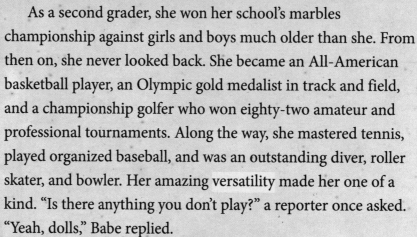

1 As far back as she could remember, Babe Didrikson Zaharias lived only for sports, and she loved and excelled in them all. "Before I was even into my teens," she wrote in her autobiography, "I knew exactly what I wanted to be when I grew up. My goal was to be the greatest athlete that ever lived."

2 As a second grader, she won her school's marbles championship against girls and boys much older than she. From then on, she never looked back. She became an All-American basketball player, an Olympic gold medalist in track and field, and a championship golfer who won eighty-two amateur and professional tournaments. Along the way, she mastered tennis, played organized baseball, and was an outstanding diver, roller skater, and bowler. Her amazing versatility made her one of a kind. "Is there anything you don't play?" a reporter once asked. "Yeah, dolls," Babe replied.

3 For more than two decades, her wide, delighted smile appeared regularly in the nation's newspapers. Sportswriters called her "The Wonder Girl," "The Super Athlete," or simply "The Babe," and the Associated Press poll of sports editors voted her Woman Athlete of the Year an unprecedented six times. In the eyes of many, she was and still is the greatest woman athlete of all time.

4 Babe was lavishly gifted, but she became a champion through relentless practice and a burning desire to excel. When she took up tennis, she played sixteen or seventeen practice sets a day. She ran the soles off a pair of tennis shoes every two weeks. "Oh, how that girl would *work* for the things she wanted," her sister Lillie recalled.

5 Babe Didrikson Zaharias won more contests and broke more records that any woman in sports history.

---

versatility   A person who has versatility has many different skills.
unprecedented   Something that is unprecedented has never happened before.
lavishly   Something that is done lavishly is done in an abundant way.

Babe mastered diving . . .

and won eighty-two golf tournaments.

6   She rose to fame in an era when women athletes had few chances for competition and were looked upon by many people as freaks or aberrations. "Girls in sports were [considered] tomboys and a little weird," according to Babe's friend and fellow golfer Peggy Kirk Bell.

7   When Babe was growing up, those attitudes were being challenged. She was nine years old in 1920, when the nineteenth amendment to the Constitution finally gave American women the right to vote. That same year, the United States sent its first women's team—swimmers—to the Olympics. Women were demanding equality in many areas of life, and young women who loved sports had more opportunities than ever before.

171

8   Even so, competitive sports were still regarded as masculine territory. An aspiring female athlete had to confront society's strict view of what a proper woman should be and should do. Young Babe Didrikson seemed to defy conventional notions of femininity. She had the natural grace and buoyancy of a born athlete, but she was also tough, strong, ambitious, and fiercely competitive, with hacked-off hair and an unadorned face. Her battle to succeed as an athlete was, at the same time, a battle for the right to be herself, and her example helped break down barriers not just for women athletes, but for everyone. "Babe was a very brave girl or she could never have become the person she was," said her friend and former teacher Ruth Scurlock.

9   Golf was the game she loved most of all, and with her wisecracks, clowning, and trick shots, she brought a new sense of theater to the golf course. In 1947, she caused a sensation when she captured the British Women's Amateur gold championship, becoming the first American to win that historic tournament since its inception in 1893. "We have not seen a fairway phantom like her—not in 47 years," marveled a London newspaper. "What a Babe!"

10   Growing up, she almost seemed to court trouble. At Magnolia Elementary School, in Beaumont, Texas, her antics often sent her to the office of the principal, Effie Piland. "One day I heard the kids outside yelling for me," Mrs. Piland recalled. "I went outside and there was Mildred (Babe's given name), sitting on top of the flagpole. She had climbed to the top and I told her to come down."

11   According to her brother Ole, Jr., Babe's stunts earned her a second nickname: "The Worst Kid on Doucette [Street]." Whenever a window was broken by a baseball, she was the one who got the blame. "She was just too active to settle down," Ole remembered. "She always wanted to be running, jumping, or throwing something."

---

unadorned   Something that is unadorned is not decorated or made fancier.
antics   Antics are funny, goofy ways of behaving.

Students at Magnolia Elementary School in Beaumont, Texas. Babe is in the front row on the far left.

12   Everyone who knew Babe recognized her passion for sports and her fierce determination to win any game she played. She could run faster, throw a ball farther, and hit more home runs than anyone her age, and she took pride in beating the boys at their own game. "She was the best at *everything* we did," said Lillie.

13   When Babe entered Beaumont High School, she went out for every sport in sight. She won a swimming match sponsored by the YWCA and, with her classmate Lois "Pee Wee" Blanchette, easily captured the doubles crown in tennis. She was a member of the girls' baseball, volleyball, and golf teams, excelling at and reveling in every sport she tried. Her physical education teacher and coach at Beaumont High, a young woman named Beatrice Lytle, gave Babe her first formal training in several sports. Years later, Lytle remembered Babe Didrikson as a superb natural athlete.

14   "I saw possibly twelve thousand young women over those years," she said. "I observed them closely and I trained a lot of them to be fine athletes. But there was never anyone in all those thousands who was anything like Babe. I never again saw the likes of her. Babe was blessed with a body that was perfect. I can still remember how her muscles *flowed* as she walked. She had a neuromuscular coordination that is very, very rare."

15 Despite her skills, Babe did not, at first, win a place on the girls' basketball team, the Miss Royal Purples. "They said I was too small," she wrote. "I couldn't accept the idea that I wasn't good enough for the basketball team. I was determined to show everybody."

16 She spent hours practicing—dribbling, pivoting, passing, shooting baskets—and she pestered the coach of the boys' team for advice. "He took the time to help me," she wrote, "because he could see I was interested. . . . I'd say, 'Coach Dimmitt, tell those women I can play basketball!'"

17 Babe eventually played on every girls' team at Beaumont High. "She wanted to excel," said her friend Raymond Alford. "She wanted to show you up. . . . I think her motives were probably a lot like mine. I knew that winning in sports was the only way I'd ever be recognized. Babe and I were both from poor families. If you did not have a car or if you did not have money, you were unacceptable. . . . Sports was a way of getting to be equal, and I think that's what carried Babe through and made her work so hard. . . . There was no other way to get ahead except sports."

Babe, at the front, prepares to shoot a basket.

18   Babe's single-minded **devotion** to sports set her apart from most of the other girls. "There was an academic group and an athletic group among the girls," recalled Ruth Scurlock, her English teacher. "Babe and her few friends in the athletic group wore denim skirts with pockets, socks like gym hose and flat oxford shoes. The others, the so-called society girls, wore their hair permanent waved. They wore silk stockings and high heels. These were the 'sissy girls' to Babe . . . but they were in the overwhelming majority and they were the leaders. It was terribly difficult for Babe to do what she wanted to do. Even in her own tough neighborhood, the other girls didn't like her because she was an athlete. Her very excellence at sports made her unacceptable to the other girls. She was an alien in her own land, believe me."

19   The most popular girls at Beaumont High belonged to a small, select group called the Kacklers Klub, which was dedicated to the support of Beaumont's male athletes. The Kacklers' motto was "Athletes are our favorite boys." And the chief requirement for membership was good looks and a pleasing personality. Babe was never invited to belong to the Kacklers, and she never expected to be. She was more interested in being cheered than in cheering others. Besides, she never wore jewelry, hated makeup, and didn't care about "fussy clothing."

20   "Babe was bucking society even then," said Ruth Scurlock. "She was simply being herself. She really had no other choice, I suppose."

21   But if Babe felt like an outsider—snubbed by the fashionable "society girls" and teased by some of the boys—she acted as though she couldn't care less. "She was just sure of herself," said one classmate. "She could do everything in athletics well, and she wasn't bashful about telling you about it."

---

devotion   Devotion is commitment to an activity.

Boxing was one of Babe's many sports.

22   She certainly wasn't bashful about standing up for herself. Once, she was challenged to a boxing match by "Red" Reynolds, the star halfback on the Royal Purple football team. "Go ahead, hit me as hard as you can," Reynolds taunted, sticking out his chin. "You can't hurt me!"

23   Babe took him at his word. She swung once, and Red dropped to the floor, senseless. "They were pouring water on me to clear the bells and birdies out of my head," he remembered. "That gal really gave me a K.O." For the rest of his life, Reynolds bragged about how he had been knocked out by the famous Babe Didrikson.

Warming up for the javelin throw

24 *After graduating from high school, Babe achieved great success as a young adult athlete. She competed on an amateur "industrial team" of the Employers' Casualty Insurance Company of Dallas. She won the 1931 Amateur Athletic Union (AAU) women's basketball championship, and in 1932, she competed in eight out of ten events she entered at the AAU Championships. Shortly after that, Babe competed at the 1932 Los Angeles Olympic Games.*

25 Six track-and-field events were open to women that year. The Olympic Committee had ruled that a single athlete could compete in no more than three events. Babe entered the javelin throw, the 80-meter hurdles, and the running high jump, events in which she had set records two weeks earlier in Evanston, Illinois.

26 The javelin throw was held late in the afternoon on the first day of competition. Each contestant was allowed three tries. Babe waited at the side of the field, swinging her arms and stretching nervously. When her turn came for her first throw, she paused briefly, left hand on her hip holding the javelin about ear level over her shoulder. Rising slightly on her toes, she started down the runway, drew back her arm, rotated to the right, and with a hop-step, let the javelin fly. As she did, her hand slipped off the cord on the handle and she felt a sharp pain in her right shoulder.

27 Instead of soaring in a high arc as it usually did, the javelin zoomed along close to the ground "like a catcher's peg from home plate to second base," Babe recalled, before finally slicing into the ground. Babe had set an Olympic record and had broken her own recognized world record by more than four feet with a throw of 143 feet 4 inches. When the new record was announced over the loudspeaker, the stadium erupted with cheers and applause. Babe trotted about the field, her hands clasped high above her head.

28   Her face was beaming, but her shoulder hurt. Years later she revealed that she'd been unable to warm up properly because of the crowd on the field. "Nobody knew it, but I tore a cartilage in my right shoulder when my hand slipped making that throw," she wrote. "On my last two turns, people thought I wasn't trying because the throws weren't much good. But they didn't have to be." No other competitor came close to Babe's new record. She had won her first Olympic gold medal.

29   Two days later, the qualifying heats for the 80-meter hurdles were held. Again, Babe was hoping to break both the Olympic record and her own world record. She did both in the qualifying heat, completing the course in 11.8 seconds—a tenth of a second faster than the time she had set in Evanston, during the Olympic Games tryouts.

30   The finals of the 80-meter hurdles were held the next day. Babe's chief rival was her teammate Evelyne Hall. As the runners knelt at the starting line, Didrikson and Hall were in lanes side by side. Babe was a bit too anxious. She jumped the gun, and everyone was called back. Jumping the gun twice meant automatic disqualification. The runners knelt again, and when the gun cracked, Babe held herself back for a split second, until she saw the other runners in front of her. Then she surged forward.

31   Evelyne Hall was ahead, leading by a stride over the first hurdles. Babe closed in on her with powerful leaps and then pulled even. The two athletes were neck and neck as they cleared the last two hurdles They appeared to be absolutely even when their feet touched the ground just before the finish line. As they hit the tape together, Babe threw up her arm and yelled to Hall, "Well, I won again!"

32   The official timer declared that both women had reached the tape in 11.7 seconds—a new world record. It looked like a dead heat. The judges huddled in confusion and took nearly half an hour to make their decision. Finally, they declared Babe Didrikson the winner. She was awarded her second gold medal.

Babe (right) on her way to a new world record of 11.8 seconds in the qualifying heat of the 80-meter hurdles.

An "eye-lash victory." Evelyne Hall (right) and Babe Didrikson breaking the tape in the finals of the 80-meter hurdles.

33 Babe's double Olympic victory—two gold medals in two events—made headlines all over the country. It now seemed possible that she could win a third track-and-field gold medal in a single Olympic year, something that no woman had done. Excitement mounted as she prepared for her third and final event, the running high jump.

34 Her chief rival was a teammate, Jean Shiley, the captain of the American team and the athlete who had previously tied Didrikson for first place. On the day of the event, all other competitors had dropped out by the time the bar had been raised to 5 feet 5 inches—nearly two inches higher than the record that Didrikson and Shiley had set jointly in Evanston. Both women cleared that height, setting a new world record. To break the tie, a jump-off had to be held. The judges raised the crossbar an inch, to 5 feet 6 inches.

35 Jean Shiley was up first. She failed to clear the bar. Then it was Babe's turn to try for her third gold medal. Sportswriter Grantland Rice described what happened: "There was a wild shout as Miss Didrikson cleared the bar by at least four inches. It was the most astonishing jump any woman ever dreamed about. But luck was against her. As the Babe fluttered to earth her left foot struck the standard a glancing blow, just six inches from the ground—and the crossbar toppled into the dust with her."

36 The judges ruled that Babe's jump was a miss. They dropped the bar to 5 feet 5 ¼ inches—lower than the first jump-off, but high enough to give each woman a chance to break the tie and set a new record.

37 This time Jean Shiley made it. Then Babe ran toward the crossbar and leaped off the ground, kicking up her feet and rolling in midair as she went over the bar.

38   It was another tie—or was it? The judges huddled. According to Olympic rules then in effect, a high jumper had to clear the bar feet first. If the jumper went over the bar head first in a "dive," the jump was disqualified. The judges ruled that Babe had dived. The first-place gold medal went to Jean Shiley, the silver to Babe Didrikson.

Babe sets a new world record in the high jump.

39   Many of the reporters who were there felt that the decision was unfair, since Babe had been jumping the same way all afternoon, using a style called the Western roll, an acceptable jumping technique that had never been challenged until the Olympics. In 1932, however, most women used the classic scissors jump, which allowed less chance of fouling. The rule that the feet must cross the bar first held for women, but not for men, and was eliminated the following year. In recognition of the controversial nature of the decision, Babe was later made coholder with Jean Shiley of the high-jump world record set that day.

40   Despite the controversies, Babe emerged as the undisputed star of the women's games. She had broken world records in each event she entered and walked away with three medals—two gold and one silver. BABE BREAKS RECORDS EASIER THAN DISHES, announced one headline. Another said, BABE GETS PRAISE ON COAST: IS CALLED THE GREATEST WOMAN ATHLETE OF THE WORLD.

41   Babe was hailed as a conquering hero when she flew back to Dallas in a privately chartered American Airways transport escorted by fifteen United States Army planes, all paid for by her employer, Employers Casualty. Ten thousand people, including the mayor, were waiting at the airport to greet her. As she stepped from the plane, carrying a javelin in her hand, the Dallas Police Department band struck up "Hail to the Chief," and the city's fire chief escorted her to his gleaming red limousine, which was draped with hundreds of roses. Members of the Golden Cyclones, the group of female athletes that Babe competed with, formed an honor guard on either side of the open car as a festive ticker-tape parade set off through the streets of Dallas, with Babe perched on top of the back seat, waving to thousands of cheering fans who lined the route.

42   Babe's parents, her brother Ole, and her sister Lillie had driven up from Beaumont in Ole's battered old jalopy to help celebrate. By the time they arrived, the parade was about to start.

---

jalopy   A jalopy is a worn out old car.

When Babe spotted them, she yelled, "Come on up here! Come on!" motioning for them to join her in the fire chief's car.

43   "[We] got up there with her," Lillie recalled, "and there were roses all over us, all over us. . . . We was so dirty and so sweaty when we finally found the landing field. We had two flat tires on the way there and the big shots, they was all looking at us country folks, but we didn't care. Babe didn't care. We had our parade through Dallas—confetti and scrap paper falling on the cars."

44   After the parade, Babe was feted at a luncheon attended by five hundred people at the Adolphus Hotel. During the speeches, when she was called to the microphone and invited to say something, she said simply, "I'm tickled to be back home," and sat down.

Homecoming: Babe's parents, Hannah (third from left) and Ole (far right), join the welcoming dignitaries in Dallas.

The conquering hero: Babe waves to her cheering fans as she rides through the streets of Dallas.

45   From Dallas, Babe flew to Beaumont for an equally stupendous welcome. Once again, thousands came to greet her, bands played, and crowds cheered as she rode through the streets in the Beaumont fire chief's red car, which was also draped in roses. This time, members of the Miss Royal Purple high school teams marched as Babe's honor guard.

46   At a reception following the parade, Babe was presented with the key to the City of Beaumont. Her former Miss Royal Purple teammates gave her a silver cup with the inscription "We knew her when." A procession of dignitaries made speeches praising her, and her old friend, sportswriter Tiny Scurlock, told the guests, "She's the same swell kid she used to be."

47   The "worst kid on Doucette" had become, at the age of twenty-one, Beaumont's most illustrious citizen.

> **procession**   A procession is a group of people who are walking, riding, or driving as part of a parade or other public event.

Collaborative Discussion

Look back at what you wrote on page 168. Tell a partner what interested you most about this text. Then work with a group to discuss the questions below. Refer to details and examples in *Babe Didrikson Zaharias* to explain your answers. Take notes for your responses. When you speak, use your notes.

1 Babe said that her goal was "to be the greatest athlete that ever lived." What did Babe have to do to achieve her goal? Cite evidence from the text to support your answer.

2 How do the photographs help you better understand details in the text? Cite specific photographs in your answer.

3 If Babe could see women's sports today, how might she describe the similarities and differences between how women athletes are treated today compared to how they were treated when she played sports? Use details from the text to support your idea.

Listening Tip

Listen for specific details. What details does the speaker use in his or her response? What details or examples can you add?

Speaking Tip

Build your ideas onto what speakers have said before you. If you do not agree with what a speaker has said, politely say so, and then explain why.

Write a List

In *Babe Didrikson Zaharias*, you read about Babe Didrikson Zaharias, a gifted athlete who broke down gender barriers in sports and became one of the top athletes of her time.

Babe Didrikson Zaharias was special in many different ways. She had great talent and ability in several sports, but she also had a strong personality. What are five character and physical traits that helped make her one of the top athletes of the twentieth century?

PLAN

Reread *Babe Didrikson Zaharias* and study the photographs. Make a list of Babe's achievements. How did she accomplish each one? Think about her character and the physical traits that helped make her a top athlete.

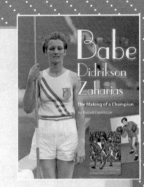

Now write your list of Babe's traits from *Babe Didrikson Zaharias.*

Make sure your list

☐ has an appropriate title.
☐ includes five character or physical traits, each beginning a new line.
☐ uses text evidence to support your chosen traits.
☐ makes connections between Babe's traits and her achievements as a top athlete of the twentieth century.
☐ uses punctuation marks correctly, including commas and quotation marks.

Notice & Note
Words of the Wiser

Prepare to Read

GENRE STUDY **Poetry** uses the sounds and rhythms of words to show images and express feelings.

- Poets use details that appeal to the senses to describe ideas.
- Poets use figurative language, such as similes and metaphors, to develop the ideas in their poems.
- Free verse poetry does not have a regular meter or consistent stanzas.

SET A PURPOSE **Think about** the titles and genre of these poems. Why do you think some poets write poetry about sports? Write your ideas below.

Meet the Author:
Kwame Alexander

CRITICAL VOCABULARY

impersonation

endure

unity

bicker

Four poems capture the spirit of sports.

SPORTS
Poetry

At the End of Warm-Ups, My Brother Tries to Dunk

by Kwame Alexander

1   Not even close, JB.
What's the matter?
The hoop too high for you? I snicker
but it's not funny to him,
especially when I take off from center court,
my hair like wings,
each lock lifting me higher and HIGHER
like a 747 ZOOM **ZOOM!**
I throw down so hard,
the fiberglass trembles.
BOO YAH, Dad screams
from the top row.
I'm the only kid
on the team
who can do that.

2   The gym is a loud, crowded circus.
My stomach is a roller coaster.
My head, a carousel.
The air, heavy with the smell
of sweat, popcorn,
and the sweet perfume
of mothers watching sons.
Our mom, a.k.a. Dr. Bell, a.k.a. The Assistant Principal,
is talking to some of the teachers
on the other side of the gym.
I'm feeling better already.
Coach calls us in,
does his Phil Jackson impersonation.

---

impersonation An impersonation is when you pretend to be someone else by speaking or acting like that person.

Love ignites the spirit, brings teams together, he says.
JB and I glance at each other,
ready to bust out laughing,
but Vondie, our best friend,
beats us to it.
The whistle goes off.
Players gather at center circle,
dap each other,
pound each other.
Referee tosses the jump ball.
Game on.

Analysis of Baseball

by May Swenson

1 It's about
the ball,
the bat,
and the mitt.
Ball hits
bat, or it
hits mitt.
Bat doesn't
hit ball,
bat meets it.
Ball bounces
off bat, flies
air, or thuds
ground (dud)
or it
fits mitt.

2 Bat waits
for ball
to mate.
Ball hates
to take bat's
bait. Ball
flirts, bat's
late, don't
keep the date.
Ball goes in
(thwack) to mitt,
and goes out
(thwack) back
to mitt.

3 Ball fits
mitt, but
not all
the time.
Sometimes
ball gets hit
(pow) when bat
meets it,
and sails
to a place
where mitt
has to quit
in disgrace.
That's about
the bases
loaded,
about 40,000
fans exploded.

4 It's about
the ball,
the bat,
the mitt,
the bases
and the fans.
It's done
on a diamond,
and for fun.
It's about
home, and it's
about run.

You Can't Put Muhammad Ali in a Poem

by Juan Felipe Herrera

1 If you did—
            it would
                    knock you down (remember Liston) &
        if
            you were
                still stand
                        ing   you would
                                have to
    bust out (remember the March on Washington)
                of your shakin' vaulted
        poor thinkin' self (oh yes!)
                    & change (that's right!)

2 this big ol' world (say it!)
            & if   you did— You (yes, you)
                would have to battle w/words & rhymes & body & time—for
    your New Idea—(did you hear that) you would
                        have to
    endure (i hear you) & propose (what?)
                a new name for all
    (a new name?)

3 it could be Peace
        it could be Unity (sounds easy)
                but this poem   cannot
                                provide this
                                or   contain this

    Word   —(Watch out!)
    here it comes! &
                (it's gonna sting like a bee)

---

endure   If you endure a difficult situation, you put up with it.

unity   Unity is what happens when different parts or groups join
together as a whole, especially in agreement or harmony.

195

Taking One for the Team

by Sarah Holbrook

1 We practiced together,
sweat and stained.
We pummeled each other
and laughed off pain.
Teams may disagree,
may tease,
may blame.
Teams may bicker and whine,
but get down for the game.

2 You had my back.
We fought the fight.
And though our score
was less last night,
we're walking tall.
Our team came through
and stuck together like Crazy Glue.
I'm proud to say
I lost with you.

> **bicker** To bicker means to argue about unimportant things.

Collaborative Discussion

Look back at what you wrote on page 188. Tell a partner two things you learned from this text. Then work with a group to discuss the questions below. Refer to details and examples in *Sports Poetry* to explain your answers. Take notes for your responses. When you speak, use your notes.

1 Reread pages 190–191. Which simile or metaphor from "At the End of Warm-Ups, My Brother Tries to Dunk" helps you visualize an image or understand a feeling?

2 Reread page 192 and notice the rhyming words *fun* and *run* in the last stanza of the poem. Why do you think the poet chose these rhyming words? What do they tell you about the game of baseball?

3 Compare and contrast the sports poems in this selection. What do they have in common? How are they different?

 **Listening Tip**

Give your full attention to the speaker when he or she is speaking. Look at the speaker to show that you are listening.

Speaking Tip

Make sure to speak at a pace that isn't too fast or too slow.

Write a Sports Poem

PROMPT

In *Sports Poetry*, you explored different ways poets structure their poems to create vivid images, feelings, and even humor.

Imagine your class is making a book of sports poetry. Choose one athlete or sport you care about. Then write a poem with at least five lines. Start your poem by using one line or an adapted line from one of the poems in *Sports Poetry*.

PLAN

Reread the poems and write down lines of poetry from *Sports Poetry* that interest you. Make notes about the figurative language, repetition, and interesting word choices you see in these lines.

WRITE

Now select one line of poetry from *Sports Poetry* to use or adapt to write your own poem about a favorite athlete or sport.

Make sure your poem
☐ has an appropriate title.
☐ includes details that appeal to the senses.
☐ begins with one line or an adapted line from a poem in *Sports Poetry*.
☐ uses figurative language, repetition, or interesting word choices.
☐ includes at least five lines.

Notice & Note
Contrasts and Contradictions

Prepare to Read

GENRE STUDY **Persuasive texts** give an author's opinion about a topic and try to convince readers to believe that opinion.

- Authors of persuasive texts may organize their ideas by explaining causes and effects.

- Persuasive texts include strong language and techniques to convince readers to believe their viewpoint. For example, appeal to emotion is a technique often used when authors share personal stories with their readers.

SET A PURPOSE **Think about** the title and genre of this text. When have you or a friend received a trophy or award? Why did you receive it and how did it make you feel? Write your ideas below.

Meet the Author:
Dr. Jonathan Fader

CRITICAL VOCABULARY

diminish

acknowledgment

reinforced

bribed

200

Who Gets a Trophy?

Selections by Betty Berdan, Katie Bugbee,
and Jonathan Fader, PhD

1   **Millions of kids across America get trophies for being on a sports team—regardless of whether they play well or win. Are participation trophies important to build kids' self-esteem, or do they send the wrong message about sports and life?**

Participation Trophies Send a Dangerous Message

by Betty Berdan

2   Like many other kids my age, I grew up receiving trophy after trophy, medal after medal, ribbon after ribbon for every sports season, science fair, and spelling bee I participated in. Today the dozens of trophies, ribbons, and medals sit in a corner of my room, collecting dust. They do not mean much to me because I know that identical awards sit in other children's rooms all over town and probably in millions of other homes across the country.

3   Trophies used to be awarded only to winners, but are now little more than party favors: reminders of an experience, not tokens of true achievement.

When awards are handed out like candy to every child who participates, they diminish in value. If every soccer player receives a trophy for merely showing up to practice and playing in games, the truly exceptional players are slighted. The same applies to teams. Regardless of individual effort or superior skills, all who participate receive equal acknowledgment.

4   Trophies for all convey an inaccurate and potentially dangerous life message to children: We are all winners. This message is repeated at the end of each sports season, year after year, and is only reinforced by the collection of trophies that continues to pile up. We begin to expect awards and praise for just showing up—to class, practice, after-school jobs—leaving us woefully unprepared for reality. Outside the protected bubble of childhood, not everyone is a winner.

5   Showing up to work, attending class, completing homework, and trying my best at sports practice are expected of me, not worthy of an award. These are the foundations of a long path to potential success, a success that is not guaranteed no matter how much effort I put in.

6   I believe that we should change how we reward children. Trophies should be given out for first, second, and third; participation should be recognized, but celebrated with words and a pat on the back rather than a trophy. As in sports, as well as life, it is fact that there's room for only a select few on the winners' podium.

diminish   When something diminishes, it becomes less important or valuable.

acknowledgment   An acknowledgment is an action or expression of recognition or appreciation.

reinforced   If something is reinforced, it is made stronger.

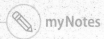

Bring on the Participation Trophies!

by Katie Bugbee

7 Two years ago, my 5-year-old son and 3-year-old daughter ran a race. It was a big pre-marathon kids' fun run event. And out of more than 300 kids, my 5-year-old son won. He actually won the whole thing.

8 My daughter came in about 300 spots behind him. And that afternoon, they both walked away with the same trophy—for participation.

9 And at the finish line, when they handed out ribbons, I thought, "Really? Here is my firstborn, pride-and-joy child, ecstatic over his big finish—and you give him some rinky-dink ribbon you give everyone else? Where is the mega-trophy with the word 'Winner' on it? You're seriously going to let this kid go home with a 2-cent ribbon? You cannot let this child go home with a 2-cent ribbon. He worked so hard—and won!"

10 But I bit my tongue and placed both of their medals around their necks as we celebrated.

11 For months, my son relived that winning moment: The first few seconds when he turned the bend and came running toward the crowd as the leader of the pack; the kid who started gaining on him; the police escort guiding his path; the shock (and tears) on his mother's face when I realized he was actually winning—just like he said he would that morning—and the cheers from the crowd.

12   And if you were to ask him about that moment, those are the details he'd tell you. The trophy—a two-inch-wide medallion hanging from a red, white, and blue ribbon—wouldn't even come up.

13   But you know who has the medal hanging on her wall? My daughter. She's not the athlete in our family. Or if she is, we just haven't figured out her sport yet. She's our witty, cheery, smart, creative child. But in an effort to get her some exercise, she gets signed up for things, and bribed to participate in things—and nothing has really stuck. She'd rather be home, playing with her toys, helping us with projects, or cheering for her brother.

14   But at the end of the season, she's really, really proud of her participation trophies. She finished.

15   So, for all the "high scorers" and MVPs out there, I applaud you. You should definitely be getting a bigger prize than those who just "showed up." But for the kids who get dragged along, encouraged to get off the sidelines and "exercise," who get cheers for actually making contact with the ball, I applaud you, too. Because you're the ones who need to be encouraged to keep trying next year. And it's just not as easy for you to show up.

16   So yes, keep giving out the participation trophies— at least in the Under 8 Leagues. And remember that they're hanging on the walls of kids who might never win the race, but are sure proud of themselves for finishing.

> **bribed** If you are bribed, someone has offered you money or something else that is valuable to get you to do something.

205

Should We Give Our Kids Participation Trophies?

by Jonathan Fader, PhD

**They've become a political controversy.
But what does psychology tell us?**

17 Last month, I was invited on a news program to discuss participation trophies. Detested by some, celebrated by others, they've become a hot topic again after a recent poll at *Reason* Magazine showed that 57% of people felt that trophies should only be given to winners.

18 But underneath all that, the question remains: should we give our kids trophies just for showing up?

19 Those perceptions change drastically among different economic and political groups, making the debate a proxy for larger political debates. As a sport psychologist, however, I actually think it's the wrong question to ask: in my opinion, trophies are a bad metric for winners and losers alike. Countless studies have shown that we're more committed to an activity when we do it out of passion, rather than an external reward such as a trophy.

20   The people who denigrate these trophies are often bent on teaching their kids that life has "winners" and "losers," but this can also be a tricky matter. The science suggests that we need to praise our kids on process, not results. For example, instead of dealing with defeat by telling our kids that "everyone's a winner at heart," we should praise them for how hard they hustled, what they did right, and how they improved.

21   But it's not just the "losers" we need to worry about; it's the "winners," too. Phrases like "You're a winner" or "You're a natural" can actually be toxic to how kids deal with losing. As the work of child psychologist Carol Dweck shows us, praising kids for their innate talents (in this study's case, their intelligence) actually makes it more difficult for them to cope when they're actually confronted with losing. Kids who are praised for their effort rather than their ability tend to strive harder, enjoy activities more, and deal with failure in a more resilient way.

So: should we give our kids participation trophies?

22   To be honest, it depends. As an unexpected surprise for someone's unwavering dedication and effort—absolutely! As a meaningless gesture for just "showing up"—maybe not. Kids are smart, and they know that being handed a participation trophy isn't the same as winning.

23   I coach tons of world-class athletes, and the pride they feel from a big win doesn't come from a ring, or a trophy, and it doesn't come from someone else telling them they're the best. That moment of pride comes from out-performing the best of the best, from knowing that years of relentless training led them to the performance of a lifetime. The pride comes from doing what they love and being the best at it.

24   And that's a feeling no trophy can provide.

Collaborative Discussion

Look back at what you wrote on page 200. Tell a partner two things you learned about Betty Berdan, Katie Bugbee, and Jonathan Fader from this text. Then work with a group to discuss the questions below. Refer to details and examples in *Who Gets a Trophy?* to explain your answers. Take notes for your responses. When you speak, use your notes.

1. How do Betty Berdan and Katie Bugbee agree and disagree on the topic of participation trophies?

2. Betty Berdan compares sports to life by saying "it is fact that there's room for only a select few on the winners' podium." What does she mean?

3. The first two articles give opinions against and for participation trophies. What opinion does Jonathan Fader offer in the last article, and how does he explain his position?

Listening Tip

When someone speaks, listen closely to what is said. Wait until the speaker finishes before you volunteer to share your own ideas.

Speaking Tip

When you speak, add to what other group members said before you. If you agree with what they said, mention that as well.

Write a Letter to the Editor

Across the country, participation trophies are distributed to young people involved in sports. Some people think these trophies are a terrific idea. Other people are concerned that they might have negative effects.

Write a letter to the editor of your local newspaper or news website. Express your opinion about participation trophies. Then support your opinion with facts and examples from *Who Gets a Trophy?*

PLAN

State your opinion about participation trophies in one sentence. Then record three details from *Who Gets a Trophy?* that support your opinion.

WRITE

Now write your letter to the editor about participation trophies. Include supporting details from *Who Gets a Trophy?*

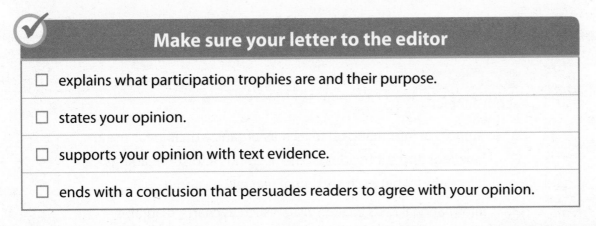

Make sure your letter to the editor
☐ explains what participation trophies are and their purpose.
☐ states your opinion.
☐ supports your opinion with text evidence.
☐ ends with a conclusion that persuades readers to agree with your opinion.

Prepare to Read

GENRE STUDY **Informational texts** give facts and examples about a topic.

- Authors of informational texts may organize their ideas using headings and subheadings. The headings and subheadings tell readers what each section of text will be about.

- Informational texts include visuals such as charts, diagrams, graphs, timelines, and maps. They also may include photographs, which help readers understand difficult concepts.

SET A PURPOSE **Think about** the title and genre of this text. What do you find interesting about extreme sports? What would you like to learn about these sports? Write your ideas below.

**Build Background:
Extreme Sports**

CRITICAL VOCABULARY

radically

mechanisms

stationary

reputable

obstacles

vaulting

taut

cove

SEVEN OF THE WILDEST SPORTS EVER

7

1 Just about everyone has had an opportunity to sample sports such as basketball, soccer, and baseball. But for the world's most daring and creative athletes, such sports are way too tame. What can you do if you're an athlete who wants to try something radically different? What's the right sport for you if you're an athlete who's driven to scale walls, plummet from breathtaking heights, or leap tall objects in a single bound? If you long to try—or maybe just watch—something truly out of the ordinary, one of these sports might be for you. Read on to discover seven wild sports.

radically Something that is radically different is very different in important ways.

① ZORBING

2   The point of zorbing is to roll down a hill. That might not sound very intense, but it can be when you do it inside a zorb—a giant plastic ball. Invented in New Zealand in the mid-1990s, this extreme adventure sport soon became a worldwide phenomenon.

3   The zorb itself is actually two balls. The inner ball is about six-and-a-half feet in diameter and can accommodate up to three passengers. It is attached to the larger outer ball by pieces of rope. A two-foot cushion of air between the inner and outer balls acts as a shock absorber. An opening in the balls allows riders to enter and exit and ensures that they have enough oxygen during the ride.

4   The inventors of the zorb initially hoped passengers could stand up inside it and walk on water. When the zorb proved too difficult to control on water, the inventors began strapping passengers in and rolling them down ski slopes and other hillsides. Where there are no natural hills, zorb operators build metal tracks, generally about 700 feet in length.

5   Zorbing always takes place on land, but for extra fun, you can have a few gallons of water added to the inner ball. Passengers have compared "wet zorbing" to being a sock in a washing machine!

② POWERBOCKING

6 If walking on stilts looks hard, how about running and jumping on them? That's the point of powerbocking, an urban street sport also known as "power-rizing" and "blade running."

7 Of course, the stilts aren't just any stilts. Patented in 2004 by German inventor Alexander Bock, these "power stilts" have flexible carbon spring mechanisms attached. The springs allow users to run at high speeds, jump extremely high, and perform a variety of stunts, such as turning a series of backflips, or leaping over cars and other stationary objects.

8 Powerbocking is easy to learn; mastering the basic moves takes as little as half an hour. Still, to enjoy powerbocking safely, you need the appropriate gear, including knee pads, elbow pads, and especially a crash helmet. It's also important to purchase sturdy, well-made stilts from a reputable dealer.

9 While many enthusiasts consider powerbocking an extreme sport, others see it as simply a creative way to get around town, several notches cooler and more exciting than riding a bike or a skateboard.

10 There's also evidence that powerbocking is great for fitness. Some aficionados claim the sport uses 95 percent of the body's muscles!

---

mechanisms A mechanism is a part of a machine that performs a specific function.

stationary If something is stationary, it's not moving.

reputable Someone who is reputable is reliable and trustworthy.

③ BLOBBING

11 It sounds more like an activity for couch potatoes than for athletes, but blobbing is actually an extreme water sport popular at summer camps across North America. The blob is a partially inflated air bag—sometimes called a water trampoline—about 33 feet long by 6 feet wide. One "blobber" sits on one end of the air bag. A second participant jumps from a platform onto the opposite side of the blob, launching the first participant high into the air and ultimately into the water.

Experienced blobbers may perform flips, twists, and other stunts as they descend.

12 Invented by sailors, blobbing first happened at sea. The original blobs were actually floating fuel tanks towed alongside ships. Sailors in search of entertainment would jump from ship to blob.

13 Eventually, in the 1980s, two summer camp owners in Austin, Texas, got the idea of adapting blobbing as a camp activity. The sport caught on and spread to other camps around the country.

14 Today, blobbing has gone competitive. Since 2011, an organization called Blob Europe has held annual Blobbing Championships in Austria and, later, in Germany. Teams of two jumpers and one blobber compete for the highest score in a variety of categories.

④ XPOGO

15 Pogo sticks aren't just for little kids anymore. Back in 1999, a Provo, Utah, athlete named Dave Armstrong picked up a traditional steel spring pogo stick—the kind young children use to jump up and down—and began teaching himself to perform tricks on it.

16 By 2004, Xpogo (as in extreme pogo) had caught on among small communities of enthusiasts around the U.S. and abroad. Manufacturers began introducing special extreme pogo sticks, designed to expand the limits of the sport. Built for adult-sized riders, the new sticks included features such as Moto-X style handlebars and bungee-like rubber "elastomers" in place of steel springs.

17 Riders could now reach heights of up to nine feet, allowing them to perform a range of new tricks, including leaping over minivans and performing the first-ever full no-hands backflip on a pogo stick.

18 Today, the sport has grown popular enough to attract thousands of participants and fans to Pogopalooza: The Xpogo World Championship Series. This annual event takes place in multiple cities across the globe. Athletes come together to compete, show off their tricks, and, of course, strive for new world records.

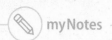

⑤ PARKOUR

19 Parkour is a training discipline that involves running, jumping, climbing, swinging, vaulting, rolling, and crawling over obstacles in the environment. Inspired by military obstacle course training, parkour was developed in France in the late 1990s. It takes its name from the French word *parcours* meaning "the way through" or "the path." Practitioners—called *traceurs*—attempt to trace a path from one point to another in the fastest and most efficient way possible.

20 A few of the many common parkour moves include vaulting over obstacles, dropping and rolling from a high surface onto a lower one, precision landing with two feet on a small or narrow surface, and running at a wall, then jumping and pushing off against the wall with the feet to reach the top. While most often practiced in urban spaces, parkour can happen in any environment with a suitable array of obstacles.

21 Traceurs use no assistive equipment, and some even practice with bare hands and feet. They may practice solo, with others, or at large gatherings called jams. Most agree on a few common principles: parkour is not competitive, not for show, and meant to be practiced in ordinary environments, rather than on courses designed for the sport.

obstacles   Obstacles are objects that are in your way and block your path.

vaulting   If you are vaulting over something, you are jumping quickly onto or over something.

⑥HIGHLINING

22 Highlining is a daring and dangerous form of tightrope walking developed by rock climbers. Practitioners string a type of rope called tubular nylon webbing from one high cliff to another, and then walk across it.

23 Most tightrope walkers carry steel poles for balance and walk on taut steel cable that doesn't move very much. Highlining is extra dangerous because highliners use only their arms for balance, while their ropes are flexible and can swing and bounce as the highliners walk.

24 The sport was born in California, where it evolved from slacklining—basically the same activity, but performed low to the ground for the purpose of developing balance and improving leg and core strength.

> **taut** Something that is stretched very tight is taut.

25 In 2012, American rock climber Dean Potter brought international attention to highlining when he crossed a 132-foot-wide canyon almost 6,000 feet deep without using a harness or safety net.

26 Not all highliners choose to walk without safety equipment, but even with a harness, this sport is not for the faint of heart or unsteady of foot. One false move—or strong gust of wind—might send a highliner tumbling off the rope and swinging back into the cliffside!

Don't try this at home!

⑦ CLIFF DIVING

27 If walking from cliff to cliff on a rope doesn't sound daring enough for you, how about diving off a cliff?

28 Practiced for at least 250 years, cliff diving might be the world's first extreme sport. This dangerous but uncomplicated sport is pretty much exactly what it sounds like. Practitioners dive headfirst off high ocean cliffs into the water below.

29 Probably the world's most famous cliff divers are the La Quebrada Cliff Divers of Acapulco, Mexico. These professional high divers perform daily for the public, diving from the cliffs of La Quebrada into a Pacific Ocean cove below. The highest cliffs they use are about 135 feet—roughly the equivalent of diving from a 13-story building! For added drama, the divers sometimes perform at night, holding torches.

30 For the La Quebrada Cliff Divers, as for all cliff divers, timing is everything. They must carefully time their dives in order to catch a wave rolling in and avoid crashing onto the rocky ocean bottom.

31 The La Quebrada Cliff Divers organization became official in 1934, but the oldest recorded cliff dive is much older than that. Back in 1770, King Kahekli, the last king of Maui, Hawaii, dove from a 63-foot cliff and hit the water without causing a splash!

> **cove**   A cove is part of the coast where the land curves in, creating a partly enclosed section of the sea.

Collaborative Discussion

Look back at what you wrote on page 212. Tell a partner something you
learned from this text. Then work with a group to discuss the questions
below. Refer to details and examples in *Seven of the Wildest Sports Ever* to
explain your answers. Take notes for your responses. When you speak,
use your notes.

1 Based on details in the text, why do you think people like to
participate in risky, wild sports?

2 How do the photographs that accompany the text help you better
understand each sport? Cite specific photographs and text to
support your answer.

3 Of the seven sports you read about, which one do you think is the
wildest? Which one would you like to try? Use details from the text
to support your opinions.

Listening Tip

Look at group
members as they
speak and notice the
facial expressions
or gestures they use
to help explain
their ideas.

Speaking Tip

As you speak, look at
the others in your
group. Does anyone
look confused? Invite
that person to ask
you a question.

221

Write an Advertisement

PROMPT

In *Seven of the Wildest Sports Ever*, you read about different sports that involve risk and danger. While explaining these activities, the article proves that many people enjoy participating in these unusual sports.

Imagine you work at an advertisement agency. Your job is to write an ad for a sports company that offers experiences with one of the extreme sports described in the selection. Pick one and come up with convincing reasons why someone should try it. Design an ad with images, a slogan, and information about the sport.

PLAN

Choose one of the sports for your advertisement. Then make notes about that sport in the space below. Include ideas for images to go with your advertisement and for a slogan to "sell" the sport to readers.

Now write your advertisement about an extreme sport from *Seven of the Wildest Sports Ever*.

Make sure your advertisement

- ☐ is about one of the sports from *Seven of the Wildest Sports Ever*.

- ☐ uses information from the text to describe the sport.

- ☐ includes a slogan that grabs people's attention.

- ☐ includes images that persuade people to try the sport.

- ☐ uses correct spelling and capitalization.

(?) **Essential Question**

How do sports test an athlete's character?

Write a Persuasive Speech

PROMPT Think of what you learned about athletes and their motivation to win, their physical and mental traits, and challenges that they faced to become champions of the game.

Imagine you are a coach for a conventional or extreme sport and you need to convince a group of parents that their children should participate in your sport. What attributes will the potential athletes gain by joining your team? How will you motivate them to become champion athletes? Write a speech that persuades parents to sign up their children for your sport.

I will write about _____.

✓ **Make sure your speech**

☐ opens with a clear statement, or claim, about the benefits of your sport.
☐ is logically organized into paragraphs based on clearly stated ideas.
☐ uses persuasive language to convince parents to sign up their children for your team.
☐ provides text evidence that supports your claims.
☐ includes a conclusion that summarizes your argument.

PLAN ·· Gather information.

Review your notes from this module. Find and underline parts or ideas that you can use in your persuasive speech. Reread the texts as necessary.

In the web below, write *The Benefits of My Sport* in the center. Then use evidence from the texts to write facts and details in each circle that support the idea that your extreme sport benefits children. Make sure to include details about the mental and physical traits that will be developed by playing your sport. Use Critical Vocabulary words where appropriate.

My Topic: _____

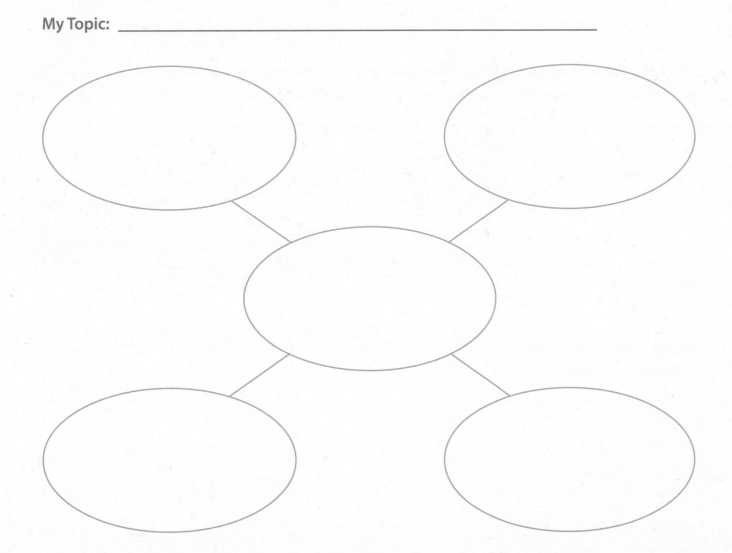

DRAFT · Write your persuasive speech.

Write an **opening statement** that clearly presents your claim about the benefits of your sport.

For the **body paragraphs**, use the information in your web to explain how your sport benefits children and provide supporting evidence from the texts.

In your **conclusion**, restate your claim in a way that convinces readers or listeners to agree with your opinion.

The revision and editing steps give you a chance to look carefully at your writing and make changes. Work with a partner to determine whether you have explained your ideas clearly to readers. Use these questions to help you evaluate and improve your speech.

PURPOSE/ FOCUS	ORGANIZATION	EVIDENCE	LANGUAGE/ VOCABULARY	CONVENTIONS
☐ Is my opinion clearly stated? ☐ Did I explain the benefits of the sport effectively?	☐ Does each paragraph have a main idea and supporting details? ☐ Did I use transition words to connect ideas?	☐ Does the text evidence I chose support my opinion?	☐ Did I use precise language to state my opinion? ☐ Did I use persuasive language that appealed to the emotions of my readers?	☐ Have I used correct punctuation, including commas, in complex sentences? ☐ Have I spelled words correctly?

Create a Finished Copy Make a final copy of your speech. You may wish to include a photo or illustration. Consider these options to share your writing.

1. Publish the speech in an online format.

2. Read your persuasive speech at a class forum.

3. Hold a panel discussion to debate your opinion about this topic.

Mummies and Bones

"And beauty immortal wakes from the tomb."

—James Beattie

? Essential Question

How can the remains of ancient peoples give us a window into their lives?

Get Curious

Video

Words About Mummies

The words in the chart will help you talk and write about the selections in this module. Which words about mummies have you seen before? Which words are new to you?

Add to the Vocabulary Network on page 231 by writing synonyms, antonyms, and related words and phrases for these words about mummies and the study of ancient peoples.

After you read each selection in this module, come back to the Vocabulary Network and keep building it. Add more boxes if you need to.

WORD	MEANING	CONTEXT SENTENCE
remains (noun)	The remains are a person's body after death.	The mummy's remains were on display at a museum in Italy.
alarmed (verb)	If you are alarmed, something has caused you to feel frightened or very concerned.	The museum director was alarmed to find the pharaoh's jewel missing.
archaeologists (noun)	An archaeologist studies societies and peoples of the past by examining what is left of their civilizations.	An archaeologist spends hours surveying an area, searching for ancient objects, such as pieces of pottery and stone tools.
relics (noun)	Relics are valued objects from the past, especially ones of historical interest.	The relics found at the archaeological site tell us about Mayan life before the arrival of Europeans.

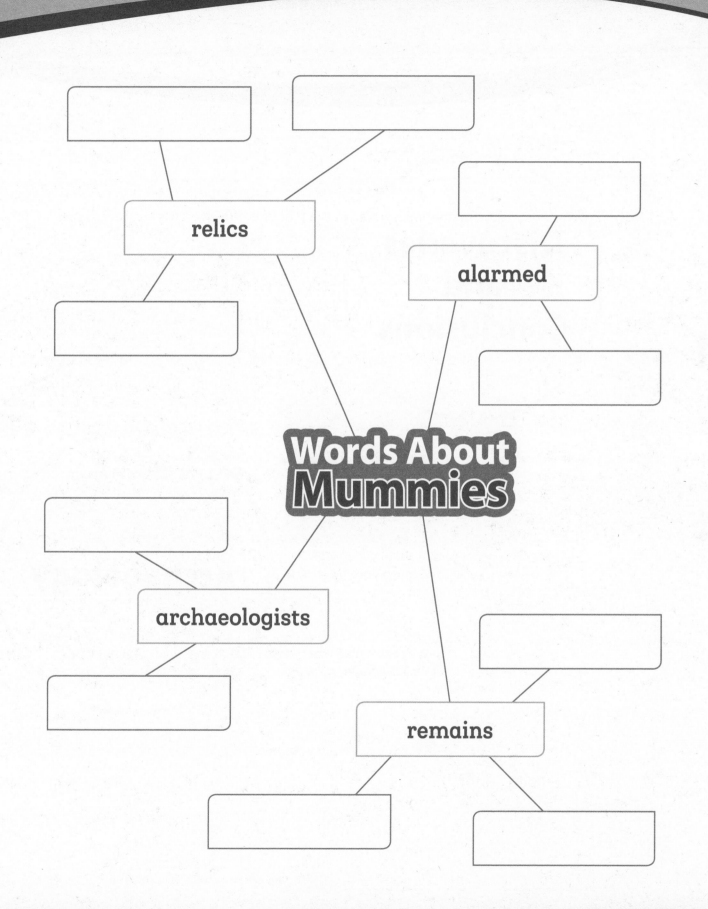

relics

alarmed

archaeologists

remains

Words About Mummies

**Discoveries
and
Conclusions**

Archaeology

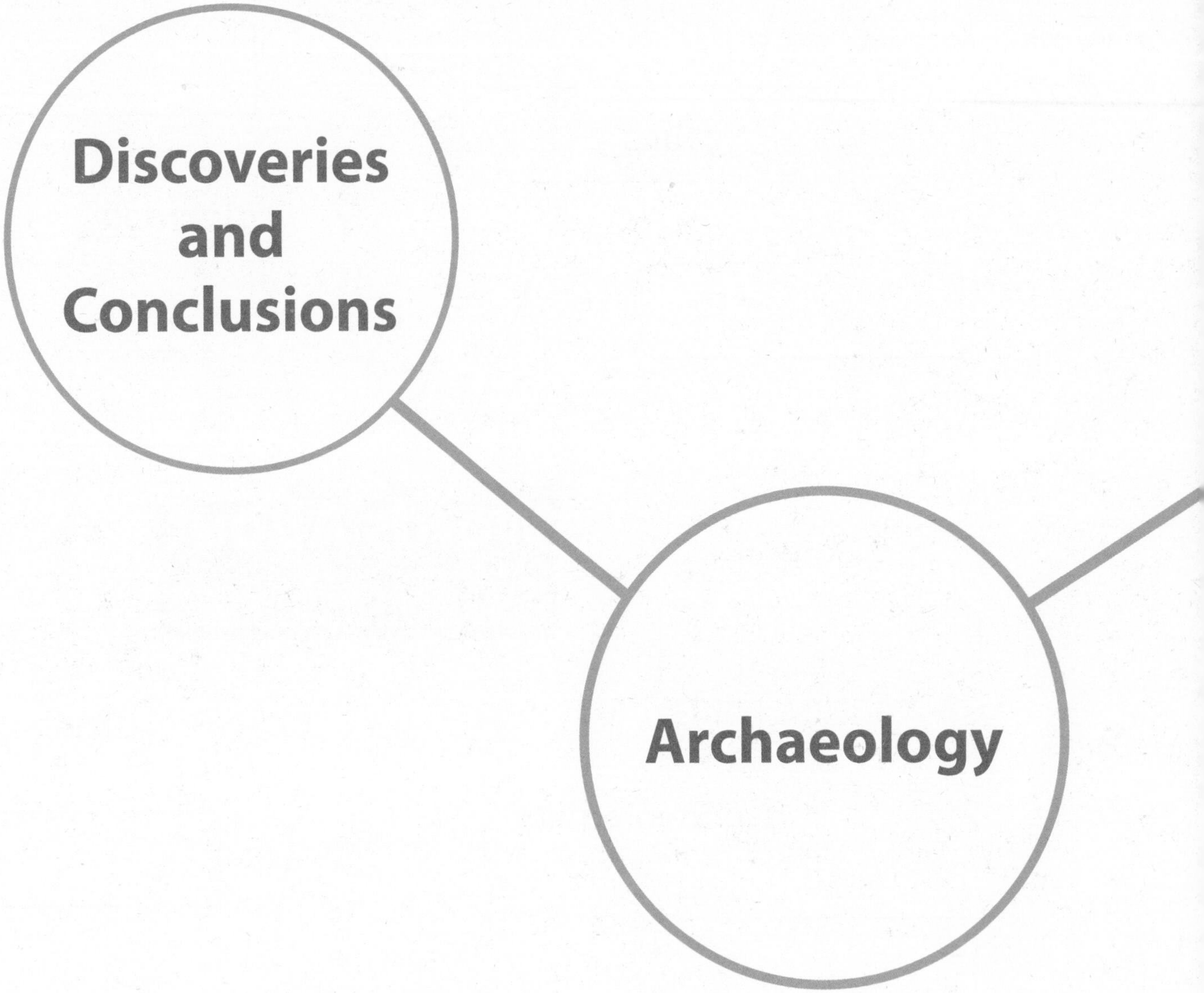

Mummies

Short Read

WHO: Inuit mummies WHEN: 1972

When hikers discovered this well-preserved mummy, they thought he was a doll. In fact, he was a human baby boy. He was buried in a freezing, rocky grave, along with other Inuit, a native group from Arctic Greenland, Canada, and Alaska. Dating back to about 1475, these centuries-old mummies have provided a wealth of information about Inuit culture in their time.

Greenland

NORTH AMERICA

WHO: Inca Ice Maiden WHEN: 1995

Many of the discoveries on this map were accidental, like the Ice Maiden . Finding her remains was the result of a trip by archaeologist Johan Reinhard and expert climber Miguel Zárate to Mount Ampato in the Peruvian Andes to photograph a volcano. They uncovered the Ice Maiden, a well-preserved 14-year-old girl who died between 1450 and 1480.

Peru

SOUTH AMERICA

Secrets of the MUmMiEs

Mummies might strike you as the stuff of horror films and scary campfire tales. But to **archaeologists** and other experts on the past, mummies and other preserved human **remains** in good condition are important tools for research and learning. The map on these pages presents exciting and important discoveries from around the world.

WHO: Tollund Man WHEN: 1950

Police in Silkeborg, Denmark, were alarmed when they received a call about a body found in a local bog. But rather than a recent murder victim, the body turned out to be a mummy more than 2,000 years old. Tollund Man is perhaps the best-preserved prehistoric mummy ever discovered. Experts who studied his body were able to determine what and when he last ate, and even that he had not shaved on the day of his death.

For more information, read *Mummy Murder Mystery* on page 273.

ASIA

 Denmark

EUROPE

 Italy

For more information, read *Bodies from the Ash: Life and Death in Ancient Pompeii* on page 237.

Egypt

AFRICA

For more information, read *King Tut: The Hidden Tomb* on page 255.

WHO: Eight "new" Egyptian mummies WHEN: 2017

Egypt has long been famous for its mummies, and some still remain to be discovered! In April 2017, archaeologist Mostafa Waziri and his team unearthed the 3,500-year-old tomb of an Egyptian nobleman called Userhat. Inside the tomb, they found several mummies and hundreds of ancient relics including wooden masks and small statues meant to serve and protect the dead in the afterlife.

AUSTRALIA

Notice & Note
3 Big Questions

Prepare to Read

GENRE STUDY **Informational text** gives facts and examples about a topic.

- Authors of informational texts may present their ideas in sequential, or chronological, order. This helps readers understand what happened and when.

- Informational texts include features such as bold print, captions, key words, and italics. They may also include sidebars that offer additional information about the topic.

SET A PURPOSE **Think about** the title and genre of this text. What do you know about the ancient city of Pompeii? What do you want to learn about its people and history? Write your ideas below.

Meet the Author:
James M. Deem

CRITICAL VOCABULARY

excavator

imprints

agony

dramatic

reproduced

volcanic

considerable

Bodies from the Ash

LIFE AND DEATH IN ANCIENT POMPEII

James M. Deem

1   *In the Roman city of Pompeii, almost two thousand years ago, wealthy families lived in grand homes, with fine clothing, art, jewelry, and servants. Mount Vesuvius stood only a few miles away.*

2   *On August 29, AD 79, the mountain erupted, and over the next few days flaming rocks and rivers of ash killed thousands—and destroyed the city. Buried under ash—and eventually forgotten—those who died lay undisturbed for centuries. Even the name of the city was no longer used on maps. However, the stories of those who had died still remained just below the surface, waiting to be discovered.*

3   *In March of 1748, near the modern-day city of Naples, Italy, on the Italian coast of the Mediterranean Sea, workers began digging into the ground around an ancient canal site. They were working to find buried treasures, as had been found elsewhere in the area. Workers found a skeleton and coins, but further exploration only found ruined buildings, and the work stopped.*

4   *More than twenty years later, in 1771, after the location had been identified as the ancient city of Pompeii, workers found a large home and two skeletons laden with riches—a gold ring, and gold, silver, and bronze coins. Twenty more skeletons were discovered in a large house called a villa, some of them wearing beautiful clothing and jewelry.*

5   *Called the Villa of Diomedes, this site became a major tourist attraction. Almost a century passed in this way, with Pompeii's greatest discoveries yet to be revealed.*

Rediscovering Pompeii

6   By the middle of the 19th century, much had been discovered at Pompeii, but nothing prepared the world for the excitement caused by a new excavator named Giuseppe Fiorelli. Appointed in 1860, he made many important changes that helped preserve Pompeii. He understood that treasure-hunting excavators had ruined a great deal of historical and scientific information. He also realized that Pompeii had much to teach the world, if the excavations were thorough and carefully recorded.

The ancient city of Pompeii is now a well-preserved tourist site.

excavator   An excavator is a person who carefully digs to uncover what is buried underground.

7   Three years later, on February 5, 1863, Fiorelli's workers came across some hollow areas in the ash that they were digging in along a lane soon to be called the Alley of the Skeletons. Peering inside the cavities, they could see bones lying at the bottom. They called Fiorelli, who was ready to take a revolutionary step in the study of human remains at Pompeii. He instructed workers to, rather than remove the skeletons, fill the hollow spaces with plaster. He had used a similar technique when workers had uncovered spaces where doors, shutters, furniture, and even tree stumps had once stood before decaying over time. When the plaster had hardened in a few days' time and the outer layer of volcanic debris was chipped away, a detailed plaster cast of the object remained. Now he hoped to apply the same technique to the hollow cavities left by the victims of Vesuvius. In this way, four people—one male and three females—who had vanished in death suddenly reappeared and took on new life as plaster mummies. Not mummies in the traditional sense, the casts preserved only imprints of the people's dying moments.

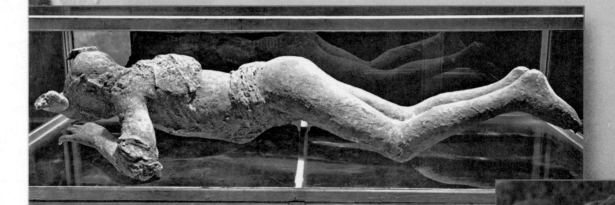

This woman's remains (above left) were discovered in 1875. Her plaster cast became so famous that it was photographed frequently, drawn by artists, and reproduced on postcards sold to tourists.

The teeth in the skull of a plaster cast (to the right) are visible.

imprints   Imprints are outlines left by something that has been pressed into softer material.

The plaster cast of this man was displayed in the Pompeii antiquarium for many years.

8   By studying these individuals and the possessions that they had with them, Fiorelli and other researchers attempted to piece together their story. They believe that the four were members of the same family, though there is no way to know this for certain. Leading the way as the group fled was the father, who carried their most valuable possessions: coins, gold jewelry, and a house key. He was followed by two younger females (his daughters) unadorned by jewelry. Bringing up the rear was a woman (his wife), who wore some jewels and carried another bag containing a few silver plates and mirrors.

9   When the surge hit them, the man was knocked to the ground. He struggled to get back up and died as he tried to cover his head with his cape. One girl landed facedown, holding a piece of her clothing across her mouth; the other was blown onto her side. Behind them, the woman, who had rolled up her dress in order to run, landed on her back.

10   Soon these casts and others were put on display for all who visited Pompeii. Everyone who saw them was impressed that the helpless victims could so easily be brought back to life with Fiorelli's creative technique.

The antiquarium at Pompeii exhibited plaster casts and other artifacts found in the ruins. It was badly damaged by Allied bombing in World War II and remains closed today.

The Plaster Bodies of Pompeii

11 From then on, whenever workers discovered a skeleton in the ash, they attempted to recapture the last moment of another victim. Not every person left a hollow space, but many did. Most of the casts they created were chilling, and provided details about not only the person's appearance but his last living moment.

12 The victims of Vesuvius in Pompeii would not have died an instantaneous death. According to scientist Paul Wilkinson, they might have had a chance to take three breaths of hot gas and ash before they stopped breathing. But those three breaths, in which they essentially lined their lungs and esophagus with superheated ash, caused them to suffocate. During that brief time, many writhed in agony, as shown by the plaster casts. Surprisingly, some others look as if they simply fell asleep.

13 The plaster casts amazed the world. Photographers took many photos of them and sold them to tourists as dramatic souvenirs of their visit to the ruins. Like the skeletons before them, some of the plaster bodies were placed in the ruins so that visitors could experience the sensation of seeing the victim in the location near where he or she had died.

agony Agony is extreme suffering.
dramatic Something that is dramatic attracts a lot of attention.

14   Eventually, an antiquarium, or museum, was started at Pompeii, which displayed many of the casts and some of the artifacts that had been found there. One writer commented that the bodies placed there "are reproduced just as they were when death struck them; some wrestling against it in despair, others yielding without resistance. It is a striking sight, and one of the greatest curiosities of Pompeii."

15   As word spread about Fiorelli's creative technique, more and more people journeyed to Pompeii to see the plaster people and the ruins of a city that provided a snapshot of life during the Roman Empire. While they were there, many also made the ascent to the top of Mount Vesuvius despite its periodic deadly eruptions. The trip for early visitors was lengthy; they either hiked to the crater or were carried in a sedan chair. Eventually, so many tourists came to Vesuvius that a funicular was built. When it was damaged by an eruption, a chairlift took its place until it was shut down in 1984.

16   Tourists may have been amazed at everything that Pompeii had to offer, but scientists were still puzzled. They wanted to know why some bodies left hollow spaces in the volcanic material, while others became only skeletons.

Visiting the top of Mount Vesuvius was so popular that a funicular was opened in 1880 to make the climb easier for tourists. But a subsequent eruption in 1944 damaged the railway so badly that it was never used again.

reproduced   Something that is reproduced is copied.
volcanic   Something that is volcanic has come from a volcano.

243

17   Over the years, they studied the debris that came from Vesuvius, pinpointed the locations where people were found, and analyzed the skeletons and plaster casts. In the end, scientists concluded that the time and place that a person died during the eruption determined whether the person's body left a cavity in the volcanic debris.

18   **Time of death.** Scientists found that a person who died during the surge of hot gas and ash after dawn on the second day of the eruption was more likely to create a cavity in the volcanic material than someone who died the first day during the pumice fall. For example, a woman fleeing the city who died in the fourth pyroclastic surge was immediately covered with hot ash that molded itself to her skin and clothing. Next her body was covered with a layer of volcanic debris in the pyroclastic flow that followed. The last two surges and flows buried her completely. Soon, the volcanic matter surrounding her body began to harden as it cooled. Eventually, the woman's body began to decay inside the hardened deposit, leaving behind a hollowed space and a skeleton where her body had once lain.

Above left, a storage room of archaeological findings in Pompeii.

Above right, a restorer works on a petrified victim of the volcanic eruption in the laboratory at the excavation site.

19 This wouldn't have happened, however, if the woman had died as she attempted to leave town on the first day of the eruption. She would have been covered mostly with pumice, rather than ash. Because the pumice was granular and did not stick to the body like ash, it would not have created a hardened mold of the woman. Her body would have become a skeleton without a well-defined cavity around it. For this reason, no plaster casts have been made from people found only in layers of pumice.

20 **Location of death.** Scientists also discovered that the place a person died determined whether a cavity would be formed. For example, a man who died inside his house, either on the first or second day, would not have been covered with ash. Instead, he was surrounded by pumice that fell through windows, doors, and courtyards, or by building material from collapsed roofs and walls. However, if the man had died in an area where the hot ash from the final surges could coat his body, a hollow cavity was formed as his body decayed.

This man died near the Nucerian Gate. Archaeologists believe that he was a beggar. He carried a bag for alms and wore good-quality sandals, a sign, some believe, that he was well taken care of.

At the archaeological site of Pompeii in 1961, workers dig out the mummified bodies of two adults and three children who died almost 19 centuries earlier.

21　　In studying the plaster casts, archaeologists have also learned something else. Because of the circumstances under which the victims died, not all of the hollow spaces that the decaying bodies created could produce an entire person. Some people, for example, were not completely covered by hot ash. As a result, only part of their body could be recreated in plaster. Others may have been completely formed, but during the centuries that followed the eruption, earthquakes may have damaged the cavities as the ground shifted and collapsed.

Sometimes only a partial mold could be created.

22　　For these reasons, some of the plaster bodies are strangely incomplete, while others look like odd sculptures. Sometimes workers even used a bit of artistic license after they chipped off the volcanic ash and cleaned up the cast. When facial features were missing on incomplete casts, workers occasionally added them, sculpting a nose or ears and carving a mouth and eyes.

Lives from the Ash

23　The plaster casts and skeletons of the victims of Vesuvius have become windows to what Pompeii life was like in AD 79. Through their studies, archaeologists and other scientists have tried to describe the life and death of the person. Although the stories they told were based on fact, writers would often add a bit of creative imagination to the retelling. For example, when the skeleton of a man was found in a sheltered area of the Herculaneum Gate in 1763, some writers imagined that he was a loyal sentry who guarded the gate until the eruption buried him alive. After all, it made for a dramatic story. The truth, however, is that the man simply took shelter near the gate, where the pyroclastic surges and flows killed him.

24   Here are a few of the people whose remains were found at Pompeii and the stories that archaeologists have told about them:

HOUSE OF THE CRYPTOPORTICUS

25   A group of skeletons was unearthed in what is now called the House of the Cryptoporticus. Although a cryptoporticus is an underground passage of a villa meant to provide shade and a space for walking, the cryptoporticus of this house had been altered to store wine jugs, called amphorae. The house itself, which was still being repaired after an earthquake in AD 62, was a restaurant with a triclinium, or dining room with three couches, in this case for warm-weather banquets.

26   In 1914, excavators uncovered ten victims, most in the garden. These people may have lived in the house; some may also have been customers of the restaurant. On the first day of the eruption, they took shelter in the cryptoporticus below the restaurant. By the next morning, they decided to make a run for safety, across the garden in the back of the house. They held tiles above their heads to protect themselves from the falling pumice. As the fourth surge overtook them, they quickly suffocated.

The inside of the House of the Cryptoporticus, a passageway that had been used as a storage area in ancient Pompeii. Ten victims of the eruption were found in and around this house.

27 Of the ten skeletons, archaeologists were able to turn four into plaster casts. Two appear to be a mother and her teenage daughter, who were embracing each other in their last moment. Another victim was a slave. His plaster cast shows that he was trying to release his ankles from the large iron bonds that shackled them. Researchers report that he was the third slave found at Pompeii with iron rings around his ankles. The fourth cast was another man, who carried two silver goblets and a simpulum, a silver ladle used in religious ceremonies.

28 What surprised archaeologists about this man was his collection of silver, which was not common outside of wealthy homes. Little silver has been found with the fleeing victims of Pompeii. Could he have been a priest from a temple where the simpulum was used? Or could he have been a thief? No one will ever know.

HOUSE OF THE GOLDEN BRACELET

29 One of the largest and most beautiful houses in Pompeii, the House of the Golden Bracelet, was both a hotel and restaurant, built on three levels. The top floor of the building was typical of Roman homes, with an atrium surrounded by many rooms. The middle floor was the most lavish, with many reception rooms, multiple dining rooms, and a bathing area. The lower floor contained a beautifully decorated dining room that led to a large garden. Excavators named the house after a beautiful solid-gold bracelet with a two-headed snake that they discovered on the arm of one skeleton inside the house; the bracelet weighed a hefty one and one-third pounds.

A worker restores an ancient fresco in the House of the Golden Bracelet.

The four bodies found in the House of the Golden Bracelet are assumed to be a family.

30   As excavators uncovered the house in 1974, they found cavities containing four skeletons at the bottom of the staircase that led to the garden. Archaeologists believe that these people were members of a young family, most likely killed the second morning of the eruption when the stairs to the second floor collapsed. No one knows if they were the owners of the house or merely residents there, but near them, scattered over the lower floor, were jewels and more than two hundred gold and silver coins. Whoever they were, they had a considerable fortune with them.

COUNTING THE DEAD

31 Since the first skeleton was found in 1748, approximately 1,150 human remains have been recovered at Pompeii. Some 394 skeletons were located in the pumice deposits from the first day, most of them inside buildings. About 655 were found in the pyroclastic flows of the second day. These were almost evenly divided between those killed on roads or other outdoor spaces and those who died in buildings. The skeletal remains of about 100 other people have also been found, but they were simply bits of bones that scientists cannot place in either group.

considerable   Something that is considerable is very large in size or amount.

Collaborative Discussion

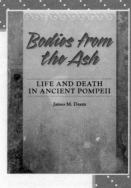

Look back at what you wrote on page 236. Tell a partner two things you learned about archaeology from this text. Then work with a group to discuss the questions below. Refer to details and examples in *Bodies from the Ash* to explain your answers. Take notes for your responses. When you speak, use your notes.

1 Which of the archaeological items described in the article would you most like to see in person? Explain why you find it interesting.

Listening Tip

If you can't hear someone in your group easily, politely raise your hand and then ask that person to speak a little louder.

2 How do the photographs and captions give you a better understanding of the plaster casts Fiorelli created in Pompeii?

Speaking Tip

When speaking, say each word clearly and at a pace that isn't too fast or too slow. Be sure each member of your group can hear you.

3 What did you learn about the people of Pompeii from this text? Explain what kinds of people lived there when Vesuvius erupted.

Write a Postcard from Pompeii

PROMPT ··

In *Bodies from the Ash*, you read about the volcanic eruption that buried the ancient city of Pompeii. You also read about how centuries later excavators found the city and have tried to understand who lived there and what happened.

Imagine that you are a tourist visiting Pompeii today. Using details from the text, write a postcard from Pompeii that describes your visit and something that is particularly interesting about one of the artifacts, buildings, or scenes that is discussed in the text.

PLAN ··

Choose an artifact, building, or scene from Pompeii. Using details from the text, captions, and photographs, make notes that describe your subject.

WRITE

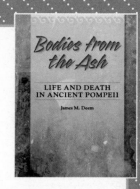

Now write your postcard describing the artifact, building, or scene from Pompeii you've chosen from *Bodies from the Ash*.

Make sure your postcard

- ☐ begins with a salutation to your friend or family.
- ☐ uses descriptive language to create a mental image of the artifact, building, or scene.
- ☐ includes evidence from the text, captions, and photographs.
- ☐ uses at least two Critical Vocabulary words.
- ☐ uses correct capitalization for proper nouns.

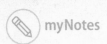
Notice & Note
3 Big Questions

Prepare to Read

GENRE STUDY **Narrative nonfiction** gives factual information by telling a story.

- Authors of narrative nonfiction may organize their ideas using headings and subheadings. The headings and subheadings tell readers what the next section of text will be about.

- Narrative nonfiction includes visuals, such as photographs, illustrations, maps, and diagrams.

SET A PURPOSE **Think about** the title and genre of this text. Have you ever heard of King Tut? What stories or facts do you know about him? Think of a question about King Tut that you would like to answer by reading this text. Write your question below.

Build Background: The Afterlife of Ancient Egyptians

CRITICAL VOCABULARY

chariots

annex

shrine

autopsy

King Tut
The Hidden Tomb

by Ruth Owen

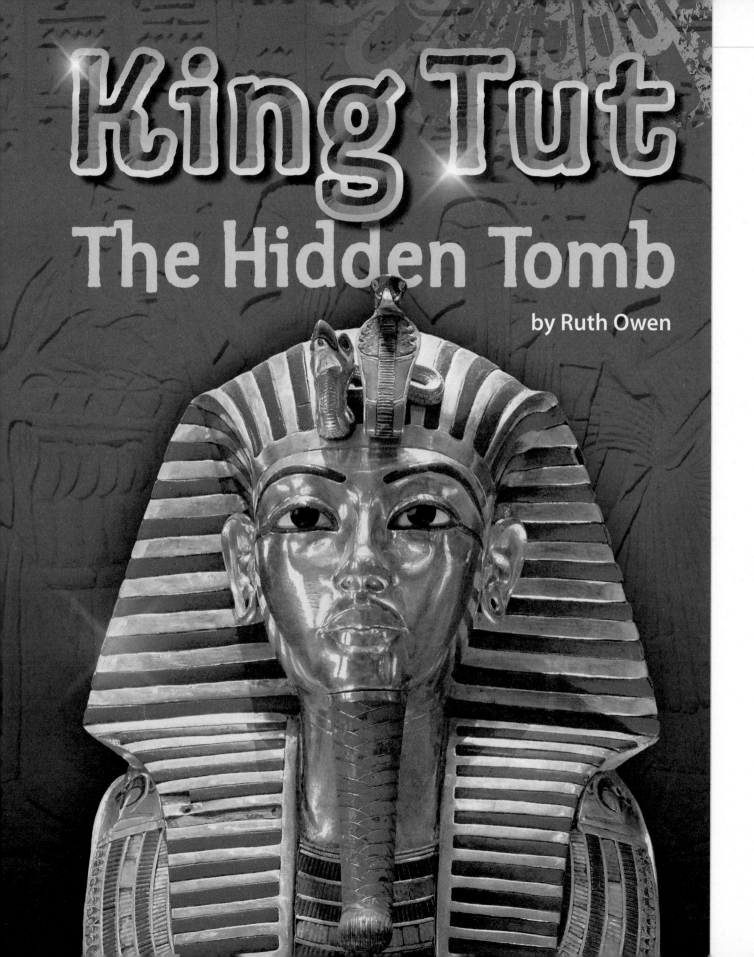

Gold Everywhere!

1 It was late afternoon on November 26, 1922, in the Egyptian desert. In an underground passageway below the Valley of the Kings, British archaeologist Howard Carter worked in tense silence. As sweat trickled down his face, he used a tool to chip a hole in a stone doorway.

Howard Carter

2 For five years, Carter had been searching for the hidden tomb of the ancient Egyptian Pharaoh Tutankhamen (too-tahn-KAH-men). Finally, Carter had discovered a doorway that might lead to the tomb. Carefully, he lifted a candle to the hole and peered into the darkness.

3 "At first I could see nothing," Carter said. "But… details from the room within slowly emerged from the mist. Strange animals, statues, and gold—everywhere the glint of gold."

4 Tutankhamen's tomb had remained hidden in the Valley of the Kings for 3,245 years. Now its ancient secrets were about to be revealed!

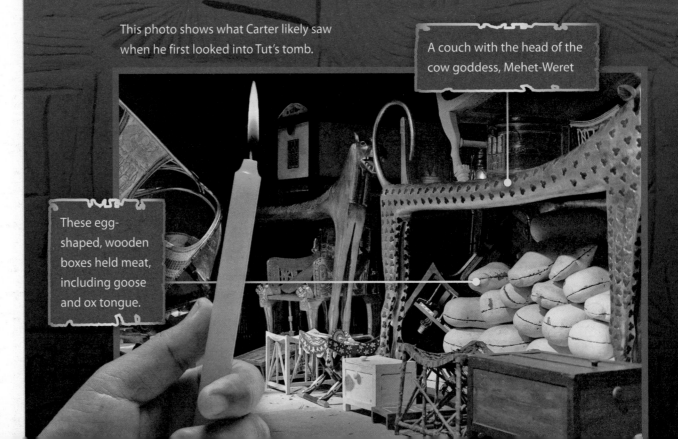

This photo shows what Carter likely saw when he first looked into Tut's tomb.

A couch with the head of the cow goddess, Mehet-Weret

These egg-shaped, wooden boxes held meat, including goose and ox tongue.

Tutankhamen

5 Pharaoh Tutankhamen was a part of a powerful civilization based in Africa from around 3000 BC to AD 300. Experts know he was born around 1341 BC. They also know Tutankhamen, or Tut for short, was the son of the ancient Egyptian king Akhenaton (*ah*-ken-AHT-on). Tut grew up in a city named after his father.

6 However, little else is known about the young prince's life. Tut most likely lived in a palace with his father, his father's many wives, and his six older sisters. When Tutankhamen was still a young child, his father died. Then, when Tut was just nine years old, he became pharaoh. As a result, Tutankhamen became known as the boy king.

This map shows the Valley of the Kings and the city of Akhetaten (today known as Amarna), where Tut grew up.

A statue of Pharaoh Akhenaton

The King Is Dead!

7   Only about ten years after becoming pharaoh, Tutankhamen mysteriously died. After his death, his body was taken to an embalmers' workshop. There it would be made into a mummy. In ancient Egypt, people believed in the afterlife, or life after death. They preserved a person's body so that he or she could live on in the afterlife.

8   First, the embalmers drained all the blood from Tut's corpse. Then, using their hands, they carefully removed his lungs, liver, stomach, and intestines from a small cut in his abdomen.

9   These organs were placed in salt to dry and preserve them. Then each organ was wrapped in linen and placed in a tiny coffin-shaped container. Salt was then heaped over the whole body to dry it. After about 35 days, the embalmers wrapped the dry, shriveled body with strips of cloth to create a mummy.

Before wrapping a body, its dry skin was rubbed with beeswax, animal fat, and plant oils to make it soft again.

This embalmer is wearing an Anubis mask. Anubis is the Egyptian god of death and embalmers. He's usually shown with the head of a wild dog.

The ancient Egyptians did not believe the brain was important. To remove it, an embalmer pushed a metal hook up the corpse's nose. Then he pulled the brain out in little pieces.

To give a dried-out body a plump, lifelike shape, it was packed with linen and sawdust.

The Valley of the Kings

10   Once Tut's body was mummified, it was placed in a coffin. Then servants carried the preserved corpse into the Valley of the Kings. Here, in a desert cemetery close to his royal ancestors, Tutankhamen was placed in an underground tomb. Like all pharaohs, Tut was considered a god who lived on Earth when he was alive. Now, in death, he would take his place alongside other gods in the afterlife.

11   To live on forever, Tut would need food to eat and clothing and jewelry to wear. He might also need furniture, including a throne to sit on and chariots to ride. In addition, Tut may want weapons and entertainment, such as games and musical instruments. Everything a pharaoh could possibly need or want in the afterlife was placed in Tut's tomb. Then the tomb was sealed . . . forever.

Tut's mummy

This painting is from the wall of Tutankhamen's tomb. It shows 12 men pulling Tut's mummy to its final resting place.

Right: Tutankhamen was buried with 412 tiny statues called shabtis. In the afterlife, the shabtis would work for the pharaoh as servants and farmers.

chariots   Chariots are ancient two-wheeled vehicles pulled by horses.

Discovery in the Desert

12 As the centuries passed, the tombs in the Valley of the Kings became hidden under layers of sand and rock. In the 1800s and early 1900s, archaeologists and treasure seekers traveled to Egypt to hunt for ancient tombs and the valuable artifacts inside them. However, no one was able to find the lost tomb of the boy king.

13 Then in early November 1922, archaeologist Howard Carter made a stunning discovery. Beneath the sand and rock, Carter uncovered a flight of 16 steps leading to an underground door.

14 Carter told his friend and employer, Lord Carnarvon, about the exciting discovery. When Lord Carnarvon arrived in Egypt a few weeks later, Carter continued the excavation. Carter soon learned that the underground door led to a passageway filled with rubble. Once the rubble was cleared away, Carter and Lord Carnarvon found themselves standing before the doorway to Tut's tomb.

From left to right: Lady Evelyn Herbert (Carnarvon's daughter), Lord Carnarvon, Howard Carter, and Arthur Callender (Carter's friend and member of the team) on the steps leading to the tomb.

Wonderful Things

15 When Carter looked into Tut's tomb for the first time, Lord Carnarvon asked if he could see anything. "Yes, yes," replied Carter. "It is wonderful!" He was right. Gold statues shined in the candlelight. No one had ever discovered a tomb filled with as many objects as Tutankhamen's.

16   In the days that followed, Carter and Lord Carnarvon explored different chambers inside the tomb, including the antechamber and the annex. Even though it was tiny, the annex was packed with hundreds of items. Some of the objects included jars of wine and oil, baskets of fruit, and furniture.

17   As he carefully searched the rooms, Carter realized that others had been there before him—tomb robbers! Carter noticed that the tomb's two outer doorways had been broken and repaired. Also, the tiny annex chamber was very messy and looked as though someone had hurriedly searched through it.

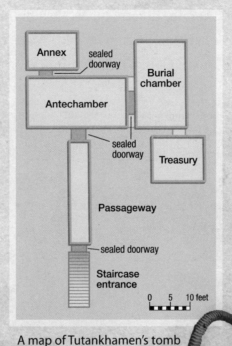

A map of Tutankhamen's tomb

A beaded collar found in Tut's tomb

A carved stone jar containing oil that came from Tut's tomb

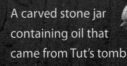

annex   An annex is a room that is attached to another larger room.

Another Sealed Door

18　Carter knew that the discovery of Tut's tomb could tell the world a lot about life in ancient Egypt. He made sure that every item was photographed and carefully cleaned and checked before it was removed from the tomb. He also made detailed drawings and notes about the artifacts.

19　　Carter soon realized that there was no sign of a mummy in the antechamber or annex. There was, however, another sealed door leading from the antechamber. Next to that door stood two life-size statues of pharaohs covered in gold. Was it possible that there was yet another room? Could Tut's mummy lie just a few feet away?

Above: A piece of jewelry found in Tut's tomb that's decorated with a blue scarab beetle

Left: Carter and Lord Carnarvon carefully removing the sealed door in the antechamber

Carter found many jewelry boxes in Tut's tomb. The boxes contained lists of their contents. When he checked what he found against the lists, he discovered many items were missing. Carter still found more than 200 pieces of jewelry.

Meeting Tutankhamen

20 When Carter finally opened the sealed door, he couldn't believe his eyes. Behind it he discovered Tut's burial chamber! In the middle of the room stood a huge, gilded wooden box, or shrine.

21 When Carter opened the doors at one end of the shrine, he found three smaller shrines inside it. Inside the inner shrine was a stone coffin, or sarcophagus. Slowly and carefully over many months, Carter and his workers removed the shrines from the tomb. Then the heavy stone lid of the sarcophagus was raised using ropes and pulleys.

22 Inside the sarcophagus were three beautiful coffins, one neatly placed inside the other. Each coffin was made in the shape of the king's body. The third and inner coffin was made of solid gold. When the lid of the golden coffin was opened, Carter found Tut's mummy inside! The mummy's head and shoulders were covered by a dazzling gold mask. Carter was speechless—the boy king had finally been found!

Solid-gold inner coffin

Carter and a worker examine the inner coffin.

Second, or middle, coffin

shrine   A shrine is a place that is treated with reverence because it is associated with a sacred person or object.

The Mummy Autopsy

23   On November 11, 1925, Carter and a small team of scientists gathered around Tut's mummy to perform an autopsy. One of the men, Professor Douglas Derry, led the work. Derry began by making a long cut down the middle of Tut. This allowed the delicate wrappings to be peeled back to reveal the pharaoh's preserved body.

24   The gold mummy mask was lifted away with extreme care. Then the wrappings around Tutankhamen's head were removed. The scientists gently examined Tut's dark brown, brittle skin. Carter was finally able to look into the face of the young pharaoh. Derry then examined the mummy's bones and teeth. He confirmed that Tut had died when he was around 19 years old. However, Derry could find no clues as to why the pharaoh had died so young.

This dagger and its cover were found placed against Tutankhamen's thigh.

Right:
Tutankhamen's mummy

autopsy   During an autopsy, a dead body is examined to figure out the cause of death.

Tut's Treasures

25　Just beyond Tut's burial chamber, Carter and his team found a room called the treasury. In it, they discovered a large canopic chest. It was made from a single block of rock. When the chest's lid was removed, it revealed four stoppers. Each was carved in the shape of Tut's head. Beneath each stopper was a hollow space containing a tiny coffin. Inside the coffins were the king's mummified lungs, liver, stomach, and intestines.

26　More than 5,000 other objects were found throughout Tut's tomb, including model boats, canes, and golden sandals. Carter also found gloves Tut had worn as a child. He even found a lock of hair belonging to Queen Tiye (TEE-ay), Tut's grandmother!

27　It took Carter almost ten years to examine all the objects and send them to the Cairo Museum. Once there, the objects helped Egyptologists learn about life—and death—in ancient Egypt. However, Carter and his team could still not figure out what happened to Tut.

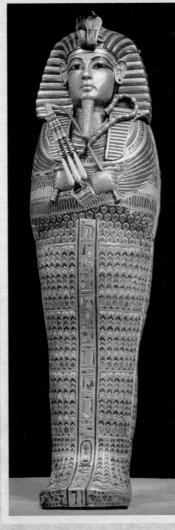

A small coffin containing one of Tut's mummified organs

A wooden sandal decorated with gold

How Did Tut Die?

28 For almost 100 years, Egyptologists have wanted to know what killed Tutankhamen. After examining his body and skull, scientists discovered several broken bones. They looked into whether a blow to the head or a chariot crash might have killed Tut.

29 Then, in 2014, scientists carried out a virtual autopsy of Tut. They examined more than 2,000 CT scans of Tutankhamen's remains. The scientists discovered that damage to Tut's skull and other fractures actually happened after his death. The breaks may have occurred when Howard Carter moved the fragile mummy.

Tut's mummy ready to be scanned in a CT machine

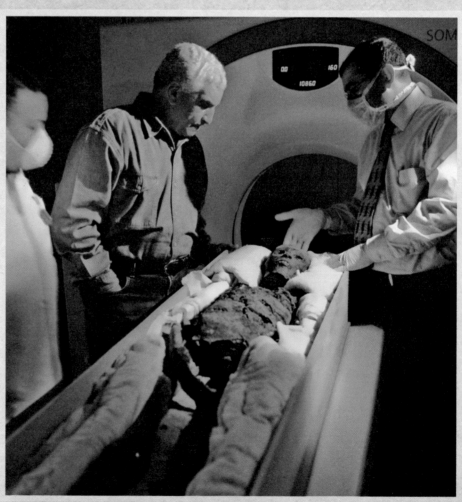

30   The scans also showed a bad fracture on Tut's left knee that happened shortly before he died. Tests have also shown that Tut had a disease called malaria. No one knows for sure, but perhaps this illness—and a serious infection from his knee injury—killed the young king.

Scientists also discovered that Tut had a badly disfigured left foot. He likely used a cane to get around. Tut probably was unable to stand up and ride in a chariot. However, this painting from Tut's tomb shows him riding in a chariot. In the afterlife, he would be able to do things he couldn't do when he was alive.

Mysteries of the Tomb

31 There are signs within Tut's tomb that suggest he died suddenly. Unlike most pharaohs' tombs, Tutankhamen's was very small and had little decoration. Usually, a pharaoh's tomb would take years to build and decorate. When Tut died unexpectedly, was his official tomb not ready? Is it possible his small, simple tomb was prepared at the last minute?

32 In 2012, special photographs were taken of the burial chamber, and the mystery took a new turn. Experts noticed traces of two blocked-up doorways in the walls. In 2015, scientists used high-tech radar to scan the walls. They discovered what looks like additional chambers. Are there more rooms beyond Tutankhamen's burial chamber? Is it possible that his small tomb was built in the entrance to a much larger tomb? And, if so, whom does it belong to? The investigation continues. . . .

Today, Tut's mummy lies in the antechamber of his tomb.

The walls of Tut's tomb are covered with dark spots of ancient mold. This suggests that the room was once damp. This mold does not appear in any other pharaoh's tomb. Was the tomb sealed up before the wall paintings had dried?

It normally took years for artists to paint an ancient Egyptian king's tomb. However, Tut's tomb paintings were rushed and likely painted in just a few days.

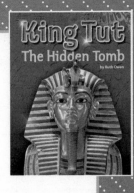

Collaborative Discussion

Look back at what you wrote on page 254. Tell a partner which two details of Howard Carter's discovery interest you the most. Then work with a group to discuss the questions below. Refer to details and examples in *King Tut: The Hidden Tomb* to explain your answers. Take notes for your responses. When you speak, use your notes.

1 What did you learn about King Tut's life and family from this text?

2 How did the theories about the death of King Tut change over time? Why did the theories change? Use vocabulary from the text in your response.

3 Which object in King Tut's tomb do you think reveals the most about who King Tut was and what he valued? Explain your answer.

Listening Tip

Give your full attention to what each member of your group has to say. Show you are listening by looking at the speaker.

Speaking Tip

Make eye contact with group members as you speak. This will help you tell whether they understand your ideas.

Write Quiz Questions

PROMPT

In *King Tut: The Hidden Tomb,* you read about Howard Carter's discovery of King Tut's tomb and how that discovery has taught us about King Tut, ancient Egypt, and the process of mummification.

Imagine you are in charge of writing five questions about King Tut for a TV quiz show. Choose the five most important facts related to King Tut. Use those facts to write quiz questions with answers that would test someone's knowledge about the subject.

PLAN

Make notes about facts in the text related to the discovery of King Tut's tomb. Then review your notes and circle the five most important facts.

WRITE

Now write your five quiz questions about King Tut's tomb.

✓	Make sure your questions
☐	are about the most important facts from the text.
☐	cannot be answered with just a yes or no.
☐	include answers that can be verified in the text.
☐	use at least one Critical Vocabulary word.
☐	end with a question mark.

Prepare to Read

GENRE STUDY **Persuasive** texts give an author's opinion about a topic and try to convince readers to believe that opinion.

- Persuasive texts include strong language and techniques to convince readers to believe their viewpoint. Authors may also use formal language to further convince the reader that they are knowledgeable about the topic.

- Persuasive texts include evidence, such as facts and examples, to support the author's viewpoint.

SET A PURPOSE **Think about** the title and genre of this text. How could a murder mystery be classified as a persuasive text? What might the author want to persuade you to believe? Write your ideas below.

**Meet the Author:
Rod Nordland**

CRITICAL VOCABULARY

profiler

homicide victim

humidity

physique

elevation

Mummy Murder Mystery

by Rod Nordland

ADAPTED FROM *THE NEW YORK TIMES* ARTICLE, "WHO KILLED THE ICEMAN? CLUES EMERGE IN A VERY COLD CASE"—MARCH 26, 2017

A reconstruction of the Iceman in the South Tyrol Museum of Archaeology in Bolzano, Italy.

1 The head of a small Italian museum called Detective Inspector Alexander Horn of the Munich Police. She asked him if he investigated cold cases.

2 "Yes I do," Inspector Horn said, recalling their conversation.

3 "Well, I have the coldest case of all for you," said Angelika Fleckinger. She is the director of the South Tyrol Museum of Archaeology, in Bolzano, Italy.

4 The unknown victim is nicknamed Ötzi. He has literally been in cold storage in her museum for a quarter-century. Often called the Iceman, he is the world's most perfectly preserved mummy. The Copper Age fellow had been frozen inside a glacier along the northern Italian border with Austria until warming global temperatures melted the ice. Two hikers discovered him in 1991.

5 The cause of death remained uncertain until 10 years later. That's when an X-ray of the mummy pointed to foul play in the form of a flint arrowhead embedded in his back, just under his shoulder. But now, Inspector Horn is armed with a wealth of new scientific information that researchers have compiled. He has managed to piece together a remarkably detailed picture of what befell the Iceman on that fateful day around 3300 BC, near the crest of the Ötztal Alps.

6   "When I was first contacted with the idea, I thought it was too difficult, too much time has passed," said Inspector Horn, a noted profiler. "But actually he's in better condition than recent homicide victims I've worked on who have been found out in the open."

7   There are a few mummies in the world as old as Ötzi, but none so well preserved. Most were ritually prepared. That usually meant removal of internal organs, preservation with chemicals, or exposure to destructive desert conditions.

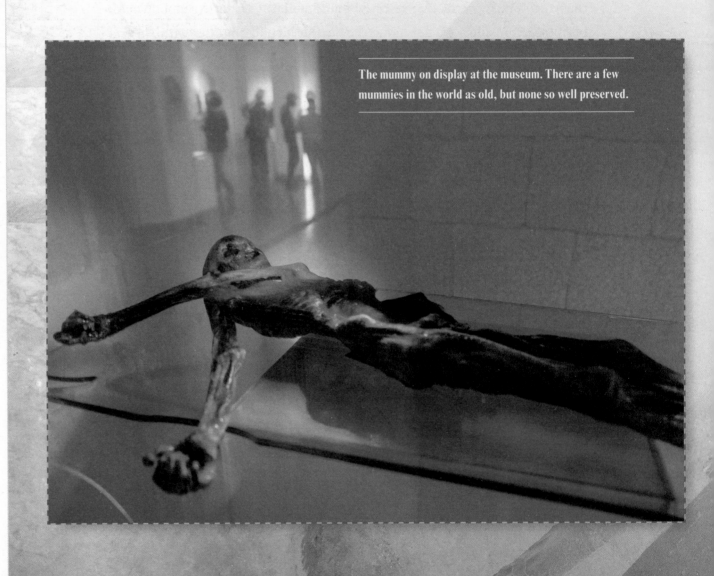

The mummy on display at the museum. There are a few mummies in the world as old, but none so well preserved.

profiler   A profiler studies a person's traits and behavior to draw conclusions about what that person is like.

homicide victim   A homicide victim is a person who has been murdered.

8 The glacier not only froze Ötzi where he had died. The high humidity of the ice also kept his organs and skin largely intact. "Imagine, we know the stomach contents of a person 5,000 years ago," Inspector Horn said. "In a lot of cases we are not able to do that even now."

9 Those contents, as it turned out, were critical in determining with surprising precision what happened to Ötzi. They even helped shed light on the possible motive of his killer.

10 The more scientists learn, the more recognizable the Iceman becomes. He was 5 feet 5 inches tall, about average height for his time. He weighed 110 pounds and had brown eyes and shoulder-length, dark brown hair. He had a size 7½ foot. He was about 45, give or take six years. That's respectably old for the late Neolithic Age—but still his prime.

11 Ötzi had the physique of a man who did a lot of strenuous walking but little upper-body work. There was hardly any fat on his body. He had all of his teeth. Between his two upper front teeth was a 3-millimeter gap. It's an inherited condition known as diastema.

12 When viewed through the window of the museum's freezer, where he is kept now, his hands appear unusually small. They also show little sign of hard use, suggesting that Ötzi was not a manual laborer.

13 Every modern murder investigation relies heavily on forensic science. But in Ötzi's case, the techniques have been particularly high-tech. They involve exotic specialties like archaeobotany and paleometallurgy.

14 From examining traces of pollen in his digestive tract, scientists were able to place the date of Ötzi's death around late spring or early summer. In his last two days, they found, he consumed three distinct meals. He walked from an elevation of about 6,500 feet, down to the valley floor and then up into the mountains again. There, he was found at the crime site, 10,500 feet up.

---

humidity When something has high humidity, it has a lot of water vapor in it.
physique Someone's physique is the form, size, and development of his or her body.
elevation An elevation is a height above a certain level.

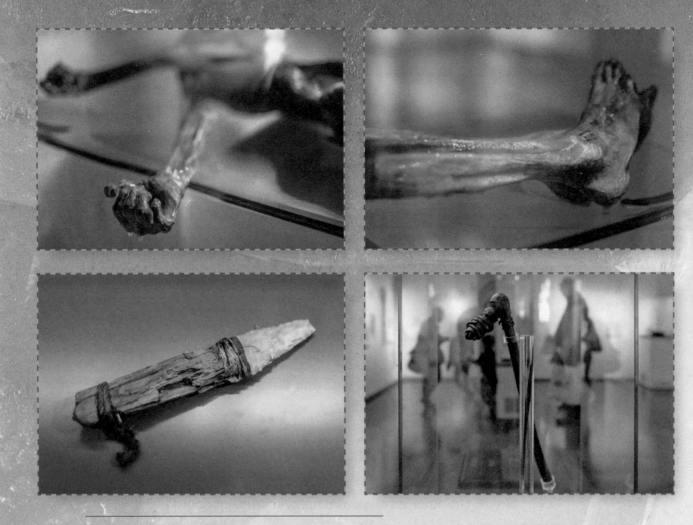

Clockwise from top left: the Iceman's hand, leg, ax and dagger

15   On his body was one prominent wound, other than the one from the arrowhead. It was a deep cut in his right hand between the thumb and forefinger. It went down to the bone and was potentially disabling. By the degree of healing seen on the wound, it was one to two days old.

16   From this, Inspector Horn surmises that Ötzi may have come down to his village and become embroiled in a fight.

17   Then he left, fully provisioned with food. He also had the embers of a fire preserved in maple leaf wrappings, and quite a lot of other equipment. He probably carried most of it in a backpack with a wooden frame. For weapons he had only a small flint dagger, a six-foot-long stave for a bow; and a beautifully crafted deerskin quiver with a dozen arrows. Only two of them had arrowheads attached.

18   Inspector Horn reckons Ötzi was in no hurry. At 10,500 feet, he made what appeared to be a camp in a protected gully on the mountain saddle. He spread his belongings around and sat down to his last meal.

19   "Roughly half an hour before his death he was having a proper meal, even a heavy meal," Inspector Horn said. The Copper Age menu was well balanced, consisting of ibex meat, smoked or raw; einkorn wheat, possibly in the form of bread; some sort of fat, which might have been from bacon or cheese; and bracken, a common fern.

20   There is even evidence that some of his food was recently cooked. "If you're in a rush and the first thing is to get away from someone trying to kill you, that's not what you do," he said. Ötzi's longbow was almost completed, he added. Yet, there was no sign that he was working on it at the time.

21   Half an hour after Ötzi dined, the killer came along and shot him in the back from a distance of almost 100 feet. The arrow went under his left armpit. It ripped through an artery. The wound would have been quickly fatal and probably not treatable even in modern times. By the angle of the wound, he was shot from below and behind. Or, he had been bent forward when he was hit from above and behind.

22   "The aim of the offender was to kill him, and he decides to take a long-distance shot—could be a learning effect from what happened one or two days before," Inspector Horn said. "Which is pretty much what you see all the time nowadays. Most homicides are personal, and follow violence and an escalation of violence. I want to follow him, find him and kill him. All the emotions we have in homicide, these things have not died out in all these years."

23   Robbery can be ruled out as a motive, Horn said. Ötzi had a copper ax. This valuable artifact was only rarely seen in burials of the period. His clothing and kit were a match for the harsh alpine climate, and probably valuable. They were made from the leather and fur of at least 10 animals of six species.

24   "This was not a robbery gone bad or something," Inspector Horn said. Clearly, the killer was trying to cover up his act. "You go back to your village with this unusual ax, it would be pretty obvious what had happened."

25   Ötzi's cold case continues to yield surprises to scientists in many disciplines who still are studying his remains. Last year, for example, they discovered that he was infected with an unusual strain of H. pylori. It is the bacteria believed responsible for ulcers today.

26   There is one thing they are unlikely to discover, as Inspector Horn noted with a chuckle. "I'm not optimistic we'll find the offender in Ötzi's case."

27   Both in life and in death, the Iceman seems uncannily familiar to his modern descendants, said the museum's deputy director, Katharina Hersel.

28   "He is so close to us. He uses the same equipment as we do when he goes to the mountain, just the materials are different," she said. "And we are still killing each other, so maybe there hasn't been so much evolution after all."

The area where the Iceman was from. The crime scene was in the mountains, 10,500 feet up.

Collaborative Discussion

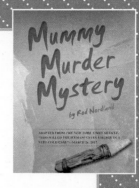

Look back at what you wrote on page 272. Tell a partner why you agree or disagree with the author's viewpoint on this murder mystery. Then work with a group to discuss the questions below. Refer to details and examples in *Mummy Murder Mystery* to explain your answers. Take notes for your responses. When you speak, use your notes.

1 What do we learn about Ötzi from this text? Summarize Inspector Horn's findings.

2 Reread page 279-280. What details support Horn's opinion that robbery was not the motive, or reason, for Ötzi's murder?

3 Do you think Horn makes a good case for what happened to Ötzi? Use details in the text to explain why or why not.

Listening Tip

Listen for the specific details the speaker uses to answer a question. What details or examples can you add?

Speaking Tip

When it is your turn to share your ideas, remember to speak clearly and make eye contact with each member of your group.

Write a Press Statement

....

In *Mummy Murder Mystery*, you learned about Ötzi and profiler Inspector Alexander Horn's theory about the cause of his death more than 5,000 years ago.

Imagine that Inspector Horn and Angelika Fleckinger are giving a press conference about Ötzi. They want to make a brief statement about who Ötzi is, why he is important, and Horn's opinion about how he died. Write a one-paragraph speech that they can read before answering questions from the press.

PLAN ....

Review the details of Inspector Horn's findings from the text. Then make notes on the most important facts about Ötzi.

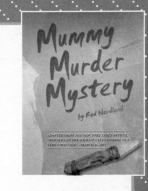

WRITE . . . .

Now write your press statement for Inspector Horn and Angelika Fleckinger.

Make sure your press statement

- ☐ is written as a script, with speaking parts for both Horn and Fleckinger.

- ☐ begins with an introduction about what they will be discussing during the press conference.

- ☐ includes well-organized details from the text that summarize Horn's findings.

- ☐ concludes by asking the press for their questions.

- ☐ includes some Critical Vocabulary and newly acquired vocabulary words from the text.

Notice & Note
Again and Again

Prepare to Read

GENRE STUDY ▶ **Mysteries** are stories in which the main character sets out to solve a mystery, crime, or another puzzle.

- Authors of mysteries tell the story through the plot, which includes a conflict, or problem, and the resolution.

- Mysteries include dialogue to develop the story. Dialogue is a conversation between characters. Authors often use informal language to make the conversation seem real.

SET A PURPOSE ▶ **Think about** the title of this text. Think about what this mystery might be about. Write your ideas below.

**Meet the Author:
Pseudonymous Bosch**

by Pseudonymous bosch

myNotes

Cass, Max-Ernest, and Yo-Yoji are friends, classmates, and fellow members of a secret organization called the Terces Society. The mission of the Terces (that's secret _spelled backward) Society is to guard an ancient secret, first discovered by an Egyptian doctor in 1212 BC. However, even the friends themselves don't know what the secret is, and their efforts to investigate it have led to numerous wild adventures—and lots of trouble— throughout their middle-school years. Now they are about to graduate, but not before completing a class trip to a natural history museum. Might the Egyptian mummy exhibit reveal clues to the Secret? Or will the trip lead the young investigators into trouble again?_

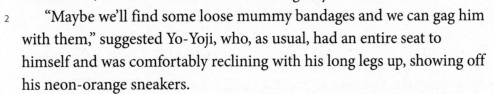

1   **M**ax-Ernest had spent the entire bus ride to the Natural History Museum trying out mummy jokes for his graduation speech. (The opportunity to make a speech was an honor bestowed on him as Bookworm of the Year, winner of the Book-a-Day Reading Challenge; also, there was the fact that nobody else had volunteered.) By the time they neared their destination, his friends were brainstorming ways to silence him.

2   "Maybe we'll find some loose mummy bandages and we can gag him with them," suggested Yo-Yoji, who, as usual, had an entire seat to himself and was comfortably reclining with his long legs up, showing off his neon-orange sneakers.

3   Cass, sitting with Max-Ernest in the seat opposite Yo-Yoji, shook her head. "Nah, he would just tell jokes with his hands. Don't forget he knows sign language."

4   Max-Ernest nodded cheerfully. _How many mummies does it take to change a lightbulb?_ he signed, mouthing the words.

5   "OK, so we tie his wrists together—" said Yo-Yoji, ignoring him.

6   "Forget it," said Cass. "He'll just tap Morse code with his foot."

7   Max-Ernest started tapping the floor: *N-O-N-E, T-H-E-Y L-I-V-E I-N E-T-E-R-N-A-L D-A-R-K-N-E-S-S.*

8   "Then we'll bury him in a sarcophagus," Yo-Yoji persisted.

9   Cass shook her head again. "With our luck, an earthquake will push it to the surface, and he'll jump out and tell some dumb joke about zombies—"

10   "Like this one?" asked Max-Ernest, grinning. "*Do zombies eat hamburgers with their fingers?*"

11   "See what I mean?"

12   "*No, they eat their fingers separately!*"

13   The plump boy who called himself Glob leaned over the seat in front of Max-Ernest. "Dude, zombies tell better jokes than you do—and I bet they give better graduation speeches, too."

14   "Leave him alone, man," said the boy sitting next to Glob, his voice muffled by the dreadlocks that covered his face. This was Daniel—more popularly known as Daniel-not-Danielle. "Zombies are cool. They kick mummy butt."

15   "They're not mutually exclusive categories, you know," said Max-Ernest. "Zombie equals dead body that comes back to life. Mummy equals dead body. Ergo, mummy that comes back to life equals—"

16   "Silence, please!"

17   It was Mrs. Johnson, standing up near the front of the bus.

18   Our friends shrank in their seats. Although they were no longer quite as scared of their principal as they once had been, she still held the power to suspend them or even to prevent them from graduating middle school. And as much as they all feared graduating, there was one thing they all feared more: *not* graduating.

19   "Thank you," said Mrs. Johnson, holding on to her turquoise-blue hat as the bus lurched to a stop in front of the old brick museum. "Let's start practicing our museum voices now. Remember, a museum is not a zoo. It is a place of quiet contemplation and reflection—"

---

mutually   If you describe two things as mutually exclusive, they cannot both be true.

contemplation   Contemplation is the act of thinking deeply about something.

UNWRAPPED: REAL MUMMIES!

DUSTY TOMBS. ANCIENT CURSES.
WALKING DEAD.

20 From King Tut to Boris Karloff,[1] mummies have long captured our imagination. Yet they are not just creatures of fantasy, haunting us on late-night television and on the streets at Halloween. They are material specimens of lost worlds—real people of the past whose bodies have been preserved so that we may study them today. What were their lives like? How did they die? What secrets do they hold in their ancient hands? Join us as these voyagers from the past take us on a journey across time.

21 **SPECIAL THANKS TO EGYPT'S SUPREME COUNCIL OF ANTIQUITIES**
EXHIBITION MADE POSSIBLE BY A GENEROUS GRANT FROM *SOLAR-ZERO* LLC

22 Contrary to Mrs. Johnson's assertion, the museum was quite loud. The marble floors and vaulted ceilings magnified the kids' every footstep, and a lot of other sounds besides.

23 Most of the museum would be closed to the public for another two hours, and museum staff were using the time to repair exhibits and take inventory. It can be startling to hear soft-spoken curators shouting instructions or grave-faced museum guards joking with each other, but it certainly makes a museum livelier. If you've never visited a museum when it is closed, I recommend it; that's when a museum really comes to life.

24 The special, behind-the-scenes tour had been arranged by Daniel-not-Danielle's father, Dr. Albert Ndefo, who happened to be the chief curator of the mummy exhibit. Dr. Ndefo—also known as Albert 3-D, in

---

[1] BORIS KARLOFF WAS AN ACTOR WHO BECAME FAMOUS IN THE 1930S PLAYING DEAD BODIES THAT COME BACK TO LIFE. IF YOU ARE UNFAMILIAR WITH HIS OEUVRE, I HIGHLY RECOMMEND THE CLASSIC HORROR FILMS *FRANKENSTEIN* AND *THE MUMMY*. (IF YOU ARE UNFAMILIAR WITH THE WORD *OEUVRE*, IT IS THE BODY OF WORK OF AN ARTIST, WRITER, OR COMPOSER—LIVING, DEAD, OR OTHERWISE.) IN *THE MUMMY*, KARLOFF PLAYS IMHOTEP, A MUMMY REAWAKENED WHEN AN ARCHAEOLOGIST ACCIDENTALLY READS AN ANCIENT EGYPTIAN SPELL.

> **specimens** Specimens are individual animals, plants, or objects that are examples of their type.

reference to his three degrees: one in archaeology, one in anthropology, and one in Egyptology—greeted them next to the eight-foot-tall stone sarcophagus that stood just inside the entrance, dwarfing anyone who passed by. "Hi, everybody, welcome to chaos. We're just doing a little rearranging before the noon rush!"

25   The Nigerian-born professor had dreadlocks like his son's, but at the moment his were tied back under an old, camouflage-patterned sun hat that looked as though it had been to the desert and back more than once. He wore a T-shirt that said **ARCHAEOLOGY—DIG IT!**, and he ushered his guests into the exhibit as if they were entering an excavation of buried ruins.

26   "Watch your backs," he warned. "The mummies most likely won't attack, but museum workers have been known to shoot poison darts."

27   As if on cue, a student bumped into a ladder, and a loose power cord fell down. Mrs. Johnson shrieked. Her students giggled.

28   "So, what is a mummy?" Albert 3-D asked rhetorically, beckoning the last few stragglers inside. "Simple: a mummy is any dead body whose tissue has been preserved beyond the usual time. In this exhibit, we have naturally occurring mummies as well as man-made ones. Mummies created in caves, in sand, in icebergs—and even, in the case of bog mummies, *underwater*.² There are specimens from Peru, Chile, Greenland, Norway, and, of course, ancient Egypt. And then there are the animal mummies. . . ."

29   The first room of the exhibit was large and gray, with few doors and fewer windows. It looked not unlike a tomb—a strange, futuristic tomb in which mummies were confined in protective glass cases. On the walls were big backlit photos of archaeological digs and ancient burial grounds that cast a ghostly fluorescent glow on the faces of the students.

30   The students fell silent as they got their first look at the mummies on display. While the bog mummies were hardly more substantial than

---

² Bog mummies, if you're curious (and I can't imagine that you aren't), are usually found in the bogs of northern Europe. The peat in the bogs acts as a unique preservative—and leaves the faces of bog mummies uniquely lifelike.

chaos   Chaos is complete disorder and confusion.
substantial   If something is substantial, it has considerable size, strength, or value.

rags, others looked strong enough to stand. Some were wrapped in the familiar linen bandages; others, in sheets. Some were naked; others were wearing elaborate jeweled garments. Some had hair; some were bald. Some were sitting up; some, lying down. One was curled in a ball; another was slumped over.

31   A few students had to look away and take deep breaths; the mummies of **UNWRAPPED: REAL MUMMIES!** were altogether more real than they had imagined.

32   Yo-Yoji shook his head. "Ridiculous, man."

33   Max-Ernest nodded uncertainly. *Ridiculous* was a word that Yo-Yoji had been using often lately, but as with many of the words he adopted, you didn't always know if it was meant in a positive or negative sense— or in some other sense comprehensible only to those fluent in the language of cool.

34   "I'll let you look around, and then we'll talk in a few minutes," said Albert 3-D. "Unless someone has a question right now?"

35   "I do," said Glob. "Is it true people fart after they die? And if a mummy farts, will it still stink a thousand years later when his coffin is opened?"

36   His classmates tittered.

37   "Hmm . . . I doubt it," Albert 3-D answered seriously. "The smell would dissipate long before then. But you're right about dead bodies. In Mayan mythology, the god of the underworld was called Cizin, meaning *stinking one.*"

38   While the rest of her class laughed, Cass slipped the ibis ring onto her finger.

39   It was a bit foolish of her to wear the ring in public, she knew, but holding a little piece of ancient Egypt in her hand gave her a sense of confidence. Maybe seeing the ibis next to other hieroglyphs in the exhibit would jog her memory; today, she was determined to identify the remaining hieroglyphs of the Secret.

---

garments   Garments are pieces of clothing.

40   Her backpack, as usual, had everything she might need:

41   Magnifying glass: check.

42   Hidden camera: check.

43   Molding wax for taking impressions: check.

44   Brush for dusting specimens: check.

45   Armed like an archaeologist in the field, Cass looked in every place she might conceivably find a hieroglyph. While the other students casually checked out the exhibit, she methodically studied photos of tomb paintings and copies of spells from the *Book of the Dead*.[3] She examined the decorations on funeral masks, and the carvings on stone sarcophagi. She inspected tiny *shabti* figures who were supposed to serve Egyptian nobles in the afterlife, and strange finger-shaped amulets meant to seal wounds and protect the dead.

46   And yet as far as she could tell, none of the hieroglyphs she saw resembled the hieroglyphs of the Secret. Then again, perhaps the sketches in her notebook were incorrect. There was no way to know.

47   Her confidence beginning to crumble, she stood, holding her notebook open in her hand and staring at a bowl of natron, the natural salt that is found in desert lakes and that was used by the Egyptians to dry out bodies before they were mummified. Could you mummify a body using normal table salt? she wondered idly. Maybe she should try it on herself. If she didn't figure out the Secret soon, she might as well be mummified.

48   As she turned away, Max-Ernest crept up behind her. He reached around and tapped her on her far shoulder—

49   She spun around, snapping her notebook shut. "What? Oh!"

50   She rolled her eyes when she saw Max-Ernest standing there, grinning at his little practical joke. "That is so not funny."

---

[3] THE EGYPTIAN *BOOK OF THE DEAD*, ALSO KNOWN AS THE *PAPYRUS OF ANI*, IS THE ESSENTIAL FUNERARY GUIDE THAT NO SELF-RESPECTING AMATEUR EGYPTOLOGIST CAN DO WITHOUT. TO QUOTE NO LESS AN AUTHORITY THAN ONE PSEUDONYMOUS BOSCH, "IT INCLUDES MANY IMPORTANT SPELLS AND INSTRUCTIONS FOR SUCCESS IN THE AFTERLIFE—A USEFUL INTRODUCTION TO ANCIENT EGYPTIAN LIFE ABOVEGROUND AS WELL!"

---

essential   Something that is essential is necessary.

51   "Did you see the ibis mummies?"[4]

52   "Uh-huh."

53   Max-Ernest eyed the notebook in her hand. "Is that where you have your notes about . . . it?"

54   "Shh!" Cass whispered sharply.

55   "If you're so worried about people knowing, are you sure you should be wearing that ring?" asked Max-Ernest, stung.

56   Cass's ears flared red. "Why don't you go think of more jokes for your graduation speech or something?"

57   Max-Ernest watched her in consternation as she moved on to another display: **HAVE YOU EVER WONDERED WHAT A MUMMY'S SKIN FEELS LIKE? TOUCH HERE TO FIND OUT!** It was an interactive wall display containing swatches of leather, plastic, and other materials. She touched a few of the swatches and made a face.

58   "What's up with her?" asked Yo-Yoji.

59   Max-Ernest shrugged. "You know Cass."

60   Although Yo-Yoji was a fellow Terces member, it was Cass's business to tell him—or not—about the latest development in her search for the Secret. And truth be told, Max-Ernest didn't want to talk much about it. He was beginning to wish she'd never found the papyrus in the first place.

61   Yo-Yoji squinted. "Is that a ring on her finger? I've never seen her wear a ring before. . . ." He looked askance at Max-Ernest. "You didn't give it to her, did you?"

62   "What? *No!* Why, were you planning on asking her to marry you?" asked Max-Ernest, recovering.

63   "Very funny . . ."

64   Yo-Yoji glanced at Cass again. It was almost as if he didn't like the idea of somebody else giving her a ring.

---

[4]YOU MAY BE INTERESTED TO LEARN THAT IBIS MUMMIES ARE QUITE COMMON. IN THE NECROPOLIS OF SAQQÂRA—THE EGYPTIANS' FAMED CITY OF THE DEAD— ARCHAEOLOGISTS DISCOVERED THE MUMMIES OF ONE AND A HALF MILLION IBISES. IT IS BELIEVED THAT THE IBISES WERE RAISED ON RANCHES SPECIFICALLY FOR THE PURPOSE OF BEING MUMMIFIED AND OFFERED TO THE GODS. UPSETTING? PERHAPS. BUT CONSIDER THE FATE OF A CHICKEN.

65 A moment later, Albert 3-D gathered all the students together and led the class toward a four-sided glass chamber that stood in the center of the exhibit's largest room.

66 "Here is our star attraction," he said, opening the door to the chamber. "We keep the door closed during museum hours—you're supposed to look in from the outside—but since the public's not here yet, I thought I'd give you a treat."

67 Inside the chamber, a stone sarcophagus lay open for viewing. Next to it were three colorfully decorated wooden coffins that descended in size like Russian nesting dolls, and four clay canopic jars, each about the size of a paint can.[5] Like many jars of this kind, these ones were topped with the heads of a person, a falcon, a baboon, and a jackal (who were supposed to guard the mummy's liver, intestines, lungs, and stomach, respectively).

68 "Please, please, don't touch anything. Despite the fact that his grave was robbed repeatedly, this handsome fellow is one of the best-preserved mummies ever unearthed. His tomb was excavated just a year ago, and it's the first time the Egyptians have allowed him to travel."

69 Everyone gathered around the sarcophagus and eagerly stared down at the perfectly desiccated citizen of ancient Egypt.

70 "He's something of a mystery mummy. We don't even know his name. Around the museum, we call him Amun, which means *the hidden one*."

71 Tightly wound linen bandages surrounded most of the mystery mummy's body, but his head was bare, and his hands stuck out of the bandages just above his waist. His hair, assuming he'd ever had any, was long gone, and his skin had turned the color of bronze sculpture. His eyes were closed, but his mouth was open, revealing a few rotten teeth and a dark hole where his tongue should have been.

72 "He looks like that painting they make Halloween masks out of," said Yo-Yoji. "What's it called?"

_____

[5] A canopic jar, as you no doubt remember from your own studies, is a jar in which the ancient Egyptians stored and preserved the organs of the dead.

73   "*The Scream*," Max-Ernest volunteered.[6] "Maybe he was screaming in pain when he died. Then his mouth stayed open when rigor mortis set in. How 'bout that?"

74   "People scream for other reasons," said Cass. "He could have been trying to warn somebody about something. Like a sandstorm or a plague of locusts—"

75   "I think he looks like he's laughing," said Glob.

76   "Actually, none of you are right," said Albert 3-D. "His mouth was opened after his death. The Egyptians opened the mouths of mummies so they could breathe in the afterlife."

77   "So how did he die, then?" asked Cass.

78   "All we know about Amun is that he was a young doctor who rose to become the pharaoh's personal physician and adviser," said Albert 3-D. "Then, suddenly . . ."

79   He ran his finger across his neck—the universal sign for execution.

80   He pointed to the smallest of Dr. Amun's coffins, where some hieroglyphs were painted in black and red beneath the stylized face of a handsome young man.

81   "Daniel, do you want to read these glyphs for your classmates?" he asked, looking expectantly at his son.

82   Daniel-not-Danielle, who had remained remarkably quiet ever since they entered the museum, shook his head. His dreadlocks swung back and forth like a spinning mop.

83   "I'll read them," said Max-Ernest.

84   Albert looked at him in surprise. "You read hieroglyphs? Your Egypt unit was more in-depth than I thought."

85   Max-Ernest shrugged. "It's kind of a hobby."

86   "Some people collect trading cards or play video games." Glob snickered. "Max-Ernest reads hieroglyphs."

87   "I do those things, too!" Max-Ernest protested.

88   "He was being sarcastic," said Cass. "Just read it."

---

[6]MAX-ERNEST MUST HAVE BEEN VERY PREOCCUPIED WITH THE MUMMY IN FRONT OF HIM. OTHERWISE, HE WOULD HAVE MENTIONED THAT THERE IS NOT JUST ONE PAINTING CALLED *THE SCREAM*; THERE ARE SEVERAL. THE ARTIST, EDVARD MUNCH, PAINTED THE SAME IMAGE MANY TIMES, AS IF HE COULD NEVER QUITE GET IT RIGHT. THE MESSAGE IS CLEAR: IF AT FIRST YOU DON'T SUCCEED . . . SCREAM. AND SCREAM AGAIN.

89   She looked over his shoulder, hoping that she might recognize one of her unidentified hieroglyphs. No luck.

90   Max-Ernest coughed exaggeratedly. "Ahem. OK, here goes—'The name of this man is . . . secret'? Is that the word?"

91   Albert 3-D nodded. "Go on."

92   "'Also secret is the reason for . . .'"

93   Max-Ernest stammered because a wild idea had just occurred to him. Could Dr. Amun be the doctor who had discovered the Secret? No, he thought, there's no way.

94   "'. . . for his death,'" read Albert 3-D, finishing the sentence. "That was very good. Have you considered going into Egyptology?"

95   "Yeah, I've considered it. But I still want to be a comedian. Or a comic magician." (Max-Ernest had a pretty good idea he was going to wind up being a writer instead, but he hadn't fully accepted it yet.)

96   "So nobody knows why Amun was executed?" asked Cass, who'd had the exact same idea about the mummy that Max-Ernest had. (Only she didn't think the idea was so wild.)

97   Albert 3-D shook his head. "The inscription continues: 'Pharaoh asked for his wisdom, but he gave pharaoh only his wit.' . . . It sounds as though he made some kind of smart remark at the pharaoh's expense —the kind of thing one of you guys might say about, oh, a teacher or a principal."

98   He grinned at Mrs. Johnson. She didn't grin back. "Whatever he did, I doubt we would think he deserved to die for it."

99   "In mummy movies, it's always the ones who are wrongfully executed who come back to life," said Yo-Yoji.

100   "Yeah, we better watch out," said Glob. "Or we're all going to die from the mummy's curse!"[7]

101   Albert 3-D chuckled. "I think the people burying him were a little worried about that, too. At the very end of the inscription, it reads: 'In life he had the magic touch. Now may his hands lie still.' Guess they were afraid he might reach out and grab them—"

[7]THE IDEA OF THE MUMMY'S CURSE BECAME POPULAR WHEN SEVERAL MEN INVOLVED IN THE DISCOVERY OF KING TUTANKHAMEN'S TOMB DIED SOON AFTER HIS DISINTERMENT. LATER, PEOPLE SPECULATED THAT THREE-THOUSAND-YEAR-OLD BACTERIA RELEASED FROM TUT'S TOMB MIGHT HAVE BEEN TO BLAME, BUT FRANKLY THERE IS EVEN LESS BASIS FOR THAT THEORY. I WOULD GO WITH THE CURSE.

102   As Albert 3-D led the class out of the sealed glass room, Cass, Yo-Yoji, and Max-Ernest leaned over the edge of the sarcophagus to examine the mummy more closely.

103   "So—do you think it's him?" Cass whispered excitedly after everybody else had left.

104   "Who?" asked Yo-Yoji.

105   "Who do you think? The doctor who discovered the . . . you know."

106   Yo-Yoji nodded. "Right! And he was killed right after he told it to the pharaoh. Or after he refused to tell him. Whatever. It's almost exactly the same story."

107   "I thought of that, too, but it would be a pretty huge coincidence," said Max-Ernest. "Of all the mummies in the world, for this one to be that one particular doctor, here in our town, in an exhibit organized by our friend's dad. I highly, highly, highly doubt that is the case."

108   "A lot of things seem *highly, highly, highly* coincidental," said Cass, irked. "That doesn't mean they're not true."

109   "Plus, the hieroglyphs only said that the reason he was killed was secret," Max-Ernest persisted stubbornly. "Not that the reason was *a* secret or *the* Secret." Actually, he remembered as he said this, in ancient Egyptian the words *a* and *the* weren't always used, so there was little difference. But he didn't correct himself; he didn't want to give Cass the satisfaction.

110   "Well, I say it's him," said Cass, leaning in even closer to the mummy.

111   She didn't know how she knew, but she knew.

112   She'd come to the museum hoping to translate the rest of the Secret, but instead she'd discovered something potentially much more significant: the man who had discovered the Secret and who, for that reason, had suffered a pharaoh's wrath.

113   It was *his* dying hand, she was certain, that had written the Secret on a piece of papyrus thousands of years ago. And it was the same hand—with its long, bony fingers—that held Cass's attention now. Though the mummy's wrists were bound to his waist, his fingers stretched upward, as if the mummy were straining to break free of the linen bandages. As if he wanted to touch her. To grasp her.

114   Transfixed, she stared at the mummy's fingers. She and Max-Ernest had found the ibis ring tied to a piece of shredded linen just like the

bandages that wrapped the mummy. Could the ring once have encircled one of the mummy's fingers? Albert 3-D had mentioned something about the mummy's tomb being robbed. . . .

115   The fingers were dark and crooked, with broken fingernails the color of wood. She didn't see any signs of scraping or stretching where a ring might have been pulled off, but she couldn't be certain the signs weren't there because—frustratingly—a few of the fingers of the mummy's left hand were blocked from view by a stray bandage. If only she could move the bandage aside for a second . . .

116   She glanced over her shoulder. Max-Ernest had turned away, and Yo-Yoji was about to walk out of the glass room.

117   Taking a breath, Cass leaned down and gently pulled the bandage away from the mummy's hand. Immediately, she noticed the index finger: below the knuckle was a faint but discernible ring where the mummy's skin had turned black. The black ring narrowed at the sides of the finger and widened on top into a black oval. It was the exact shape of the ibis ring—

118   "Cassandra! Max-Ernest! Yoji! Get away from there!" Mrs. Johnson's voice broke Cass's concentration. "What part of 'do not touch' do you not understand?"

119   Cass spun around, her arms flailing in her attempt to distance herself from the mummy.

120   Too late, she realized her sweatshirt sleeve had caught on something.

121   She heard a snap, like the sound of a twig breaking, and the next thing she knew, a slim, dark projectile was flying through the air.

122   It arced over Max-Ernest's head, and as they all watched openmouthed, it landed

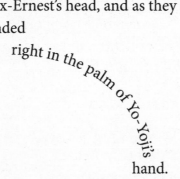

right in the palm of Yo-Yoji's hand.

123   He stared at it as if he had caught a live grenade.

124   It was the mummy's finger.

---

discernible   If something is discernible, it's noticeable or recognizable.

MUMMIES

Milwaukee Public Museum

by Richard Hedderman

125 When children ask if it's frightening
     when they come alive, I tell them yes,
     of course it is, it's absolutely terrifying,
     and believe me, you don't want to be around

126 when it happens, especially at night.
     When they ask if the mummies walk
     with their arms outstretched like mummies
     in the movies, I tell them no, it's nothing

127 like that. You see, I explain, the muscles
     of their arms have atrophied from thousands
     of years of disuse they just can't walk
     around the way mummies do in movies.

128 In fact, I explain, their feet have been so
     lovingly and carefully bound by strips
     of flax linen, that it's difficult for them
     to walk at all, which explains the halting gait,

129 the fear that at any moment they will stumble
     and pitch forward, landing in a heap of rags.
     Can they talk? No, they can't talk, not after
     all those years in tombs choked with the dust

130 of centuries and the weight of eternity
     upon them. Can they see, they want to know.
     Not anymore, I say, for long ago
     their eyes were replaced with onions or stones,

131 stones as white as the sun. Finally, I explain,
     they long only to wander forth as they used to,
     and once again admire their reflections
     in the shimmering Nile of the gallery floor.

atrophied   Something that has atrophied has wasted away because it hasn't been used.
halting   When something is done in a halting way, it is done slowly and with a lot of hesitation.

Collaborative Discussion

Look back at what you wrote on page 284. Tell a partner something you liked about the mystery. Then work with a group to discuss the questions below. Refer to details and examples in *You Have to Stop This* and "Mummies" to explain your answers. Take notes for your responses.

1 What did you learn about the mummy exhibit from the text? Does it make you want to visit a mummy exhibit? Explain your answer.

2 How would you describe the narrator of *You Have to Stop This*? Give examples from the text to describe the narrator's tone and voice.

3 The poet who wrote "Mummies" says he wrote the poem based on questions children have asked him about mummies. After reading the poem, what questions might you ask if you visited his museum?

Listening Tip

If you can't hear someone in your group easily, ask that person to speak a little louder.

Speaking Tip

Build your ideas onto what speakers have said before you. If you agree with what a speaker has said, say so, and then add your ideas.

Write the Beginning of a New Chapter

PROMPT ....

In *You Have to Stop This*, you read two chapters from a mystery surrounding a class field trip to a mummy exhibit at a museum.

The book excerpt ends with a cliff-hanger—a point in the story where the reader is anxious to know what happens next. So . . . what happens? Does the mummy come to life? Does Mrs. Johnson take Cass aside for a lecture? Pick one of those ideas or come up with your own and write at least four lines of dialogue that start the next chapter.

PLAN ....

Write the name of each character and the role he or she plays in the story. Then decide which characters you want to include in your chapter. Write a short summary of what happens next.

WRITE

Now write your beginning for the next chapter.

✓ Make sure your summary

☐ includes dialogue between two or more characters.

☐ tells what happens next.

☐ is logical, or makes sense with what has happened in the story.

☐ matches the voice and tone of the characters from the excerpt.

☐ uses punctuation correctly, including commas and quotation marks.

? Essential Question

How can the remains of ancient peoples give us a window into their lives?

Write a Personal Narrative

PROMPT Think about what you learned in this module about ancient peoples.

Imagine you are at an archaeology summer camp where you accompany archaeologists on a dig. While there, you make a remarkable discovery! Write a personal narrative that describes what you found, how you found it, and what your discovery tells us about ancient peoples.

I will write about my discovery of _____.

✓ **Make sure your narrative**

☐ begins with an introduction that includes specific details about where the dig takes place.
☐ includes specific descriptive details about how you found it and what it looks like.
☐ explains what your discovery tells about ancient peoples.
☐ uses information from at least two texts.
☐ tells why the discovery was important to you.

What kind of discovery will you make in your personal narrative? Look back at your notes, and revisit the texts as necessary.

In the chart below, plan your personal narrative. Identify the location of the archaeological dig and decide on what your discovery will be. Then use evidence from the texts to fill in the details about the archaeology summer camp and the discovery you make. Use Critical Vocabulary words where appropriate.

My Discovery: _____.

Archaeological site:
Discovery:
Details about the discovery:
Notes from the texts I can use in my narrative:

DRAFT ⋯⋯⋯⋯⋯⋯⋯⋯⋯⋯⋯⋯⋯⋯⋯⋯⋯ Write your personal narrative.

Write the **beginning** of your personal narrative. Describe the archaeological site and introduce the people on the dig. Be sure to use descriptive language that helps readers create images in their minds.

For the **middle** of your personal narrative, describe the events at camp and the details of your discovery. Use vivid language, or descriptive words, to convey what you see and how others react to the discovery.

In your **ending**, tell what you learned about ancient peoples from your discovery, what you will do next, or how your discovery made you feel.

REVISE AND EDIT

The revision and editing steps give you a chance to look carefully at your writing and make changes. Work with a partner to determine whether you have clearly explained what your discovery reveals about ancient peoples to readers. Use these questions to help you evaluate and improve your narrative.

PURPOSE/ FOCUS	ORGANIZATION	EVIDENCE	LANGUAGE/ VOCABULARY	CONVENTIONS
☐ Does my narrative include details of my discovery and what it reveals about ancient peoples?	☐ Does my narrative have a beginning, a middle, and an end? ☐ Do the events in my narrative follow a logical order?	☐ Does the text evidence make my story realistic and believable? ☐ Did I include details from at least two texts in my narrative?	☐ Did I use vivid words to describe the setting and my discovery? ☐ Did I use signal words and linking words to create a smooth flow of ideas?	☐ Have I used proper spelling? ☐ Do my subjects and verbs agree? ☐ Have I used pronouns correctly?

PUBLISH

Create a Finished Copy Make a final copy of your personal narrative. You may wish to include an illustration of your discovery. Consider these options to share your personal narrative.

1. Create a front and back cover for your personal narrative and bind all the pages to create a book.

2. Publish your personal narrative on a school website.

3. Collect the personal narratives from the class and bind them in a magazine called *Archaeology Discoveries Today*.

Get Out the Vote

VOTES FOR WOMEN

4. BUCKINGHAM STREET STRAND

MEETING

To demand the Enfranchisement
of Women, and to protest against
the exclusion of Women from a
share in Law-Making

AT

ESSEX HALL ESSEX ST. STRAND

ON MONDAY, NOV. 25

AT 8 P.M.

MRS. DESPARD
MISS IRENE MILLER
MRS. EDITH HOW MARTYN
MISS NEILANS

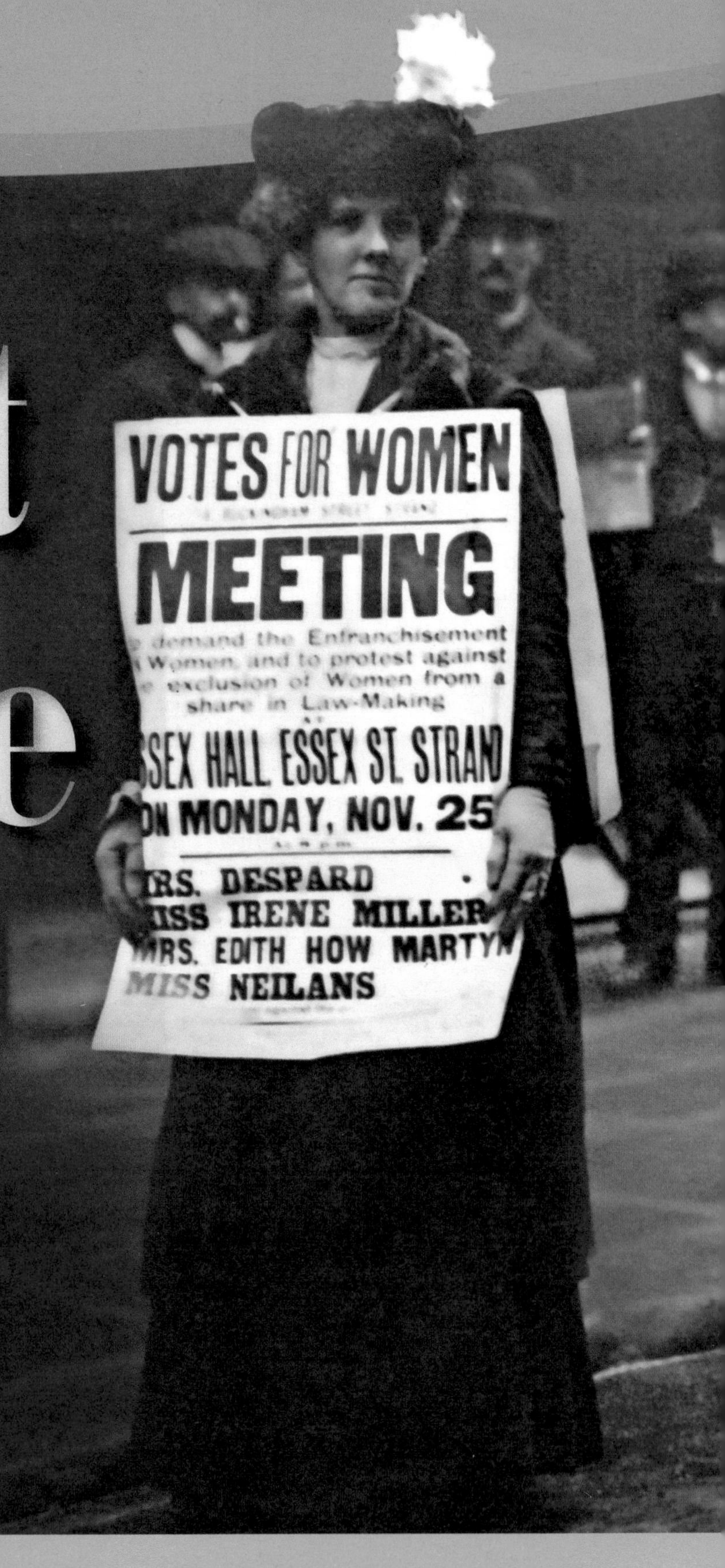

"Without a struggle, there can be no progress."

—Frederick Douglass

Why does voting matter?

Get Curious Video

Words About Voting

The words in the chart will help you talk and write about the selections in this module. Which words about voting have you seen before? Which words are new to you?

Add to the Vocabulary Network on page 311 by writing synonyms, antonyms, and related words and phrases for each word about voting.

After you read each selection in this module, come back to the Vocabulary Network and keep building it. Add more boxes if you need to.

WORD	MEANING	CONTEXT SENTENCE
prohibits (verb)	If a law prohibits something, it forbids it or makes it illegal.	President Johnson signed the Voting Rights Act of 1965, which prohibits discrimination in voting.
eligible (adjective)	If you are eligible to do something, you're qualified or able to do it.	After he turned 16 and passed his driving and written test, he was eligible to get his driver's license.
naturalized (verb)	Naturalized citizens of a country are people who have legally become citizens of that country, even though they were not born there.	Five years after she moved to the United States from China, my aunt became a naturalized U.S. citizen.
suffrage (noun)	Suffrage is the right of people to vote.	Universal suffrage gives all people, regardless of race or gender, the right to vote.

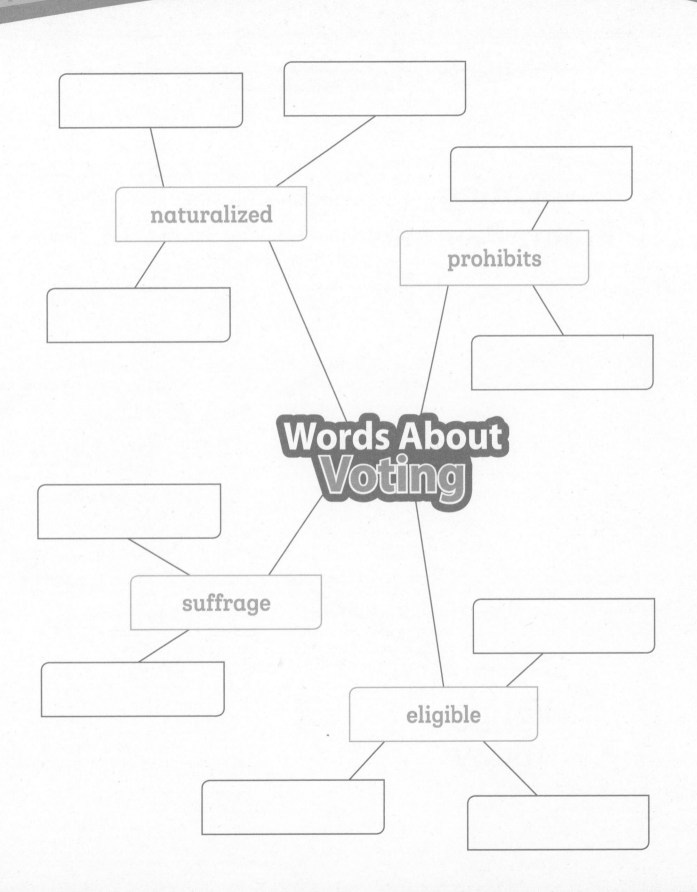

naturalized

prohibits

Words About Voting

suffrage

eligible

Voting Rights Pioneers

Right to Vote

Voting Today

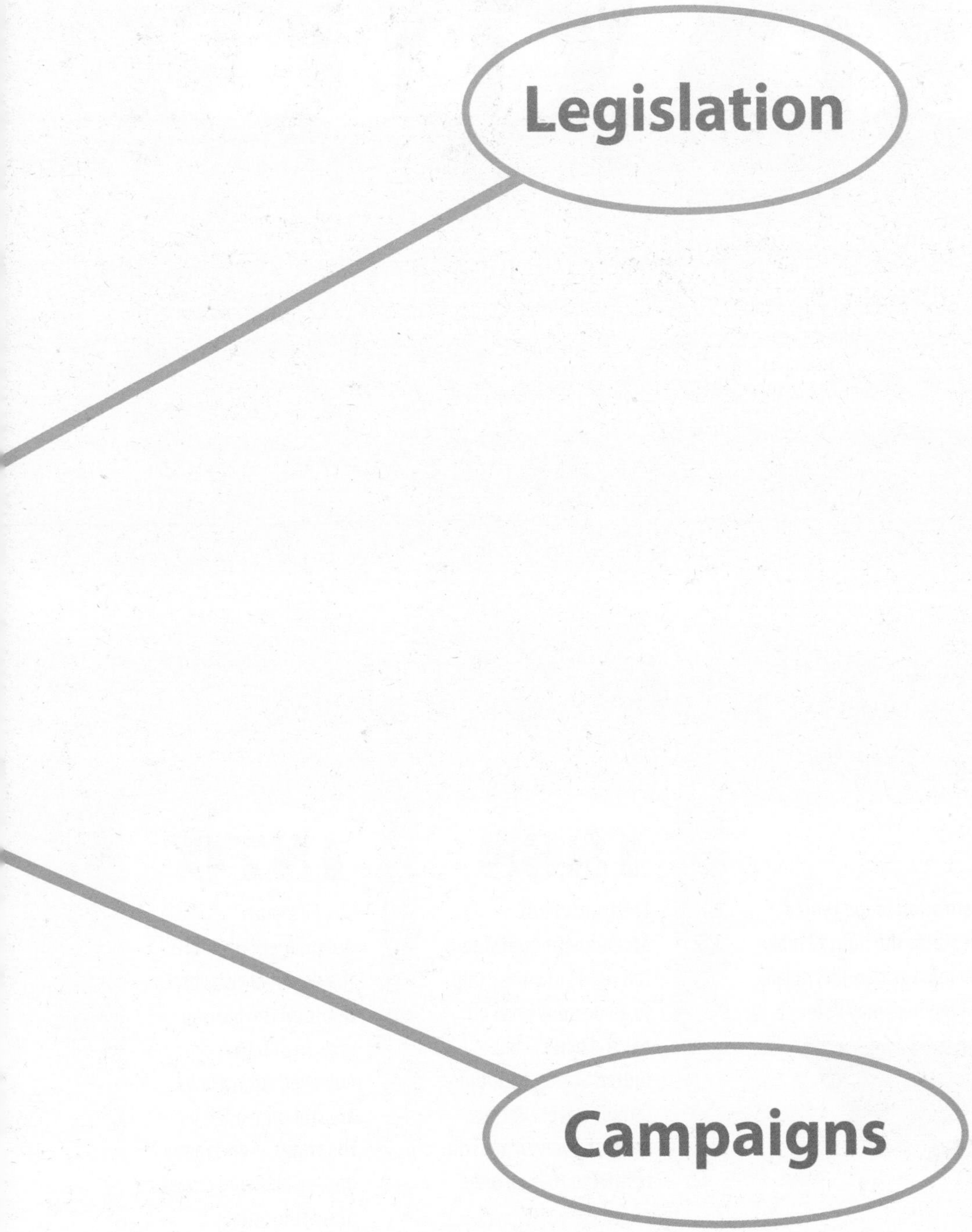

Legislation

Campaigns

Short Read

Our Right to Vote

The right to vote is the cornerstone of any democracy. Though our country was founded on the principle that all humans are created equal, for many years only native-born white men who owned land and/or paid taxes were **eligible** to vote. This timeline presents landmark events in the history of voting rights in the United States.

1787

The newly adopted Constitution of the United States of America grants states the right to make their own voting laws. In most states, this means that only white male landowners may vote.

1868

The Fourteenth Amendment guarantees full rights of citizenship to all persons born or naturalized in the United States, including former slaves. Voting rights, however, are still restricted to men only.

1870

The Fifteenth Amendment prohibits the denial of citizenship rights on the basis of race. In practice, however, voting laws are still controlled by the states—and many oppose allowing citizens of color to vote.

1971

The Twenty-sixth Amendment lowers the voting age from 21 to 18 years of age.

1920

The Nineteenth Amendment extends suffrage to women of all races. In practice, women of color face the same barriers as their male counterparts.

1924

All Native Americans are granted citizenship and the right to vote.

2006

President George W. Bush extends the Voting Rights Act of 1965 for 25 years (its fourth extension).

1965

The Voting Rights Act of 1965 protects voter registration and voting for minority citizens.

1986

The Uniformed and Overseas Citizens Absentee Voting Act grants voting rights to members of the U.S. military and other citizens living on military bases, on ships, or overseas.

VOTE

Prepare to Read

GENRE STUDY A **biography** is the story of a real person's life written by someone other than that person.

- Authors of biographies may organize their ideas using headings and subheadings. The headings and subheadings tell readers what the next section of text will be about.

- Biographies include third-person pronouns, such as *he, she, him, her, his, hers, they, them,* and *their.*

SET A PURPOSE **Think about** the title and genre of this text. Why might someone want to vote? What might keep someone from being able to vote? Write your ideas below.

Meet the Author:
Mary Kay Carson

CRITICAL VOCABULARY

activist

restrictions

clergy

abolition

obtain

petitions

lectures

swarmed

Why Couldn't Susan B. Anthony Vote?

And Other Questions About Women's Suffrage

by Mary Kay Carson

Why couldn't Susan B. Anthony vote?

1   Susan B. Anthony helped make the United States a better country. She wanted all people to be treated fairly. Today we'd call her a social activist. In the 1800s, when Anthony lived, she was called a reformer. A reformer is someone devoted to bringing about change, or reform, to improve society.

2   The nineteenth century was a time of many reform movements in America. Susan B. Anthony worked alongside others to end slavery, fought to reform child labor, and sought restrictions on alcohol because of the problems it caused some families. But Susan B. Anthony was a woman. At that time, she could not be a governor or run for congress. As a woman, Anthony could not even vote. Not being able to vote meant that reformers like Anthony had little power to change things. The female half of America had no say in how their country was run. Their choices for presidents, senators, and town sheriffs didn't count. Anthony felt this was unfair and wrong. Changing that fact became her life's work.

3   Susan B. Anthony traveled across the country giving speeches and gathering signatures on formal requests sent to officials, called petitions. People made fun of Anthony and her new ideas. Leaders, clergy, and newspaper writers criticized her. She was arrested for attempting to vote. But Susan B. Anthony was a crusader. She battled for women's rights for more than half a century. Her dedication led to a huge change in America. Women became voters.

Susan B. Anthony

Why is voting important?

4   Voting is how citizens shape their government. The United States has a government that rules by laws. Elected representatives make most of those laws. America is also a democracy, so the people get to choose their representatives. Senators, governors, mayors, and presidents are all voted into office by people in public elections. These elections decide who leads and who gets to make laws. Everyone is affected by the decisions elected officials make and the laws they create. That's why voting matters.

---

activist   If you are an activist, you work hard to support a cause you believe in.

restrictions   Restrictions are rules that limit what you can do.

clergy   Members of the clergy serve as leaders in churches.

What is women's suffrage?

5 The nation's founders believed that Americans should govern themselves. They wrote a constitution that called for a president and a legislature, or a group who makes laws, who would be elected by the people. But they had a narrow view of who those voters should be. Suffrage is having the right to vote in public elections. Early suffrage was limited to white men aged twenty-one or older who owned land. That left out a lot of people—women, enslaved people, nonwhite immigrants, Native Americans, people of certain religions, and poor people who didn't own land. Who can and can't vote has changed throughout American history.

6 By the mid-1800s, nearly all white men could vote in America. But those of other races, and the entire female half of the population, could not. Voting was only available to a minority of Americans until the twentieth century.

7 Women's suffrage is the right of women to vote. The women's suffrage movement sought equal voting rights for women. This was the goal of the so-called suffragists. Their struggle started in the early 1800s. It was a time when Americans began educating their daughters, not just their sons. Women were learning about social issues and joining in political discussions. But many women felt that their opinions carried no weight. Suffragists decided that the power to vote would help them gain other rights. Voting would allow them to better fight for issues that were important to them.

During the 1910s, suffragists marched in parades to rally support for their right to vote.

Was young Susan allowed to have toys and play games?

8   Susan Brownell Anthony was born in Massachusetts in 1820. When she was six, her family moved fifty miles to Battenville, New York, where her father ran cotton mills. Susan grew up with two brothers and four sisters. The Anthony family was part of the Quaker religious group, whose beliefs were different from most at the time. Quakers are pacifists, meaning they do not believe in war or violence for any reason. They also believe that men and women of all races are equal.

9   Quaker families wore plain clothes, didn't sing, dance, or drink alcohol. It's likely Susan's father didn't allow toys, games, or music in their house either. He believed these amusements kept the children from concentrating on God. Hard work was expected. From early girlhood Susan sewed, cooked, cleaned, and did other chores. She also worked in her father's mills sometimes. The Anthonys taught their children that being useful to the world was a Quaker's duty. "Go and do all the good you can," Susan's mother would say. Although the Anthony family was strict, they were caring and supportive. Susan's brothers later fought to end slavery, and her sisters became suffragists, too.

10   New England, Pennsylvania, Ohio, and Indiana all had large Quaker communities during the 1700–1800s. Quakers worked in many reform movements, including the abolition of slavery, better treatment of prisoners, and education for children of all races and sexes. They started many schools and universities. Today's Quakers are still involved in humanitarian work around the world.

Why did Susan's father take her out of school?

11   For most children in the early 1800s, school took place in a one-room schoolhouse. Kids as young as five learned alongside teenagers. While everyone shared the same classroom, students weren't all taught together. Boys sat on one side and girls sat on the other. Younger kids sat up front near the teacher, and older students sat in the back. The teacher, or schoolmaster, decided what each student learned. Everyone worked at their own level, and older kids often helped younger ones. Many schoolmasters had only finished eighth grade, and perhaps had trained for a few weeks learning how to teach.

abolition   Abolition is the act of stopping something.

Susan B. Anthony's schoolhouse may have looked like this one, photographed in the 1890s.

12   Susan was an eager student and had learned to read before she turned four. She started going to class at the local school where her brothers and sisters went. One day Susan came home upset. According to a family story, the schoolmaster had refused to teach her long division because she was a girl. Maybe the male teacher felt girls didn't need to learn such advanced math. Many people back then believed that too much learning harmed girls' brains and would make them bad mothers. Or perhaps the schoolmaster was covering up for not knowing how to do long division himself. Either way, Susan's father pulled her out of school. As a Quaker, he believed all children should receive equal education.

13   Mr. Anthony started a home school for his kids and the girls who worked in his mills. He hired Mary Perkins, a well-educated woman who used modern teaching methods. She taught the children to recite poems and showed them books with pictures—things they wouldn't do in regular school. Each student even had his or her own stool to sit on—no more squeezing together on long benches. Female teachers weren't common in the early 1800s. Perkins was likely the first educated and independent unmarried woman Susan had ever met. Susan's teacher was a new kind of role model for young women. Susan studied with Perkins until age seventeen, when her father sent her to a Quaker boarding school in Philadelphia.

Who was Elizabeth Cady Stanton?

14   Elizabeth Cady Stanton came from a well-off family and was an educated woman. She married an abolitionist leader, and together they attended the 1840 World Anti-Slavery Convention in London, England. Stanton was shocked to find that women weren't allowed to speak at the convention. Female attendees even had to sit apart from the men. How could abolitionists seeking rights for enslaved people not want the same rights for their daughters, mothers, sisters, and wives? Stanton knew then that only by voting could women obtain their rights.

15   Susan B. Anthony and Elizabeth Cady Stanton first met in 1851. The two became fast friends and worked together for the next fifty years. Stanton was a keen thinker and skilled writer. She was also the mother of seven children. Anthony had the energy and freedom to travel and give talks, but struggled with putting her ideas into words. Stanton wrote most of the suffrage speeches and petitions that Anthony would deliver. "I forged the thunderbolts, she fired them," said Stanton. It was a partnership that forever changed the world.

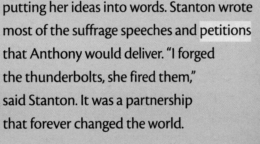

In 1848 Elizabeth Cady Stanton spoke at the first Woman's Rights Convention in Seneca Falls, New York.

obtain   If you obtain something, you make an effort to get it.
petitions   Petitions are formal requests made to an official person or organization.

What happened at Seneca Falls, New York, in 1848?

16   A few years before she met Anthony, Stanton and fellow abolitionist Lucretia Mott got to talking during the 1840 World Anti-Slavery Convention. Neither liked being silenced because of their sex, so they decided to hold a convention of their own. The result was the first Woman's Rights Convention in the United States. Mott and Stanton held it in Seneca Falls, New York, on July 19–20, 1848. About three hundred people attended, most of them women. They listened as Stanton read the "Declaration of Sentiments." The document she had written updated phrases from the Declaration of Independence. "All men are created equal" was changed to "all men and women are created equal." Stanton's speech called for women to be able to own property, sign contracts, attend college, and keep the money they earned. But the most radical idea that Stanton proposed during the convention was voting rights for women. The suffrage movement was heating up.

Why was the Fifteenth Amendment so disappointing to the suffragists?

17   The fight to end slavery had been part of Susan B. Anthony's life from early on. Like many Quaker families, the Anthonys were abolitionists. They held anti-slavery meetings at their home. Susan B. Anthony began working for the American Anti-Slavery Society in 1856. She arranged meetings, made speeches, put up posters, handed out leaflets, and was threatened by pro-slavery mobs.

18   As reformers, most people in the women's rights movement were also involved in anti-slavery efforts. It was no coincidence. Rights for the enslaved and rights for women were connected in many minds. If one person should not own another person, then that also extended to wives being the property of their husbands. If people of all races should be educated citizens, why couldn't women go to college?

19   When the Civil War ended and slavery was abolished in 1865, African Americans were far from equal members of society. Black people couldn't even vote. When reformers pushed for voting rights for African Americans, Anthony and others called for something more. They wanted universal suffrage—the right of all races and sexes to vote.

20   A few years after the Civil War ended, the government changed the U.S. Constitution. They added an amendment, or change, to the nation's most important set of laws. The Fifteenth Amendment granted voting rights to African Americans—but just men. Suffragists were furious and felt betrayed. They'd fought to end slavery, but didn't get any support for women's rights in turn. "Many abolitionists have yet to learn the ABC of woman's rights," wrote Anthony. She and Stanton realized change would have to be up to women themselves. In 1869, Anthony and Stanton formed the National Woman Suffrage Association. Men could join, but couldn't be leaders in the group. Susan B. Anthony began working for a different change to the Constitution— an amendment that guaranteed all women the right to vote.

How did Susan B. Anthony fight for women's suffrage?

21   The fact that women couldn't vote made fighting for their rights extra difficult. Women couldn't vote pro-suffrage leaders into office. Politicians serve the people who elect them, and those people didn't include women. Suffragists needed the backing of the American public. Opening minds and changing opinions were the tools that Susan B. Anthony used to gain their support. She was a tireless speaker. Anthony spent decades traveling from one town to another giving lectures. Her most famous lecture, "Woman Wants Bread, Not the Ballot," challenged her opponents head-on. Many believed that women only cared about feeding their families and had no interest in elections. Anthony argued that her lecture's title—and the idea—was wrong. She said that voting, or giving them the ballot, was a woman's only way of "securing bread and a home for herself."

22   Anthony was often scorned, and her talks were criticized. One newspaperman called her lectures "devilish" and out to "poison the morals of . . . wives, mothers and daughters." Strangers called her hateful names and made fun of how she looked and spoke. One of her talks was sabotaged by boys dumping spicy hot pepper powder onto a hot stove, right outside the room where she was speaking. When the spice started burning, everyone left coughing from the fumes.

lectures   Lectures are speeches usually given to instruct an audience.

23   While suffragists didn't have radio, television, or the Internet to help them spread the word, magazines did exist. Susan B. Anthony published a weekly journal called *The Revolution* from 1868 to 1870. It demanded equal rights for women. The motto printed on its front page read: "The true republic—men, their rights and nothing more; women, their rights and nothing less."

24   Susan B. Anthony also worked to change laws. In 1877 she presented the U.S. Congress with suffrage petitions from twenty-six states with ten thousand signatures. She became one of the first female American politicians. Anthony traveled to Washington, D.C., every year through the late 1800s to ask Congress to pass a suffrage amendment. They told her "no" more than thirty times.

Why was Susan B. Anthony arrested in 1872?

25   The Fifteenth Amendment gave citizens the right to vote no matter their "race, color, or previous condition of servitude." Suffragists argued that since they were citizens and came in all races and colors, the amendment included women. All they needed was to get the Supreme Court to agree. When a criminal court decides someone is guilty, the guilty party can appeal, asking for a higher court to change the decision. As the highest court, the Supreme Court has the final say. Suffragists urged women across the nation to try to vote during the 1872 presidential election. The plan was to appeal the guilty verdicts of women arrested to the Supreme Court.

26   Susan B. Anthony and her sisters were among a group of fifty women demanding to register to vote in Rochester, New York. After voting for president Ulysses S. Grant, Anthony wrote her friend Elizabeth Cady Stanton to say, "I have been and gone and done it!" Two weeks later a deputy U.S. Marshal arrested Anthony. Her crime? Knowingly voting while female.

27   Susan B. Anthony did not get a fair trial. The judge wouldn't let Anthony speak in court, or testify. He said women were incompetent, and not smart or trustworthy enough. The judge also didn't allow the all-male jury to discuss the case. He told them to find her guilty. He fined Anthony one hundred dollars, but refused to jail her when she wouldn't pay it—this prevented the case from going on to the Supreme Court, which he knew was the suffragists' ultimate goal. Many considered the trial "a mere farce." The trial made headlines, and Anthony ensured that newspapers across the country got copies of what was said in the court. It convinced many Americans that women were being treated unfairly. Two years later, another woman who had tried to vote did get her case heard by the Supreme Court. But the court decided against her, saying that women didn't get to vote just because they were citizens. The Supreme Court also said that it was up to each state to decide who could and couldn't vote.

While not allowed to speak during the trial, Anthony was asked during sentencing if she had anything to say. Anthony stunned the courtroom by arguing that her rights had been trampled. She said that the laws were "all made by men, interpreted by men, administered by men, in favor of men, and against women."

Did any state allow women to vote?

28   The Supreme Court's ruling that each state had to decide who could vote weakened the Fifteenth Amendment. Southern states started making up all kinds of rules to keep once-enslaved men from voting. Black voters had to own property, pass a reading test, or pay a special fee. Susan B. Anthony had seen it coming. This is what happens when you deny universal suffrage, she said. Not only were women denied the vote, but so were many of the African American men the Fifteenth Amendment was written for.

29   But women's rights workers also took advantage of the new power of states. Some western territories had been allowing women to vote, including Wyoming, Colorado, Utah, and Idaho. Anthony traveled far from home during the late 1800s to help western women earn at least some voting rights. Not all of these states gave full voting rights to women. Some allowed voting only in local or state elections. Still, it was something. It proved that women were responsible voters.

30   By the turn of the century, Susan B. Anthony had become an honored public figure. Theodore Roosevelt himself congratulated her on her eighty-sixth birthday in 1906. But true as always to the cause, she objected to the compliment. "I would rather have President Roosevelt say one word to Congress in favor of amending the Constitution to give women the suffrage than to praise me endlessly!" Anthony knew she wouldn't be there to see victory herself. Her health was failing. Elizabeth Cady Stanton had already died in 1902. A new generation was leading the battle now. Anthony had no doubt that they would see it through. These women are "true and devoted to the cause," she told those gathered in honor of her eighty-sixth birthday. "Failure is impossible." A few weeks later, Susan B. Anthony died at home in Rochester, New York, on March 13, 1906.

Women in the Wyoming Territory could vote as early as 1869. When Wyoming became a state in 1890, it was the first to give women the right to vote.

What is the Nineteenth Amendment?

31   In 1918, the House of Representatives met to decide on women's suffrage. All kinds of people turned out to watch the vote. Could the suffragists get the 274 votes needed to create an amendment to the Constitution? Representative Frederick C. Hicks of New York left his dying wife to go to Washington for the vote. She had asked him to. Without his vote, it is likely that the amendment's creation wouldn't have been approved by the House of Representatives. Unfortunately, it took the Senate more than a year to join the House in approving the amendment. Four decades after Susan B. Anthony first wrote and introduced the amendment giving women the vote, it passed in both the Senate and House on June 4, 1919. All it needed was approval by three-fourths of the states. In 1919 there were forty-eight states, so the suffragists needed thirty-six states to approve, or ratify, the amendment. Then they would finally have the vote. Within ten months, thirty-five states had ratified it. It would take another five months to get the crucial thirty-sixth state.

32   The Tennessee summer of 1920 was long and hot. Suffragists poured into the capital city of Nashville for the vote on August 18. They and their supporters wore yellow roses to identify themselves. Nashville also swarmed with people opposed to women voting. They wore red roses. It all came down to the youngest member of the Tennessee assembly, Harry T. Burn. The twenty-four-year-old stood up to vote wearing a red rose in his lapel. Burn had planned on voting no. But in his pocket was a letter from his mother asking him to vote yes. He followed her advice. The Nineteenth Amendment was now a law, stating: "The right of citizens of the United States to vote shall not be denied or abridged by the United States or by any state on account of sex."

Do all women around the world have the right to vote?

33   One hundred years after Susan B. Anthony's birth, all American women were finally able to vote. On November 2, 1920, women in all forty-eight states voted for president. Newspaper headlines announced, "Women by Thousands Pour Into Polling Places." The female voters helped elect Warren G. Harding the twenty-ninth president of the United States.

swarmed   If a place swarmed, it was very crowded and busy.

329

34   Susan B. Anthony didn't live to see women get the vote in America. But other nations did grant full female suffrage in her lifetime. New Zealand granted voting rights equal to men in 1893. Women in many European countries could vote before the Nineteenth Amendment gave women in the United States their full voting rights.

35   Although American women weren't first, they were far from last. Women in Kazakhstan couldn't vote until 1994, and Kuwait didn't have female suffrage until 2005. Some countries continue to deny women voting rights. Suffrage is limited for both men and women in the United Arab Emirates. In Lebanon, women—but not men—must prove they have completed elementary school to vote. The struggle for equal rights between men and women goes on around the globe. If Susan B. Anthony were alive today, she would no doubt be working to change that. There is still good to do and ways to be useful to the world.

Susan B. Anthony Timeline

1820	Susan Brownell Anthony born on February 15 in Adams, Massachusetts.
1848	First Woman's Rights Convention is held in Seneca Falls, New York.
1851	Anthony meets fellow reformer and suffragist Elizabeth Cady Stanton (1815–1902).
1861–1868	The American Civil War is fought (1861–1865), slavery is abolished, and African Americans are given citizenship (1868).
1868	Anthony begins publication of *The Revolution*.
1870	The Fifteenth Amendment passes, giving black men the right to vote.
1870	Stanton and Anthony form the National Woman Suffrage Association.
1872	Anthony is arrested for voting in the presidential election.
1878	A woman suffrage amendment is first introduced in the U.S. Congress.
1881	Anthony, Stanton, and Matilda Joslyn Gage publish *History of Woman Suffrage*, which eventually included six volumes.
1890	Wyoming grants women suffrage in its state constitution, and over the next three decades about half of the states give some voting rights to women.
1893	New Zealand becomes the first country to grant full voting rights to women.
1906	Susan B. Anthony dies at home in Rochester, New York, on March 13 at age 86.
1912–1917	Hundreds of thousands of women across the nation sign suffrage petitions and march in rallies. Police arrest women who are picketing outside the White House. Many are abused in jails.
1920	The Nineteenth Amendment grants full voting rights to all American women.

Respond to the Text

Collaborative Discussion

Look back at what you wrote on page 316. Tell a partner two things you learned from this text. Then work with a group to discuss the questions below. Refer to details and examples in *Why Couldn't Susan B. Anthony Vote?* to explain your answers. Take notes for your responses. When you speak, use your notes.

1 Look back at pages 320-321. What idea about equality did Susan B. Anthony learn in childhood? How did she use this idea later in life, as a reformer and suffragist?

Listening Tip

Keep your eyes on your group members as they speak. Give each speaker all of your attention.

2 Look back at pages 323-324. How were the anti-slavery movement and the women's suffrage movement similar?

Speaking Tip

As you speak, glance at each member of your group. If someone looks confused, pause and invite that person to ask you a question.

3 Look back at pages 324-326. What did Susan B. Anthony do to promote the idea that women should be allowed to vote?

Write an Informative Sign

In *Why Couldn't Susan B. Anthony Vote?*, you read about Anthony's childhood and her achievements as an adult. Even today, her life and work inspire people to act for the good of others.

Every year, Susan B. Anthony's grave welcomes many visitors who honor her memory as someone who fought for equal rights. What facts, quotations, or ideas about Anthony do you think would inspire those visitors? Write a paragraph that will be printed on an informative sign near Susan B. Anthony's grave. Don't forget to use some of the Critical Vocabulary words in your writing.

PLAN ....

List three details about Susan B. Anthony's life that you think are inspiring. Refer to the text as you decide what to include.

WRITE

Now write your informative sign about Susan B. Anthony.

Make sure your informative sign

- [ ] begins with a topic sentence.

- [ ] includes details about the life and work of Susan B. Anthony.

- [ ] organizes information in a logical order.

- [ ] concludes with an inspiring quotation or sentence about Susan B. Anthony.

Notice &
Note
3 Big Questions

Prepare to Read

GENRE STUDY An **autobiography** is the story of a real person's life written by that person.

- Authors of autobiographies use literary language and devices to present major events in their life. For example, dialogue might be used to dramatize a scene from the author's life, even though the words actually spoken were slightly different.

- Autobiographies include first-person pronouns, such as *I, me, my, mine,* and *we.*

SET A PURPOSE **Think about** the title and genre of this text. What do you think the author wants to tell you about her life? What do you think the author means by "road to freedom"?

Meet the Author:
Lynda Blackmon Lowery

CRITICAL VOCABULARY

confrontation

register

legislation

Turning 15 On The Road To Freedom

MY STORY OF THE 1965 SELMA VOTING RIGHTS MARCH

by Lynda Blackmon Lowery
as told to Elspeth Leacock
and Susan Buckley

Illustrated by PJ Loughran

1   It was my grandmother who first took me to hear Dr. King—that's Dr. Martin Luther King Jr. That was back in 1963, when I was just thirteen years old. The church was packed. When Dr. King began to speak, everyone got real quiet. The way he sounded just made you want to do what he was talking about. He was talking about voting—the right to vote and what it would take for our parents to get it. He was talking about nonviolence and how you could persuade people to do things your way with steady, loving confrontation. I'll never forget those words—"steady, loving confrontation" — and the way he said them. We children didn't really understand what he was talking about, but we wanted to do what he was saying.

2   "Who is with me?" Dr. King asked, and all of us stood up, clapping. By the time we left that meeting, Dr. King had a commitment from me and everyone else in that church to do whatever it would take, nonviolently, to get the right to vote.

confrontation   A confrontation is a face-to-face meeting between opposing groups.

DR. MARTIN LUTHER KING JR., MARCH 25, 1965

3   At that time I was already in the movement—the civil rights movement. I was mostly following the high school kids around—especially Bettie Fikes. She had this beautiful voice and I wanted to sing like her. Bettie and her friends were trying to integrate Selma by going to whites-only places. They sat at the whites-only Dairy Queen and the lunch counter at Woolworth's department store. They tried to sit downstairs at the movie theater. (Blacks could only sit in the balcony then.)

4   They said I couldn't take part in these sit-ins because I was too young, but I had a job to do. My job was to go for help. I was called the "gopher," because I always had to "go for" someone's mama when Bettie and her friends were put in jail.

5   That all changed on January 2, 1965. That's when Dr. King came back to Selma for a big mass meeting at Brown Chapel. We called it Emancipation Day because it was all about freedom. There were about seven hundred people there, and I was one of them. It was an awesome thing, a fearsome thing to see so many people. They had come from all around. And they had to travel some dangerous roads to get to Selma— little country roads where the Ku Klux Klan was riding around.

6   The music was fantastic. By then we had formed a freedom choir, and I was part of it. I got to sing in the choir with Bettie Fikes, and you know how I felt about that.

7   When Dr. King walked in, everyone stood and cheered. He talked about the vote and how we would get it. He told us we must be ready to march. His voice grew louder as he continued. "We must be ready to go to jail by the thousands." By the end he shouted, "Our cry … is a simple one. Give us the ballot!"

8   To tell you the truth, I just felt that once our parents got the right to vote, everything would be a whole lot better. There's power in a vote. For years black people tried to register to vote, but they were mostly turned away. Just for trying to register, they could lose their jobs. You see, whenever a black person tried to register, someone would take a picture and then show it to that person's boss. White people could fire black people whenever and however they wanted.

9   That's why the civil rights leaders needed us children to march. After Dr. King's speech, our local leaders planned two or three marches for us every day. They would say, "We're going to march to the courthouse tomorrow. If you're with us, come here to Brown Chapel at nine thirty."

10   The very first time I heard that, I said, "I'm going to march."

11   On the day of a march, you would go to school for attendance, then slip out and make it down to Brown Chapel. Our teachers were the ones who unlocked the back door and let us out of school. They supported us—they had our backs.

12   Our teachers were excellent, but these smart people could not vote. They couldn't pass the voter registration test. The tests were written to keep black people from voting. (White people didn't usually take those tests at all.) The registrars asked ridiculous questions such as, "How deep is the Alabama River?" and "How many jelly beans are in this gallon jar?" The questions had nothing to do with voting or the Constitution or citizenship.

13   Two or three times a day, a group of us students would leave Brown Chapel heading downtown. I don't think we were ever fewer than about fifty kids on a march. Before we left, the adults would tell us, "You're going to go to jail. Do not fight back. You might be pushed; you might be hit. Just turn the other cheek. Do not fight back. Don't worry about it. We'll take care of you."

register   When you register for something, you sign up for it.

14   Most of the time, once we got downtown the police let us march for four or five blocks. Then they would march us right onto yellow school buses. If you didn't get on the bus fast enough, the police would shock you with a cattle prod. That's a stick with an electrical charge, sort of like a Taser is now. Farmers used them to push cattle to move quicker or to get out of the way. That's what they used on us, like we were cattle.

15   At first they would take us to the old National Guard Armory, where we had to stand for hours all packed together, or sit on the concrete floor. But after a week or so of that, they started taking us right to jail.

CIVIL RIGHTS DEMONSTRATORS REST ON A WALL ON THE WAY FROM SELMA TO MONTGOMERY, ALABAMA DURING THE HISTORIC 1965 MARCH.

CIVIL RIGHTS MARCHERS WALK FROM SELMA TO MONTGOMERY, ALABAMA, IN 1965.

AFTERWORD

16   By the age of 15, Lynda Blackmon Lowery had been jailed nine times for her participation in the voting rights movement. "The first time we actually went to jail, I was kind of scared," she recalls. "But we had each other's back."

17   In March 1965, Lowery celebrated her 15th birthday while participating in a famous series of three marches from Selma, Alabama to Montgomery, Alabama. She was the youngest person to complete the entire 54-mile journey.

18   Along the way, Lowery survived the horrific events of Bloody Sunday—March 7, 1965—during which Alabama State Troopers attacked the unarmed marchers with billy clubs and tear gas. Lowery was hit in the face and head and received 35 stitches in all. "I still have a knot in my head from that," she states.

19   Later that year, the marchers' heroic efforts were rewarded by the passage of the Voting Rights Act. Among other things, this landmark civil rights legislation made voter literacy tests illegal and required investigation into the "poll taxes" (fees charged for voting). Federal authorities stepped in to supervise in counties where people of color were routinely prevented from registering to vote.

legislation   Legislation is the creation of rules or laws.

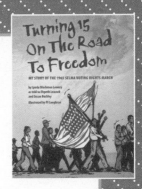

Collaborative Discussion

Look back at what you wrote on page 334. Tell a partner two facts about the civil rights movement that you learned from this text. Then work with a group to discuss the questions below. Refer to details and examples in *Turning 15 on the Road to Freedom* to explain your answers. Take notes for your responses. When you speak, use your notes.

1 What is one word you would use to describe Lynda Blackmon Lowery? Find an example from the text that supports your idea.

2 How does Lowery's personal story help you understand the civil rights movement?

3 How would you explain Dr. King's phrase "steady, loving confrontation"? Use examples from the text.

Listening Tip

Listen closely to what each speaker says. If someone is speaking too softly, politely ask that person to speak a little louder.

Speaking Tip

When you speak, make it easy for others to understand you. Say each word clearly, and do not speak too fast or too slow.

Write an Explanation for a Job Application

When people apply for jobs, they are sometimes asked if they have ever been convicted of a crime. If they answer yes, they usually are given a chance to explain why. In *Turning 15 on the Road to Freedom*, you read that Lynda Blackmon Lowery was arrested and jailed nine times as a youth. Even though her arrests were for a good cause, some people might question such a record.

Imagine that you are Lowery and are applying for a job. Write a paragraph to justify, or explain, the nine arrests from your youth.

As you make notes about Lowery's arrests for your paragraph, think about these questions: Why did she get arrested? What was she doing and why?

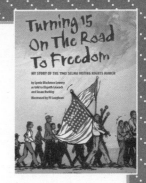

WRITE

Now write an explanation for a job application about Lowery's arrests from *Turning 15 on the Road to Freedom.*

Make sure your explanation
☐ is written in the first person, using pronouns such as *I* and *me*.
☐ uses a formal tone that is appropriate for a job application.
☐ provides a strong justification of Lynda Blackmon Lowery's good character.
☐ presents details in a logical order.
☐ uses transition words to connect details.

Prepare to Read and Listen

GENRE STUDY A **speech** is a nonfiction persuasive text that is delivered orally to an audience.

- Speeches present ideas and opinions intended to persuade the audience to agree.

We Shall Overcome

An **audio recording of a speech** shows the speaker's tone of voice and emphasis of certain phrases and words.

SET A PURPOSE **Think about** the title of this text and audio recording. What do you think the speech will be about?

Meet the Author:
Lyndon B. Johnson

CRITICAL VOCABULARY

dignity

denial

assaulted

oppressed

convocation

majesty

We Shall Overcome

President Johnson's Speech to Congress

On March 7, 1965, civil rights marchers were badly injured by state troopers on "Bloody Sunday" in Selma, Alabama. The events in Selma prompted U.S. President Lyndon B. Johnson to take a stand for African Americans' voting rights. On March 15, Johnson delivered a historic speech urging Congress to pass legislation ensuring equal voting rights for all citizens. The Voting Rights Act was signed into law on August 6, 1965.

March 15, 1965

[As delivered in person before a joint session at 9:02 p.m.]

1 Mr. Speaker, Mr. President, Members of the Congress:

2 I speak tonight for the dignity of man and the destiny of democracy.

3 I urge every member of both parties, Americans of all religions and of all colors, from every section of this country, to join me in that cause.

4 At times history and fate meet at a single time in a single place to shape a turning point in man's unending search for freedom. So it was at Lexington and Concord. So it was a century ago at Appomattox. So it was last week in Selma, Alabama.

5 There, long-suffering men and women peacefully protested the denial of their rights as Americans. Many were brutally assaulted. One good man, a man of God, was killed.

6 There is no cause for pride in what has happened in Selma. There is no cause for self-satisfaction in the long denial of equal rights of millions of Americans. But there is cause for hope and for faith in our democracy in what is happening here tonight.

dignity A person's dignity includes his or her value and self-respect.

denial The denial of something is the refusal to grant it.

assaulted If you assaulted someone, you physically attacked that person.

7   For the cries of pain and the hymns and protests of oppressed people have summoned into convocation all the majesty of this great Government—the Government of the greatest Nation on earth.

8   Our mission is at once the oldest and the most basic of this country: to right wrong, to do justice, to serve man.

9   In our time we have come to live with moments of great crisis. Our lives have been marked with debate about great issues; issues of war and peace, issues of prosperity and depression. But rarely in any time does an issue lay bare the secret heart of America itself. Rarely are we met with a challenge, not to our growth or abundance, our welfare or our security, but rather to the values and the purposes and the meaning of our beloved Nation.

10   The issue of equal rights for American Negroes is such an issue. And should we defeat every enemy, should we double our wealth and conquer the stars, and still be unequal to this issue, then we will have failed as a people and as a nation.

11   For with a country as with a person, "What is a man profited, if he shall gain the whole world, and lose his own soul?"

12   There is no Negro problem. There is no Southern problem. There is no Northern problem. There is only an American problem. And we are met here tonight as Americans—not as Democrats or Republicans—we are met here as Americans to solve that problem.

13   This was the first nation in the history of the world to be founded with a purpose. The great phrases of that purpose still sound in every American heart, North and South: "All men are created equal"—"government by consent of the governed"—"give me liberty or give me death." Well, those are not just clever words, or those are not just empty theories. In their name Americans have fought and died for two centuries, and tonight around the world they stand there as guardians of our liberty, risking their lives.

oppressed   People who are oppressed are treated in a cruel and unfair way.
convocation   A convocation is the meeting of a large group of people.
majesty   If something has majesty, it is dignified and impressive.

14   Those words are a promise to every citizen that he shall share in the dignity of man. This dignity cannot be found in a man's possessions; it cannot be found in his power, or in his position. It really rests on his right to be treated as a man equal in opportunity to all others. It says that he shall share in freedom, he shall choose his leaders, educate his children, and provide for his family according to his ability and his merits as a human being.

15   To apply any other test—to deny a man his hopes because of his color or race, his religion or the place of his birth—is not only to do injustice, it is to deny America and to dishonor the dead who gave their lives for American freedom.

16   Our fathers believed that if this noble view of the rights of man was to flourish, it must be rooted in democracy. The most basic right of all was the right to choose your own leaders. The history of this country, in large measure, is the history of the expansion of that right to all of our people.

17   Many of the issues of civil rights are very complex and most difficult. But about this there can and should be no argument. Every American citizen must have an equal right to vote. There is no reason which can excuse the denial of that right. There is no duty which weighs more heavily on us than the duty we have to ensure that right.

18   Yet the harsh fact is that in many places in this country men and women are kept from voting simply because they are Negroes.

19   Every device of which human ingenuity is capable has been used to deny this right. The Negro citizen may go to register only to be told that the day is wrong, or the hour is late, or the official in charge is absent. And if he persists, and if he manages to present himself to the registrar, he may be disqualified because he did not spell out his middle name or because he abbreviated a word on the application.

20   And if he manages to fill out an application he is given a test. The registrar is the sole judge of whether he passes this test. He may be asked to recite the entire Constitution, or explain the most complex provisions of State law. And even a college degree cannot be used to prove that he can read and write.

21   For the fact is that the only way to pass these barriers is to show a white skin.

22   Experience has clearly shown that the existing process of law cannot overcome systematic and ingenious discrimination. No law that we now have on the books—and I have helped to put three of them there—can ensure the right to vote when local officials are determined to deny it.

23   In such a case our duty must be clear to all of us. The Constitution says that no person shall be kept from voting because of his race or his color. We have all sworn an oath before God to support and to defend that Constitution. We must now act in obedience to that oath.

24   The last time a President sent a civil rights bill to the Congress it contained a provision to protect voting rights in Federal elections. That civil rights bill was passed after 8 long months of debate. And when that bill came to my desk from the Congress for my signature, the heart of the voting provision had been eliminated.

25   This time, on this issue, there must be no delay, no hesitation and no compromise with our purpose.

26   We cannot, we must not, refuse to protect the right of every American to vote in every election that he may desire to participate in. And we ought not and we cannot and we must not wait another

8 months before we get a bill. We have already waited a hundred years and more, and the time for waiting is gone.

27   So I ask you to join me in working long hours—nights and weekends, if necessary—to pass this bill. And I don't make that request lightly. For from the window where I sit with the problems of our country I recognize that outside this chamber is the outraged conscience of a nation, the grave concern of many nations, and the harsh judgment of history on our acts.

28   But even if we pass this bill, the battle will not be over. What happened in Selma is part of a far larger movement which reaches into every section and State of America. It is the effort of American Negroes to secure for themselves the full blessings of American life.

29   Their cause must be our cause too. Because it is not just Negroes, but really it is all of us, who must overcome the crippling legacy of bigotry and injustice.

30   And we shall overcome.

We Shall Overcome

As you listen to *We Shall Overcome: President Johnson's Speech to Congress,* notice how President Johnson changes the tone of his voice. How does this add meaning to the words he says? What mood or feeling is created? How is hearing the speech different from reading it?

When Johnson says, "There is only an American problem," what happens next? How does the audience react? Explain how the audio affects your understanding of the audience for this speech.

We Shall Overome

Respond to the Text and Audio

Collaborative Discussion

Work with a group to discuss the questions below. Refer to details and examples in *We Shall Overcome: President Johnson's Speech to Congress* and the recorded speech to support your ideas. Take notes for your responses. During the discussion, listen actively and pay attention to the speakers.

1. What is President Johnson's opinion on equal voting rights? How does he communicate this opinion?

Listening Tip

Listen closely to information and ideas a speaker shares. Wait for the speaker to finish before you volunteer your own ideas.

2. How does President Johnson describe the civil rights issue in the United States? Include examples from his speech in your answer.

Speaking Tip

If you agree with another speaker, say so. Build your own ideas onto what other speakers have already said.

3. In his speech, President Johnson says, "I speak tonight for the dignity of man and the destiny of democracy." What does he mean?

Write Notes for a Newspaper Article

PROMPT

By reading *We Shall Overcome: President Johnson's Speech to Congress* and listening to the recording, you learned about the historic speech that President Johnson delivered to the nation during the civil rights movement.

Imagine that you are a reporter on the scene who is assigned to write a newspaper article that summarizes President Johnson's speech. Your article should identify the purpose of the president's speech and summarize its key ideas. Decide on the article's headline and its hook, or first sentence that grabs readers' attention. Don't forget to use some of the Critical Vocabulary in your writing.

PLAN

Make notes about the key ideas in President Johnson's speech to help you choose a headline, hook, and two quotations that sum up the speech.

We Shall Overome

WRITE

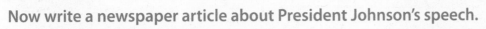

Now write a newspaper article about President Johnson's speech.

Make sure your newspaper article
☐ identifies the purpose of President Johnson's speech.
☐ summarizes the key ideas of the speech.
☐ includes a headline that identifies the topic of the article in a catchy way.
☐ includes a hook that will grab readers' attention and make them want to keep reading.
☐ includes two quotations that best summarize the speech.

Notice & Note
3 Big Questions

Prepare to Read

GENRE STUDY An **informational article** gives facts and examples about a topic.

- Authors of informational articles may organize their ideas by stating a problem and explaining its solution.

- Social studies texts also include words that are specific to the topic. These are words that name things or ideas.

- Authors of informational articles may organize their ideas using headings and subheadings. The headings and subheadings tell readers what the next section of text will be about.

SET A PURPOSE **Think about** the title of this text. Why do you think people vote? Why might people not vote? Write your ideas below.

Meet the Author:
Bethany Brookshire

CRITICAL VOCABULARY

quavered

implored

political scientist

polls

official

contrast

apathy

economist

fatigue

WHY VOTE?

BY BETHANY BROOKSHIRE

4 REASONS WHY MANY PEOPLE DON'T VOTE

Scientists have insight into why millions of people who are eligible to vote, won't.

1 In my senior year of high school, I was sitting in my government class as my teacher begged us to vote. He had to know that he and I would never vote the same way. But he met my eyes along with those of every other student in that class. His voice quavered as he implored us—for the sake of our country—to vote.

2 My teacher was begging because millions of people who can vote, don't. Voter turnout in the United States is incredibly low compared to similar countries, notes Donald Green. He's a political scientist at Columbia University in New York City. In fact, U.S. voter turnout ranks 31 out of 35 developed countries—nations with advanced economies and a heavy use of technology. That's according to a Pew Research Center study released in the summer of 2017.

3 It's a little surprising that so many Americans don't vote. Most are fairly interested in politics, notes Mert Moral. He's a political scientist at the State University of New York at Binghamton. "If you look at survey data, you find more Americans are equally, if not more, engaged than their counterparts [in other countries]," he says. "They have bumper stickers. They talk about politics. They are interested in political topics at the local level."

4 So why don't people vote? Scientists have been looking into this. There are four reasons they offer to explain why many people do not show up at the polls.

---

quavered   If your voice quavered, it sounded shaky and unsteady.

implored   If you implored someone, you begged that person to do something.

political scientist   A political scientist analyzes government systems and behaviors to predict future behavior.

polls   People go to the polls to vote.

Why don't people vote?

5 **1 Registration takes work** In many countries, being registered to vote is automatic. If you are a citizen, you are signed up to vote. Not so in the United States. It is up to each person there to sign up, notes Barry Burden. He's a political scientist at the University of Wisconsin–Madison. To register, someone must go to an official site, such as a library or a government office, then fill out paperwork. A 2012 Pew Research Center study reported that 51 million citizens—nearly one-in-four citizens eligible to vote—had not registered.

6 Easier registration could mean more voting. Burden and his colleagues showed that during the 2004 and 2008 presidential elections, a "one-stop shop" where people could register and vote at the same time increased voter turnout. By contrast, making it easier for people to vote by letting them vote before Election Day (known as early voting), actually lowered the voting rate. The researchers published their findings in 2013 in the *American Journal of Political Science*.

"MILLIONS OF PEOPLE WHO CAN VOTE,
DON'T."

official Something that is official has been approved by someone in authority.
contrast A contrast signals a different situation or idea.

7 **2 Education** Data show that the single biggest predictor of whether someone will vote is whether they hold a college degree, Burden notes. College graduates make more money, on average. They are more likely to look for information about politics. And they are more likely to have friends who vote. People without a college degree, he says, are less likely to seek out political information. They also are less likely to have friends who care about politics or talk about voting.

8 **3 Two parties may not be enough** The United States has two main political parties: Republicans and Democrats. Other political parties exist, such as the Green Party and the Libertarians. Few people, however, vote for candidates of those "other" parties. This is because U.S. elections only reward what is known as "first past the post." The one who gets the most votes wins.

9   In many other countries, such as the United Kingdom, people don't vote for individuals. They vote for parties to sit in a Parliament. The party that dominates the Parliament gets to pick the Prime Minister. But even a non-dominant party can get one or more members in Parliament—if that party gets enough votes. "A party that got 25 percent of the vote could get 25 percent of the seats," Burden says. "That's very encouraging."

10   In contrast, it wouldn't matter if the presidential candidate for the Green Party or the Libertarian Party got 25 percent of the U.S. vote. If 25 percent wasn't the highest percentage of votes, their candidate wouldn't become president. No one else from their party would automatically get a seat in Congress either. Americans vote for candidates for particular, individual seats.

11   Americans also vote for Congressional candidates only in their particular geographical area. So a candidate from a third party would have to win the majority of votes from their particular area to get the seat in Congress. And many candidates from that party would have to win in many different areas to get enough seats in Congress to pass laws that reflect their party's values.

12   Such minor-party candidates seldom raise much money to campaign. Meanwhile, the two big political parties tend to raise lots of money to help their candidates. So third or fourth parties can't get organized and don't put forward many (or sometimes any) candidates. After all, what's the point of putting in a lot of effort if you have little chance of winning?

13   This promotes a system where candidates tend to be members of only the major political parties. And in a two-party system, voters might not find that either candidate represents their views. And where they don't, Moral says, voters might just stay home.

14   "A third-party candidate can't win an election here," he says. So where they don't like the Republican or Democrat running for office, Moral says, people may not bother to vote at all.

"A THIRD-PARTY CANDIDATE
CAN'T WIN
AN ELECTION HERE."

15 **4 Apathy and burnout** Who your friends are can affect whether you vote. "We use voting as a tool to transmit to others who we are," explains Eyal Winter. An economist, he works at the University of Leicester in England and the Hebrew University of Jerusalem in Israel. Voting—and then telling others that you did, or publicly stating that you plan to—is a way to show loyalty to your social group and its values, he says.

16 But some people just don't care about politics, which can lead to voter *apathy*. And if a social group doesn't regard politics as very important, its members may not bother to vote, Winter notes. In fact, he says, one might argue that in terms of any one citizen, "it makes no sense to vote." Only very rarely has a single vote changed the outcome of an election. And where that happened, it usually was only in very small, local elections.

17 Not only that, but where elections occur often people may experience voter burnout. "One of the things that makes the U.S. strange is that there's a lot of elections," says Burden. "We ask voters to make a lot of decisions." Getting out to the polls can be a hassle. What's more, learning about every single issue takes time. If people are asked to vote too often, or choose a position on too many subjects, they might just opt out of the whole process. "We have a complicated system and I think that produces fatigue," Burden says.

18 There are many other reasons people might not vote—from anger at the government to concern that being a registered voter will make the government more likely to call them up for jury duty. What could change their minds?

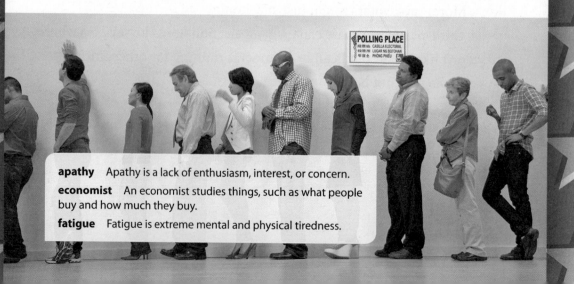

apathy   Apathy is a lack of enthusiasm, interest, or concern.
economist   An economist studies things, such as what people buy and how much they buy.
fatigue   Fatigue is extreme mental and physical tiredness.

4 RESEARCH-BACKED WAYS TO GET PEOPLE TO VOTE

Scientists are finding ways to increase voter turnout.

19 Every two years, on the first Tuesday (that falls after a Monday) in November, Americans should head to the polls to take part in a national election. Some important elections may take part in the off-years as well. But not everyone who is eligible to vote will do so. In fact, millions of people won't. And that's a problem because people who don't vote lose out on a prime chance to register their views. Also, voting isn't just important. It is a privilege and a right that many people throughout the world lack.

20 One person's vote probably won't change the course of an election. But a few thousand votes—or even a few hundred—certainly can. Consider, for instance, the famous election between George W. Bush and Al Gore in 2000. Once the polling was over, Florida had to recount its votes. In the end, Bush won by 537 votes. That difference decided who became president of the United States.

21   Even in polling for local offices—such as a school board—the result of a vote can change everything from what schools neighborhood children will attend to what their textbooks will cover. There are many reasons why people don't vote. And to counter the anger, apathy, fatigue, and other factors that deter many folks from voting, organizations big and small mount campaigns urging people to go to the polls. Facebook users may plead with their friends. Politicians may hire phone banks to call thousands of people in states where a race appears to be very competitive. Celebrities may beg over YouTube. Does any of this really work?

22   Political scientists have studied ways to change people's voting behavior. These four methods seem to stand out in terms of being most effective.

23   **1 Educate early and well** Messages that people receive early in life have a strong impact on whether people vote, notes Donald Green. Parents and teachers should therefore let kids know "voting is important," he argues. "It's what makes you a functioning adult." Teachers might help deliver this message in classes where students learn about how their country and government function. That happened to me in high school when my own teacher one day begged me and my classmates to vote.

24   People with college degrees are also more likely to vote. Perhaps society should make it easier for people to afford college. "A person who gets a college education ends up in a different life circumstance," explains Barry Burden. College graduates tend to associate more with people who vote—and then they vote, too. They also stand to earn more (paying more taxes), data have shown. So a more educated population should be a win-win for society.

25   **2 Peer pressure** A healthy dose of name and shame can have a big effect on Election Day. Green and his colleagues demonstrated this in a study published in 2008 in *American Political Science Review*. They applied a little social pressure to voters.

26   Right before Michigan's 2006 Republican primary, the researchers selected a group of 180,000 potential voters. They mailed about 20,000 voters a letter asking them to do their "civic duty" and vote.

They mailed another 20,000 a different letter. It asked them to do their civic duty, but added that they were being studied—and that their votes were a matter of public record. (In some states, such as Michigan, voting records are publicly available after an election.) A third group got the same messages as the second group. But they also got a note that showed them their previous voting record, and the previous voting records of the people in their household. A fourth group got the same information as the third group, as well as being shown the publicly available voting records of their neighbors. The last 99,000 people or so were a control—they got no mailings at all.

27   After all the votes were counted, the scientists saw a 1.8 percentage point increase in turnout by people who had been reminded to vote over those who did not get such a mailing. For the group told their votes were a matter of public record, there was a 2.5 percentage point increase. But the biggest increase was among those shown voting records. Turnout increased by 4.9 percentage points among people shown their previous voting records. And if voters were also shown their neighbors' voting records, turnout at the polls rose a whopping 8.1 percentage points.

"DOES ANY OF THIS
REALLY WORK?"

28   Although shaming may get out the vote, Green cautions that it likely also burns bridges. "I think it produces backlash," he says. In the 2008 study, many of the people who received the letter that showed the voting records of their neighbors called the number on the mailing and asked to be left alone.

29   Peer pressure doesn't always have to be mean, though. Asking friends directly to pledge to vote—and then making sure they do—might be effective, Green says. The most effective thing to do, he says, may be to say to a close friend or coworker, "let's walk to the polls together."

30   **3 Healthy competition** "People are going to participate when they think they are going to make a difference," says Eyal Winter. He notes that there is higher voter turnout when an election is close and there's no telling who might win. Winter compares elections to football or baseball games. When two close rivals face off, their competitions will draw much bigger crowds than when one team is sure to roll right over another.

"PEOPLE ARE GOING TO PARTICIPATE WHEN THEY THINK THEY ARE GOING TO MAKE A DIFFERENCE."

31   To find out whether a close election might make more people vote than a race where one politician is far behind another, Winter and his colleague looked at U.S. elections for state governors from 1990 to 2005. When surveys before the election showed that results were likely to be very close, voter turnout increased. Why? People now felt their vote might make a bigger difference.

32   More voters also turned out for the side with the slight majority in the poll. "It's nicer to support your team when you're expected to win," Winter explains. He and his colleague Esteban Klor—a political scientist at the Hebrew University of Jerusalem—published their findings in 2006 on the *Social Science Research Network*.

33   **4 Personal touch** Hundreds of studies have been done on what gets people to vote. Some of the studies might be partisan—focusing on people who support a particular party. Others might focus on both major parties or even on people in general. Such research has probed everything from the how much money to spend on voicemail messages to crafting the ideal subject line for an email.

34   Many of these ideas are described in *Get Out the Vote: How to Increase Voter Turnout*. This book was written by Green and his colleague Alan Gerber of Yale University in New Haven, Connecticut. The 2015 version of the book includes chapters on social media, mailing letters to people's houses and putting signs along highways. Letters and signs, computerized phone calls, and Facebook posts all seem to help a little. But the most effective methods employ face-to-face and one-on-one discussions of the candidates, Green says. For politicians this means walking door-to-door (or having volunteers do it).

35   But maybe someone just wants to get a sister or friend to vote. In that case, Green says the most effective message might be to convey your own enthusiasm for the candidates, the issues and how much you'd like to see that person vote.

36   Appealing directly to friends and family might help them get to the polls on Election Day. But keep in mind that everyone has their own opinions on the candidates. Even if you get your friends and family members to vote, they might not vote the way you'd like them to.

Collaborative Discussion

Look back at what you wrote on page 358. Tell a partner two facts you learned about voting. Then work with a group to discuss the questions below. Refer to details and examples in *Why Vote?* to explain your answers. Take notes for your responses. When you speak, use your notes.

1   In your opinion, which of the reasons in the article best explains why many Americans do not vote? Why was this reason most convincing?

2   Do you think more people would vote if the United States had more than two main political parties? Explain using evidence.

3   Imagine that you are an election official and you find out that only a small percentage of people in your community voted in the last election. Based on the article, what would you do to increase voter turnout?

Listening Tip

Pay attention to what each member of your group says. Show you are listening by looking at whomever is speaking.

Speaking Tip

Do not speak until your group's leader calls on you. Then speak clearly as you make eye contact with each member of your group.

371

Write a Billboard Advertisement

PROMPT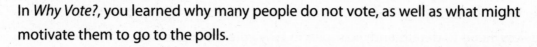

In *Why Vote?*, you learned why many people do not vote, as well as what might motivate them to go to the polls.

Imagine that you have been hired to design and write a billboard advertisement that will be displayed a few months before a major U.S. election. Your goal is to increase voter turnout by persuading people to vote in the election. Write a billboard advertisement that would inspire people to vote. Don't forget to use some Critical Vocabulary words in your writing.

PLAN

Make notes about ways to increase voter turnout. Also list facts and details from the text that could persuade people to vote.

Now write your billboard advertisement about voting using information from *Why Vote?*

Make sure your billboard advertisement

☐ addresses at least one of the ideas to encourage voter turnout.

☐ stresses the importance and benefits of voting.

☐ grabs people's attention with a slogan or short message.

☐ uses engaging graphics or pictures that support voting.

Essential Question

Why does voting matter?

....

Write a Letter to the Editor

Prompt Think about what you learned about voting in this module.

Only about 60 percent of eligible U.S. voters participate in a presidential election. Write a letter to the editor of your local newspaper that explains why voting is an important American right that all eligible voters should excercise. Give reasons for this point of view and use evidence from at least two texts to support your reasons.

I will write a letter to the editor about _____.

✓ **Make sure your opinion letter**

☐ includes an introduction that states your topic and reason for writing to the editor.
☐ provides reasons that explain your opinion and supporting details from at least two texts.
☐ uses transition words to connect your opinion and text evidence.
☐ includes language that persuades readers of the newspaper to agree with your opinion.
☐ includes a conclusion that restates your opinion and reasons.

Why do you believe that Americans should vote? People throughout American history have been motivated to fight for the right to vote. What were those motivations? Revisit the texts and look for details that support your opinion.

In the chart below, write your opinion. Then write details from the texts you have read that support your opinion. Use Critical Vocabulary words where appropriate.

My Topic: _____

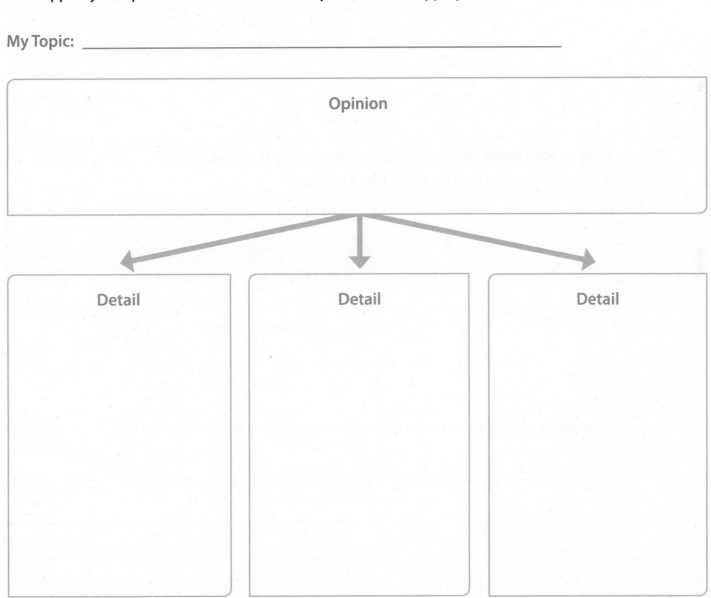

Opinion

Detail

Detail

Detail

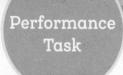
DRAFT ·· Write your letter to the editor.

Begin by writing an **introduction** that states your opinion about the importance of Americans voting in elections. Remember that your audience is the readers of the newspaper.

For the **body of your letter**, provide reasons why Americans should vote. Use evidence from two or more texts to support your reasons.

In your **conclusion**, restate your opinion and supporting reasons to persuade readers to agree with your opinion.

The revision and editing steps give you an opportunity to look carefully at your writing and make changes. Work with a partner to determine whether your opinion statement is clearly written and the details support your opinion. Use these questions to help evaluate and improve your letter.

PURPOSE/ FOCUS	ORGANIZATION	EVIDENCE	LANGUAGE/ VOCABULARY	CONVENTIONS
☐ Does my letter clearly state my opinion? ☐ Will my letter persuade readers to agree with my opinion?	☐ Have I included an introduction and conclusion for my letter? ☐ Are my reasons supported by relevant details from two or more texts?	☐ Does all of the text evidence I chose support my opinion and reasons?	☐ Do I use transition words to connect the evidence to my opinion? ☐ Do I include Critical Vocabulary words when appropriate?	☐ Have I used correct spelling? ☐ Have I used commas, parentheses, and dashes correctly?

PUBLISH .... Share your work.

Create a Finished Copy Make a final copy of your opinion letter. Consider these options to share your letter:

1. Share your letter with a small group of students in your class. Discuss what makes the letter persuasive.

2. Gather the letters your class has written into a collection titled *Why Voting in Elections Is Important*.

3. Share your article with friends online so they can be inspired to participate in elections and learn about voting rights in the United States.

Glossary

This glossary contains meanings and pronunciations for some of the words in this book. The Full Pronunciation Key shows how to pronounce each consonant and vowel in a special spelling. At the bottom of the glossary pages is a shortened form of the full key.

Full Pronunciation Key

CONSONANT SOUNDS

b	**bib**, ca**bb**age	s	mi**ss**, **s**au**c**e, **sc**ene, **s**ee
ch	**ch**ur**ch**, sti**tch**		
d	**d**ee**d**, mail**ed**, pu**dd**le	sh	di**sh**, **sh**ip, **s**ugar, ti**ss**ue
f	**f**ast, **f**i**f**e, o**ff**, **ph**rase, rou**gh**	t	**t**ight, stopp**ed**
		th	ba**th**, **th**in
g	**g**a**g**, **g**et, fin**g**er	*th*	ba**th**e, **th**is
h	**h**at, **wh**o	v	ca**v**e, **v**al**v**e, **v**ine
hw	**wh**ich, **wh**ere	w	**w**ith, **w**olf
j	**j**u**dg**e, **g**em	y	**y**es, **y**olk, on**i**on
k	**c**at, **k**i**ck**, s**ch**ool	z	ro**s**e, si**z**e, **x**ylophone, **z**ebra
kw	**ch**oir, **qu**ick		
l	**l**id, need**l**e, ta**ll**	zh	gara**g**e, plea**s**ure, vi**s**ion
m	a**m**, **m**an, du**mb**		
n	**n**o, sudd**en**		
ng	thi**ng**, i**nk**		
p	**p**op, ha**pp**y		
r	**r**oar, **rh**yme		

VOWEL SOUNDS

ă	p**a**t, l**au**gh	ŭ	c**u**t, fl**oo**d, r**ou**gh, s**o**me
ā	**a**pe, **ai**d, p**ay**		
â	**ai**r, c**a**re, w**ea**r	û	c**i**rcle, f**u**r, h**ea**rd, t**e**rm, t**u**rn, **u**rge, w**o**rd
ä	f**a**ther, k**o**ala, y**a**rd		
ĕ	p**e**t, pl**ea**sure, **a**ny		
ē	b**e**, b**ee**, **ea**sy, pian**o**	yo͞o	c**u**re
ĭ	**i**f, p**i**t, b**u**sy	yo͞o	ab**u**se, **u**se
ī	r**i**de, b**y**, p**ie**, h**igh**	ə	**a**go, sil**e**nt, penc**i**l, lem**o**n, circ**u**s
î	d**ea**r, d**ee**r, f**ie**rce, m**e**re		
ŏ	h**o**rrible, p**o**t		
ō	g**o**, r**o**w, t**oe**, th**ough**		
ô	**a**ll, c**au**ght, f**o**r, p**aw**		
oi	b**oy**, n**oi**se, **oi**l		
ou	c**ow**, **ou**t		
o͝o	f**u**ll, b**oo**k, w**o**lf		
o͞o	b**oo**t, r**u**de, fr**ui**t, fl**ew**		

STRESS MARKS

Primary Stress ´: biology [bī•**ŏl**´•ə•jē]

Secondary Stress ´: biological [bī´•ə•**lŏj**´•ĭ•kəl]

A

abolition (ăb′•ə•lĭsh′•ən) *n.* Abolition is the act of stopping something. Many people, like Frederick Douglass, worked for the abolition of slavery.

acknowledgment (ăk•nŏl′•ĭj•mənt) *n.* An acknowledgment is a sign that someone gives you to show that they see, recognize or appreciate you. The huge round of applause he received after his speech was an acknowledgment that his speech was well received.

Word Origins

acknowledgment This word is from the Old English word *oncnāwan*, meaning "to know" or "to recognize."

---

activist (ăk′•tə•vĭst) *n.* If you are an activist, you work hard to support a cause you believe in. You can be an activist for cleaner parks in your community.

aeronautics (âr′•ə•nô′•tĭks) *n.* Aeronautics is the science of air travel. She enjoyed aeronautics so much that she became an airplane pilot.

agony (ăg′•ə•nē) *n.* Agony is extreme suffering. She is in agony after falling from her bike and injuring her knee.

alarmed (ə•lärmd′) *v.* If you are alarmed, something has caused you to feel frightened and very concerned. The museum director was alarmed to find the pharaoh's jewel missing.

aloofness (ə•lōōf′•nəs) *n.* Someone who shows aloofness seems disinterested or unfriendly. Because she sat alone and did not talk to anyone, she had a reputation for aloofness.

annex (ăn′•ĕks′) *n.* An annex is a room that is attached to a larger room. The apartment includes an annex that is connected to the living room and kitchen.

anticipates (ăn•tĭs′•ə•pāts′) *v.* Someone who anticipates an event is aware of what will happen and takes action to be prepared for it. She anticipates that there will be flooding later tonight, so she has piled sandbags in front of her house.

antics (ăn′•tĭks) *n.* Antics are funny, goofy ways of behaving. When I am with my friends, we get up to all kinds of antics, including taking silly selfies.

apathy (ăp′•ə•thē) *n.* Apathy is a lack of enthusiasm, interest, or concern. If people feel apathy about something, they do not care about it at all.

aquatic (ə•kwăt′•ĭk) *adj.* A plant or animal that is aquatic lives in or around water. Scientists who study aquatic plants and animals use special equipment to explore the ocean.

archaeologist (är′•kē•ŏl′•ə•jĭst) *n.* An archaeologist studies societies and peoples of the past by examining what is left of their civilizations. An archaeologist spends hours surveying an area, searching for ancient objects like pieces of pottery and stone tools.

ōō b**oo**t / ou **ou**t / ŭ c**u**t / û f**u**r / hw **wh**ich / th **th**in / *th* **th**is / zh vi**si**on / ə **a**go, sil**e**nt, penc**i**l, lem**o**n, circ**u**s

ascent (ə•sĕnt′) *n.* An ascent is an upward movement. The two friends are racing as they make their ascent to the top of the climbing wall.

> ### Word Origins
>
> **ascent** The word *ascent* is derived from the word *ascend*, which is the Latin word *ascendere*, meaning "to climb."

assaulted (ə•sôl′•tĭd) *v.* If you assaulted someone, you physically attacked that person. When our friend saw a man being assaulted, he immediately called the police.

atrophied (ăt′•rə•fē) *v.* Something that has atrophied has wasted away because it hasn't been used. A leg with muscles that have atrophied appears thinner than normal.

attributes (ə•trĭb′•yōots) *n.* Your attributes are traits or qualities that help define you. My cousin's determination and focus were the two main attributes that helped her win the game.

autopsy (ô′•tŏp′•sē) *n.* During an autopsy, a dead body is examined to determine the cause of death. The marine biologists will have to do an animal autopsy on the beached whale to determine the cause of death.

B

barriers (băr′•ē•ərz) *n.* Barriers are obstacles or things that make it difficult to achieve a goal. Sprained ankles are often barriers to playing a sport.

bicker (bĭk′•ər) *v.* To bicker means to argue about unimportant things. Our friends always bicker over their favorite sports team.

bribed (brībd) *v.* If you are bribed, someone has offered you money or something else that is valuable to get you to do something. The boys bribed the goats to come closer by offering them some apples.

C

chaos (kā′•ŏs′) *n.* Chaos is complete disorder and confusion. It is amazing how much chaos a toddler can create in a short period of time.

chariots (chăr′•ē•əts) *n.* Chariots are ancient two-wheeled vehicles pulled by horses. Ancient Romans used chariots during battle, hunting, and special events.

classifying (klăs′•ə•fī•ĭng) *v.* If you are classifying things, you are dividing them into groups of like things. To keep his sewing area neater, he began classifying his buttons by color.

clergy (klûr′•jē) *n.* Members of the clergy serve as leaders in churches. Members of the clergy often wear special clothing to distinguish themselves from the congregation.

colonize (kŏl′•ə•nīz′) *v.* To colonize a place means to go there and take control of it. We decided to colonize this area of the beach for our family campout.

ă rat / ā pay / â care / ä father / ĕ pet / ē be / ĭ pit / ī pie / î fierce / ŏ pot / ō go / ô paw, for / oi oil / ŏŏ book /

commission (kə•**mĭsh'**•ən) *n.* A commission is a group formed to make official decisions. The town commission met to discuss the new regulations.

condense (kən•**dĕns'**) *v.* To condense something is to change it from a gas to a liquid. Cooler temperatures cause water vapor in the air to condense into water droplets.

conduct (kən•**dŭkt'**) *v.* If you conduct something, you organize or do it. She is about to conduct an interview for a kids' news channel.

confrontation (kŏn'•frŭn•**tā'**•shən) *n.* A confrontation is a face-to-face meeting between opposing groups. My younger sister and her friends had a confrontation with some classmates because they would not let her friends play.

considerable (kən•**sĭd'**•ər•ə•bəl) *adj.* Something that is considerable is very large in size or amount. There are a considerable number of clothes in the laundry hamper.

consumption (kən•**sŭmp'**•shən) *n.* If something is ready for consumption, people can hear or read about it. My mom and I were really excited to try the new virtual reality games as soon as they were ready for public consumption.

contemplation (kŏn'•təm•plā'•shən) *n.* Contemplation is the act of thinking deeply about something. She looked out the window in deep contemplation, trying to decide what to do with her future.

contrast (kən•**trăst'** or **kŏn'**•trăst') *n.* A contrast signals a different situation or idea. Yesterday it was dark and stormy. By contrast, today it is sunny and bright.

convocation (**kŏn'**•və•kā'•shən) *n.* A convocation is the meeting of a large group of people. During the convocation of young environmentalists, the students applauded when the mayor proposed banning the use of plastic bags.

cove (kōv) *n.* A cove is part of the coast where the land curves in, creating a partly enclosed section of the sea. The cove is a nice, calm, and private place to swim because there is less wind and fewer waves crash up against you.

craters (**krā'**•tərz) *n.* Craters are bowl-shaped indentations on a surface, such as on the moon or a volcano. The moon's surface has craters, which were likely formed by asteroids or meteors crashing into it.

> **Word Origins**
>
> **craters** The word *crater* comes from the Greek word *krater*, meaning "large bowl."

D

denial (dĭ•**nī'**•əl) *n.* The denial of something is the refusal to grant it. Our dog should be used to denial by now, but he still begs for table scraps at every meal.

devotion (dĭ•**vō'**•shən) *n.* Devotion is commitment to an activity. Service dogs have total devotion to helping others.

ōō b**oo**t / ou **ou**t / ŭ c**u**t / û f**u**r / hw **wh**ich / th **th**in / *th* **th**is / zh vi**si**on / ə **a**go, sil**e**nt, penc**i**l, lem**o**n, circ**u**s

dignity (dĭg'•nĭ•tē) *n.* A person's dignity includes his or her values and self-respect. He was filled with dignity as he gave the valedictory speech at his graduation.

diminish (dĭ•mĭn'•ĭsh) *v.* When something diminishes, it becomes less important or valuable. Phones diminish in value because there is always a newer version coming out to replace the old one.

discernible (dĭ•sûr'•nə•bəl) *adj.* If something is discernible, it's noticeable or recognizable. The pufferfish is well-known for its discernible spines.

disruption (dĭs•rŭpt'•shən) *n.* A disruption is a disturbance that causes an interruption. The earthquake caused a severe disruption to traffic on the road.

dramatic (drə•măt'•ĭk) *adj.* Something that is dramatic attracts a lot of attention. The group of skydivers created a rather dramatic scene in the sky.

Word Origins

dramatic The word *dramatic* is derived from the Greek word *dramatikos*, meaning "pertaining to plays."

E

economist (ĭ•kŏn'•ə•mĭst) *n.* An economist studies things such as what people buy and how much they buy. The economist tracks trends on what consumers buy each month.

elevation (ĕl'•ə•vā'•shən) *n.* An elevation is a height above a certain level. From the high elevation of the cable car, you get a clear view of the landscape.

eligible (ĕl'•ĭ•jə•bəl) *adj.* If you are eligible to do something, you're qualified or able to do it. After he turned 16 and passed his driving and written test, he was eligible to get his driver's license.

enabling (ĕn•ā'•blĭng) *v.* If someone is enabling you to do something, he or she is allowing or helping you to achieve it. Teaching his son to ride a bike is enabling his son to explore the neighborhood independently.

endure (ĕn•dŏor') *v.* If you endure a difficult situation, you put up with it. The athlete had to have a great deal of stamina and determination to endure the intense heat during the marathon.

engage (ĕn•gāj') *v.* When you engage in something, you take part in it. Everyone was happy to engage in planting new trees as part of the Earth Day activities last year.

entice (ĕn•tīs') *v.* To entice someone to do something is to persuade them by offering pleasure or advantage. He used a dog treat to entice his dog to behave well and obey his commands.

ă rat / ā pay / â care / ä father / ĕ pet / ē be / ĭ pit / ī pie / î fierce / ŏ pot / ō go / ô paw, for / oi oil / ŏŏ book /

essential (ĭ•sĕn′•shəl) *adj.* Something that is essential is necessary. Toothpaste, a toothbrush, and dental floss are essential for keeping your teeth clean and healthy.

excavator (ĕk′•skə•vā′•tər) *n.* An excavator is a person who carefully digs to uncover what is buried underground. An excavator uses special tools to carefully uncover objects that have been buried in the ground for many years.

extinction (ĭk•stĭngk′•shən) *n.* The extinction of a species is the death of all of its remaining living members. The Bengal tiger is an endangered subspecies facing extinction.

extravagant (ĭk•străv′•ə•gənt) *adj.* Something that is extravagant is excessive or expensive. On the Fourth of July, many people come to our town to watch the extravagant display of fireworks.

F

fatigue (fə•tēg′) *n.* Fatigue is extreme mental and physical tiredness. He suffered from fatigue because he stayed up too late.

fluctuating (flŭk′•cho͞o•ā′•tĭng) *v.* Something that is fluctuating is changing often and in irregular ways. The flowers' reflection on the water was fluctuating in the afternoon light.

G

garments (gär′•mənts) *n.* Garments are pieces of clothing. When she gets dressed, she has many garments from which to choose.

geology (jē•ŏl′•ə•jē) *n.* People who study geology study Earth's structure, surface, and origins. Studies on the geology of the Zhangye Danxia Landform in China show it formed partly due to erosion.

H

halting (hôl′•tĭng) *adj.* When something is done in a halting way, it is done slowly and with a lot of hesitation. My grandfather moves in a halting way because he is not sure of his footing when walking down steps.

homicide victim (hŏm′•ĭ•sīd′ vĭk′•tĭm) *n.* A homicide victim is a person who has been murdered. After the police learn of a homicide victim, they investigate to find out how and why the person was killed.

humidity (hyo͞o•mĭd′•ĭ•tē) *n.* When something has high humidity, it has a lot of water vapor in it. There was a lot of humidity in her bedroom.

I

ideal (ī•dē′•əl) *n.* An ideal is a person or thing you regard as the perfect example. My ideal of what I should drink on a hot summer day is a cold glass of lemonade.

---

o͞o b**oo**t / ou **ou**t / ŭ c**u**t / û f**u**r / hw **wh**ich / th **th**in / *th* **th**is / zh vi**si**on / ə **a**go, sil**e**nt, penc**i**l, lem**o**n, circ**u**s

impersonation (ĭm•**pûr′**•sə•nā′•shən) *n.* An impersonation is when you pretend to be someone else by speaking or acting like that person. My impersonation of a super hero always makes my family laugh out loud.

implications (ĭm′•plĭ•**kā′**•shəns) *n.* The implications of a statement are the conclusions that can be drawn but are not directly stated. If you wake up one morning and notice that there is a fallen tree and the streets are wet, the implications are that it rained and stormed the night before.

implored (ĭm•**plôrd′**) *v.* If you implored someone, you begged that person to do something. He implored his grandmother to let him go to the concert.

imprints (**ĭm′**•prĭntz′) *n.* Imprints are outlines left by something that has been pressed into softer material. The aquatic trilobites left behind imprints in the wet mud.

induces (ĭn•**doo′**•səs) *v.* If something induces a reaction, it causes it to happen. Many believe that a glass of warm milk before bed induces a good night's sleep.

inevitable (ĭn•**ĕv′**•ĭ•tə•bəl) *adj.* Something inevitable is certain to happen. In the Midwest, it is inevitable that many leaves change from green to different shades of yellow and orange during the fall.

inhabit (ĭn•**hăb′**•ĭt) *v.* If you inhabit a place, you live in it. Many types of fish and other creatures inhabit the ocean.

Word Origins

inhabit The word *inhabit* comes from the Latin word *inhabitare*; *in–* meaning "in" and *habitare* meaning "to dwell." Thus, the word *inhabit* means "to dwell in" or "to live in."

---

invertebrates (ĭn•**vûr′**•tə•brĭt or ĭn•**vûr′**•tə•brāt′) *n.* Invertebrates are animals that lack a vertebral column, or spine. Invertebrates found in the ocean include the octopus, starfish, and jellyfish.

isolation (ī′•sə•**lā′**•shən) *n.* To be in isolation is to be alone. You would be living in isolation if you were alone on an island in the middle of the ocean.

J

jalopy (jə•**lŏp′**•ē) *n.* A jalopy is an old car. When he was seventeen, my dad paid twenty dollars for an old jalopy so he could take my mom on their first date.

justify (**jŭs′**•tə•fī′) *v.* To justify something is to prove that it is worthwhile or necessary. She listed all the exciting activities she planned to do with her friend's family to justify why she should stay at their lake house for the weekend.

Word Origins

justify The word *justify* comes from the Old French word *justifier* and the Latin word *justificare*, both meaning "to act justly toward" or "to make just." The word *just* comes from the Latin *justus* meaning "law, right."

ă rat / ā pay / â care / ä father / ě pet / ē be / ĭ pit / ī pie / î fierce / ŏ pot / ō go / ô paw, for / oi oil / oŏ book /

L

languid (lăng′•gwĭd) *adj.* If you are languid, you are slow and relaxed. Turtles move at a languid pace, while rabbits move quickly.

launched (lônchd) *v.* If you've launched a rocket or satellite, it means you've sent it into space. Over the years, NASA has launched many rockets into space.

lavishly (lăv′•ĭsh•lē) *adv.* Something that is done lavishly is done in an elaborate and impressive way. The room was lavishly decorated with bouquets of fresh flowers and sparkling chandeliers.

leagues (lēgz) *n.* A league is a group of sports clubs that play against each other for a championship. My sisters belong to two different softball leagues, and they compete against each other every Saturday.

lectures (lĕk′•chərz) *n.* Lectures are speeches usually given to instruct an audience. At the community college, lectures given by the history professor are always interesting.

— Word Origins —

lectures The word *lecture* comes from the Latin *lectus*, the past participle of the Latin verb *legere*, meaning "to read."

legacy (lĕg′•ə•sē) *n.* A legacy is an ongoing impact of something from the past. The musician Mozart did not live a very long time, but he left behind a legacy of music that continues to influence classical music today.

legislation (lĕj′•ĭs•lā′•shən) *n.* Legislation is the creation of rules or laws. The Constitution states that Congress can form and pass legislation, or laws.

M

majesty (măj′•ĭ•stē) *n.* If something has majesty, it is dignified and impressive. The majesty of the landscape inspired many paintings.

mania (mā′•nē•ə or mān′•yə) *n.* If you have mania for something, you have great enthusiasm for it. The fans' mania for their favorite football team makes them cheer loudly during the entire game.

manipulation (mə•nĭp′•yə•lā′•shən) *n.* Manipulation is the act of handling something, usually with skill. The glassblower uses heat and careful manipulation of the glass to create the object.

mechanism (mĕk′•ə•nĭz′•əm) *n.* A mechanism is a part of a machine that performs a specific function. A mechanism in the clock makes the hands move.

ōō **boo**t / ou **ou**t / ŭ **c**ut / û **fur** / hw **wh**ich / th **th**in / *th* **th**is / zh vi**s**ion / ə **a**go, sil**e**nt, penc**i**l, lem**o**n, circ**u**s

module (mŏj′•ool) *n.* A module is a self-contained part of a spacecraft that can operate away from the rest of the spacecraft. During the Apollo 11 mission, the astronauts used a lunar module called *Eagle* to land on the surface of the moon.

mollusks (mŏl′•əsks) *n.* Mollusks, such as a snails and octopuses, are invertebrates with soft bodies. These mollusks are tightly attached to the rock.

motivation (mō′•tə•vā′•shən) *n.* Your motivation is your reason for caring about something. The scientists' motivation for conducting medical research is to save lives.

mutually (myoo′•choo•ə•lē) *adv.* If you describe two things as mutually exclusive, they cannot both be true. Being a good student and a good athlete are not mutually exclusive. You can be both.

N

naturalized (năch′•ər•ə•līzd′) *adj.* Naturalized citizens of a country are people who have legally become citizens of that country, even though they were not born there. Five years after she moved to the United States, my aunt became a naturalized U.S. citizen.

O

objectivity (ŏb′•jĕk•tĭv′•ĭ•tē) *n.* If you have objectivity about something, you can think about it without emotion. The court judge is considered fair by everyone because he displays complete objectivity.

obstacles (ŏb′•stə•kəls) *n.* An obstacle is an object that is in your way and blocks your path. The boulders were the obstacles that blocked the highway and caused a huge traffic jam.

obtain (əb•tān′) *v.* If you obtain something, you make an effort to get it. After graduation, you will obtain a diploma.

official (ə•fĭsh′•əl) *adj.* Something that is official has been approved by someone in authority. His signature on the contract made the agreement official.

opposition (ŏp′•ə•zĭsh′•ən) *n.* Opposition to an idea means disagreement with it. The protesters demonstrated to show their opposition to the new government decisions.

oppressed (ə•prĕsd′) *adj.* People who are oppressed are treated in a cruel and unfair way. Oppressed people are those who haven't been granted certain rights, such as the right to vote.

option (ŏp′•shən) *n.* An option is a choice. We had the option of doing yoga or aerobics in gym class today. We chose aerobics.

orbit (ôr′•bĭt) *n.* An object is said to be in orbit when it's moving in a circular motion around a planet, moon, or star. The International Space Station has been in orbit around Earth since 1998.

ă r**a**t / ā p**ay** / â c**a**re / ä f**a**ther / ĕ p**e**t / ē b**e** / ĭ p**i**t / ī p**ie** / î f**ie**rce / ŏ p**o**t / ō g**o** / ô p**aw**, f**or** / oi **oil** / oo b**oo**k /

ordeal (ôr•**dēl'**) *n.* An ordeal is generally an unpleasant experience. It was an ordeal for the babysitter to calm down the active children.

organism (**ôr'**•gə•nĭz'•əm) *n.* An organism is any living thing, including animals, plants, fungi, and bacteria. A chameleon is an example of a unique organism that has the ability to change colors.

oversees (ō'•vər•**sēz'**) *v.* A person or group that oversees an effort is responsible for it. Our teacher oversees our work to make sure we are completing our assignments correctly.

P

perplexing (pər•**plĕks'**•ĭng) *v.* If something is perplexing, it is hard to understand or know how to deal with. Even though they were skilled hikers, they found the map of the area perplexing and did not know which way to go.

petitions (pə•**tĭsh'**•əns) *n.* Petitions are formal requests made to an official person or organization. We signed petitions to protect forest preserves in our county.

physique (fĭ•**zēk'**) *n.* Someone's physique is the form, size, and development of his or her body. Everyone has their own unique body physique.

pipeline (**pīp'**•līn') *n.* A pipeline carries gas or oil long distances underground. Construction work has started on the underground pipeline.

plague (plăk) *v.* Things that plague you cause you continual trouble, discomfort, or distress. A runny nose and fever are some of the symptoms that plague people who have the flu.

--- **Word Origins** ---

plague The word *plague* comes from the Middle English word *plage*, which is from the Latin word *plaga*, meaning "blow."

political scientist (pə•**lĭt'**•ĭ•kəl **sī'**•ən•tĭst) *n.* A political scientist analyzes government systems and behaviors to predict future behavior. The political scientist is giving a speech on government systems around the world.

polls (pōlz) *n.* People go to the polls to vote. They went to the polls to cast their votes.

priorities (prī•**ôr'**•ĭ•tēz) *n.* Things that are priorities are very important to you. Reading to us is one of Mom's top priorities.

probing (**prōb'**•ĭng) *v.* Probing is searching into something for the purpose of answering questions. Scientists are probing the octopus's habitat in search of answers about its environment.

procession (prə•**sĕsh'**•ən) *n.* A procession is a group of people who are walking, riding, or driving as part of a parade or other public event. When we visited London, we watched the procession of the Changing of the Guards at Buckingham Palace.

ōō b**oo**t / ou **ou**t / ŭ c**u**t / û f**u**r / hw **wh**ich / th **th**in / *th* **th**is / zh vi**si**on / ə **a**go, sil**e**nt, penc**i**l, lem**o**n, circ**u**s

productivity (prō′•dŭk•tĭv′•ĭ•tē) *n.* Productivity is the effectiveness of a company's efforts. Robots help the company build cars faster, which increases its productivity.

profiler (prō′•fĭl′•ər) *n.* A profiler studies a person's traits and behavior to draw conclusions about what that person is like. A profiler helps catch criminals by asking questions and gathering information about a person.

prohibitive (prō•hĭb′•ĭ•tĭv) *adj.* Something prohibitive is extremely expensive or unaffordable. Even though he wants to buy the car, he knows that the cost of owning a car is prohibitive on a student's budget.

prohibits (prō•hĭb′•ĭtz) *v.* If a law prohibits something, it forbids it or makes it illegal. President Johnson signed the Voting Rights Act of 1965, which prohibits discrimination in voting.

proposal (prə•pō′•zəl) *n.* A proposal is an idea that people discuss and decide on. She presented her proposal for the new classroom design.

Q

qualify (kwŏl′•ə•fī′) *v.* If you qualify for something, you have the training, skill, or ability for a specific purpose. If you have strong swimming skills and first aid training, you can qualify for a job as a pool lifeguard.

quarry (kwôr′•ē) *n.* Quarry is something that is hunted. Some predator birds hunt their quarry, or prey, in the lake.

quavered (kwā′•vərd) *v.* If your voice quavered, it sounded shaky and unsteady. Her voice quavered with emotion when she told her mom that she got a bad grade on the test.

R

radically (răd′•ĭ•kəl) *adv.* Something that is radically different is very different in important ways. Homes can be radically different across the world and can be specific to the climate people live in.

realm (rĕlm) *n.* The term realm is used by scientists to describe a region of Earth's surface. Colorful coral and fish live in the underwater realm.

receptivity (rĭ•sĕp•tĭv′•ə•tē′) *n.* Receptivity is the ability to receive, or take something in. The students' receptivity to the idea is positive.

register (rĕj′•ĭ•stər) *v.* When you register to do something, you sign up for it. They got there early to register for the race.

reinforced (rē′•ĭn•fôrsd′) *v.* If something is reinforced, it is made stronger. The coach reinforced Claire's fitness routine by showing her some new exercises and encouraging her to stick with it.

relics (rĕl′•ĭks) *n.* Relics are valued objects from the past, especially ones of historical interest. The relics found at the archaeological site tell us about Mayan life before the arrival of Europeans.

Word Origins

relics The word *relics* comes from the Latin word *reliquiae*, meaning "sacred" remains" or "remains of a martyr."

ă r**a**t / ā p**ay** / â c**a**re / ä f**a**ther / ĕ p**e**t / ē b**e** / ĭ p**i**t / ī p**ie** / î f**ie**rce / ŏ p**o**t / ō g**o** / ô p**aw, fo**r / oi **oi**l / o͝o b**oo**k /

remains (rĭ•**mānz'**) *n.* The remains are a person's body after death. The mummy's remains were on display at a museum in Italy.

reproduced (rē'•prə•**dōōst'**) *v.* Something that is reproduced is copied. The fruit reproduced by the artist was so realistic that we thought the painting was a photograph.

reputable (**rĕp'**•yə•tə•bəl) *adj.* Someone who is reputable is reliable and trustworthy. My mom got her prescription from a reputable pharmacist who was able to answer all her questions.

respirators (rĕs'•pə•**rā'**•tərz) *n.* A respirator covers your mouth and helps you breathe. Painters should always wear respirators to protect their lungs.

restrictions (rĭ•**strĭk'**•shənz) *v.* Restrictions are rules that limit what you can do. There are certain restrictions on parking throughout the city.

rivals (**rī'**•vəlz) *n.* Rivals compete against each other to win something or prove that they are better. The two teams had been rivals for many years and always played hard against each other.

S

satellite (**săt'**•l•īt') *n.* A satellite is a human-made object that has been placed in space to collect information or for communication. The first artificial satellite in space was only 22.8 inches in diameter.

shrine (shrīn) *n.* A shrine is a place that is treated with reverence because it is associated with a sacred person or object. The mummy of King Tut was found inside a large shrine.

--- Word Origins ---

shrine The word *shrine* comes from the Old English word *scrin*, meaning "coffer for precious objects." A *coffer* is a chest or case. A *shrine* generally refers to a place or the tomb of a saint or important person.

simulators (**sĭm'**•yə•lā'•tərz) *n.* Simulators are devices that artificially create the effect of being in certain conditions, such as being in space. Flight simulators give people the chance to feel what it is like to fly a plane without ever leaving the ground.

specimens (**spĕs'**•ə•mənz) *n.* Specimens are individual animals, plants, or objects that are examples of their type. The butterfly and beetle specimens are mounted and displayed inside a frame.

stationary (**stā'**•shə•nĕr'•ē) *adj.* If something is stationary, it's not moving. Her driving instructor had her practice parking between stationary cones without hitting them.

statistics (stə•**tĭs'**•tĭks) *n.* Statistics are facts or data that are combined and considered together. If you review the statistics of the soccer match, you can understand why the red team won.

ōō b**oo**t / ou **ou**t / ŭ c**u**t / û f**u**r / hw **wh**ich / th **th**in / *th* **th**is / zh vi**s**ion / ə **a**go, sil**e**nt, penc**i**l, lem**o**n, circ**u**s

submerged (səb•**mûrjd'**) *adj.* If something was submerged, it was placed below the surface of water or another liquid. The boat has been submerged in the ocean for many years.

substantial (səb•**stăn'**•shəl) *adj.* If something is substantial, it has considerable size, strength, or value. The elephant uses its substantial strength to easily uproot the tree.

suffrage (**sŭf'**•rĭj) *n.* Suffrage is the right of people to vote. Universal suffrage gives all people, regardless of race or gender, the right to vote.

swarmed (swôrmd) *v.* If a place swarmed, it was very crowded and busy. Fans swarmed around their favorite singer for an autograph.

T

taut (tôt) *adj.* Something that is stretched very tight is taut. The strings on a guitar need to be very taut to make a higher pitch and looser if you want a lower pitch.

U

unadorned (ŭn'•ə•**dôrnd'**) *adj.* Something that is unadorned is not decorated or made fancier. The unadorned cake was ready to be decorated for Sam's birthday party.

unfurl (ŭn•**fûrl'**) *v.* When you unfurl something, such as an umbrella, you unfold it so that it spreads out. She will unfurl the umbrella when it starts to rain.

unity (**yoō'**•nĭ•tē) *n.* Unity is what happens when different groups with the same values and goals join together as one. They came together in unity to celebrate the decision to make their community better.

Word Origins

unity The word *unity*, comes from the Latin word *unus*, meaning "one."

---

unprecedented (ŭn•**prĕs'**•ĭ•dĕnt'•tĭd) *adj.* Something that is unprecedented has never happened before. She hopes to become the first female to play professional football, which would be an unprecedented moment in history.

V

vast (văst) *adj.* Something vast is very large. I felt very small as I looked out over the vast ocean.

vaulting (**vôl'**•tĭng) *v.* If you are vaulting, you are jumping onto or over something. To get better at their sport, high jumpers practice vaulting over higher and higher bars.

venture (**vĕn'**•chər) *n.* A venture is a risky project or undertaking. Some people believe that starting a business is a risky venture because many businesses do not last more than five years.

versatility (**vûr'**•sə•təl•ə•tē) *n.* A person who has versatility has many different skills. She had tremendous versatility and could do many things.

ă r**a**t / ā p**ay** / â c**a**re / ä f**a**ther / ĕ p**e**t / ē b**e** / ĭ p**i**t / ī p**ie** / î f**ie**rce / ŏ p**o**t / ō g**o** / ô p**aw**, f**o**r / oi **oi**l / ŏŏ b**oo**k /

via (**vī′**•ə or **vē′**•ə) *prep.* If you send something via a particular person or thing, that person or thing is taking or carrying it for you. We traveled through the desert via camel, while others traveled via truck.

volcanic (vŏl•**kăn′**•ĭk) *adj.* Something that is volcanic has come from a volcano. During an eruption, gray volcanic ash shoots out of a volcano and fills the sky.

--- Word Origins ---

volcanic The word *volcanic* is derived from the word *volcano*. *Volcano* comes from the Latin word *Vulcanus*, which refers to the Roman mythologocial god Vulcan. Vulcan is the god of fire and metalworking.

W

warden (**wôrd′**•n) *n.* A warden is responsible for enforcing the laws and rules regarding a place, people, or things. A warden helps protect the land and wildlife in a national forest.

Z

zoology (zō•**ŏl′**•ə•jē) *n.* Someone who studies zoology studies animals. He studies zoology and is particularly interested in sharing what he has learned about alligators.

ōō b**oo**t / ou **ou**t / ŭ c**u**t / û f**u**r / hw **wh**ich / th **th**in / *th* **th**is / zh vi**s**ion / ə **a**go, sil**e**nt, penc**i**l, lem**o**n, circ**u**s

Index of Titles and Authors

Acknowledgments

"Analysis of Baseball" from *May Swenson: New and Selected Things Taking Place* by May Swenson. Text copyright © 1978 by May Swenson. Reprinted by permission of The Literary Estate of May Swenson. All rights reserved.

"Astronaut School" by Elizabeth Preston from *Ask* magazine. Text copyright © 2017 by Carus Publishing Company. Reprinted by permission of Cricket Media. All Cricket Media material is copyrighted by Carus Publishing Company d/b/a Cricket Media, and/or various authors and illustrators. Any commercial use or distribution of material without permission is strictly prohibited. Please visit http://www.cricketmedia.com/licensing for licensing and http://www.cricketmedia.com for subscriptions.

"At the End of Warm-Ups, My Brother Tries to Dunk" from *The Crossover* by Kwame Alexander. Text copyright © 2014 by Kwame Alexander. Reprinted by permission of Houghton Mifflin Harcourt Publishing Company.

Excerpt from *Babe Didrikson Zaharias: The Making of a Champion* by Russell Freedman. Text copyright © 1999 by Russell Freedman. Reprinted by permission of Houghton Mifflin Harcourt Publishing Company.

"Behavior Psychology: 4 Research-backed ways to get people to vote" by Bethany Brookshire from *Science News for Students*, November 7, 2016. Text copyright © 2016 by Bethany Brookshire. Reprinted by permission of Science News for Students.

"Behavior Psychology: 4 Reasons Why Many People Don't Vote" by Bethany Brookshire from *Science News for Students*, November 7, 2016. Text copyright © 2016 by Bethany Brookshire. Reprinted by permission of Science News for Students.

Excerpt from "La Belle Époque" by Albert Camus, 15 April 1953. Text copyright © 1965, 2008 by Editions Gallimard, Paris. Reprinted by permission of The Wylie Agency, on behalf of the Literary Estate of Albert Camus.

Excerpt from *Bodies from the Ash* by James M. Deem. Copyright © 2005 by James M. Deem. Reprinted by permission of Houghton Mifflin Harcourt Publishing Company.

Excerpt from "Bring on the Participation Trophies!" by Katie Bugbee. Text copyright © 2007–2018 by Care.com. Reprinted by permission of Care.com.

"Crash Test Mummy" by Zachary Petit from *National Geographic Kids,* September 2014. Text copyright © 2014 by Zachary Petit. Reprinted by permission of National Geographic Society.

"Daybreak" from *A New Selected Poems* by Galway Kinnell. Text copyright © 2000 by Galway Kinnell. Reprinted by permission of Houghton Mifflin Harcourt Publishing Company.

"Earth Day on the Bay" by Gary Soto. Copyright © 2016 by Gary Soto. Reprinted by permission of Gary Soto.

"Fannie Lou Hamer" by Pauline Bickford-Duane from *Cobblestone* magazine, February 2014. Text copyright © 2014 by Carus Publishing Company. Reprinted by permission of Cricket Media. All Cricket Media material is copyrighted by Carus Publishing Company d/b/a Cricket Media, and/or various authors and illustrators. Any commercial use or distribution of material without permission is strictly prohibited. Please visit http://www.cricketmedia.com/licensing for licensing and http://www.cricketmedia.com for subscriptions.

Excerpt from "I Jumped at the Offer" from *Almost Astronauts: 13 Women Who Dared to Dream* by Tanya Lee Stone. Text copyright © 2009 by Tanya Lee Stone. Reprinted by permission of Candlewick Press and Stimola Literary Studio on behalf of Tanya Lee Stone.

Excerpt from "It's More Than Just Rain or Snow or Springtime" from *How to Read Literature Like a Professor: For Kids* by Thomas C. Foster. Text copyright © 2003, 2013 by Thomas C. Foster. Reprinted by permission of HarperCollins Publishers and Sanford J. Greenburger Associates, Inc.

"A Jelly-Fish" by Marianne Moore from *The Lantern 17*, Spring, 1909. Text copyright by the Literary Estate of Marianne Moore. Reprinted by permission of David M. Moore Esq. on behalf of the Literary Estate of Marianne Moore.

Excerpt from *King Tut: The Hidden Tomb* by Ruth Owen. Copyright © 2017 by Bearport Publishing Company, Inc. Reprinted by permission of Bearport Publishing Co. All rights reserved.

"The Largest of Them All: Whale Sharks" from *Seeking Giant Sharks: A Shark Diver's Quest for Whale Sharks, Basking Sharks, and Manta Rays* by Mary M. Cerullo. Copyright © 2015 by Compass Point Books, a Capstone imprint. Reprinted by permission of Capstone Press.

"Maggie and Milly and Molly and May" from *Complete Poems* by E.E. Cummings, edited by George J. Firmage. Text copyright ©1956, 1984, 1991 by the Trustees for the E.E. Cummings Trust. Reprinted by permission of Liveright Publishing Corporation.

"The Moon Landing Inspired Me to Become an Astronaut" by Mark Polansky. Copyright © 2015 by The Atlantic Monthly Group, Inc. Reprinted by permission of The Atlantic Monthly Group, Inc., permission conveyed through Copyright Clearance Center, Inc.

"Mummies: Milwaukee Public Museum" from *Rattle #49*, Fall 2015. Text copyright © 2017 by Richard Hedderman. Reprinted by permission of Richard Hedderman.

"Mummy Murder Mystery" by Rod Nordland from *The New York Times*, March 26, 2017. *The New York Times*. Text copyright © 2017 by the New York Times. Reprinted by permission of PARS International Corp on behalf of The New York Times. Protected by the Copyright Laws of the United States. The printing, copying, redistribution, or retransmission of this Content without express written permission is prohibited. All rights reserved.

Excerpt from *Neil Armstrong: One Giant Leap for Mankind* by Tara Dixon-Engel and Mike Jackson. Text copyright © 2008 by Tara Dixon-Engel and Mike Jackson. Reprinted by permission of Sterling Publishing Co., Inc.

"Neither Out Far Nor In Deep" from *The Poetry of Robert Frost* by Robert Frost, edited by Edward Connery Lathem. Text copyright © 1969 by Henry Holt and Company. Text copyright ©1936 by Robert Frost. Text copyright © 1964 by Lesley Frost Ballantine. Reprinted by permission of Henry Holt and Company. All rights reserved.

"The Noisy Ocean" by Lori Wollerman Nelson from *Ask* magazine, November 2012. Text copyright © 2012 by Carus Publishing Company. Reprinted by permission of Cricket Media. All Cricket Media material is copyrighted by Carus Publishing Company d/b/a Cricket Media, and/or various authors and illustrators. Any commercial use or distribution of material without permission is strictly prohibited. Please visit http://www.cricketmedia.com/licensing for licensing and http://www.cricketmedia.com for subscriptions.

Excerpt from *The Octopus Scientists: Exploring the Mind of a Mollusk,* by Sy Montgomery. Text copyright © 2015 by Sy Montgomery. Reprinted by permission of Houghton Mifflin Harcourt Publishing Company.

"Participation Trophies Send a Dangerous Message" by Betty Berdan from *The New York Times,* October 6, 2016. *The New York Times*. Reprinted by permission of PARS International Corp on behalf of The New York Times. Protected by the Copyright Laws of the United States. The printing, copying, redistribution, or retransmission of this Content without express written permission is prohibited. All rights reserved.

"Safeguarding the California Coast" from *Heroes of the Environment* by Harriet Rohmer, illustrated by Julie McLaughlin. Text copyright © 2009 by Harriet Rohmer. Illustrations copyright © 2009 by Chronicle

Credits